Bloom's Major Literary Characters

King Arthur

Nick Adams

George F. Babbitt

Elizabeth Bennet

Leopold Bloom

Sir John Falstaff

Huck Finn

Frankenstein

Jay Gatsby

Hamlet

Hester Prynne

Raskolnikov and Svidrigailov

Bloom's Major Literary Characters

Frankenstein

Edited and with an introduction by
Harold Bloom
Sterling Professor of the Humanities
Yale University

CHELSEA HOUSE
PUBLISHERS
A Haights Cross Communications ◀ Company
Philadelphia

A Haights Cross Communications ⌐⌐ Company

Introduction © 2004 by Harold Bloom.

10 9 8 7 6 5 4 3 2 1

Library of Congress Cataloging-in-Publication Data

Frankenstein / edited and with an introduction by Harold Bloom.
   p. cm. — (Bloom's major literary characters)
 Includes bibliographical references (p.) and index.
 ISBN 0-7910-7882-5
 1. Shelley, Mary Wollstonecraft, 1797-1851. Frankenstein. 2. Science
fiction, English—History and criticism. 3. Horror tales, English—
History and criticism. 4. Frankenstein (Fictitious character) 5.
Scientists in literature. 6. Creation in literature. 7. Monsters in
literature. I. Bloom, Harold. II. Major literary characters.
 PR5397.F73F68 2004
 823'.7—dc22

                                               2003025730

Contributing editor: Janyce Marson

Cover design by Keith Trego

Cover: © CORBIS SYGMA

Layout by EJB Publishing Services

Chelsea House Publishers
1974 Sproul Road, Suite 400
Broomall, PA 19008-0914

www.chelseahouse.com

Contents

HAROLD BLOOM

The Analysis of Character

"Character," according to our dictionaries, still has as a primary meaning a graphic symbol, such as a letter of the alphabet. This meaning reflects the word's apparent origin in the ancient Greek character, a sharp stylus. *Charactēr* also meant the mark of the stylus' incisions. Recent fashions in literary criticism have reduced "character" in literature to a matter of marks upon a page. But our word "character" also has a very different meaning, matching that of the ancient Greek *ēthos*, "habitual way of life." Shall we say then that literary character is an imitation of human character, or is it just a grouping of marks? The issue is between a critic like Dr. Samuel Johnson, for whom words were as much like people as like things, and a critic like the late Roland Barthes, who told us that "the fact can only exist linguistically, as a term of discourse." Who is closer to our experience of reading literature, Johnson or Barthes? What difference does it make, if we side with one critic rather than the other?

Barthes is famous, like Foucault and other recent French theorists, for having added to Nietzsche's proclamation of the death of God a subsidiary demise, that of the literary author. If there are no authors, then there are no fictional personages, presumably because literature does not refer to a world outside language. Words indeed necessarily refer to other words in the first place, but the impact of words ultimately is drawn from a universe of fact. Stories, poems, and plays are recognizable as such because they are human utterances within traditions of utterances, and traditions, by achieving authority, become a kind of fact, or at least the sense of a fact. Our sense that literary characters, within the context of a fictive cosmos, indeed are fictional personages is also a kind of fact. The meaning and value of every character in a successful work of literary representation depend upon our ideas of persons in the factual reality of our lives.

Literary character is always an invention, and inventions generally are indebted to prior inventions. Shakespeare is the inventor of literary character as we know it; he reformed the universal human expectations for the verbal imitation of personality, and the reformation appears now to be permanent and uncannily inevitable. Remarkable as the Bible and Homer are at representing personages, their characters are relatively unchanging. They age within their stories, but their habitual modes of being do not develop. Jacob and Achilles unfold before us, but without metamorphoses. Lear and Macbeth, Hamlet and Othello severely modify themselves not only by their actions, but by their utterances, and most of all through *overhearing themselves*, whether they speak to themselves or to others. Pondering what they themselves have said, they will to change, and actually do change, sometimes extravagantly yet always persuasively. Or else they suffer change, without willing it, but in reaction not so much to their language as to their relation to that language.

I do not think it useful to say that Shakespeare successfully imitated elements in our characters. Rather, it could be argued that he compelled aspects of character to appear that previously were concealed, or not available to representation. This is not to say that Shakespeare is God, but to remind us that language is not God either. The mimesis of character in Shakespeare's dramas now seems to us normative, and indeed became the accepted mode almost immediately, as Ben Jonson shrewdly and somewhat grudgingly implied. And yet, Shakespearean representation has surprisingly little in common with the imitation of reality in Jonson or in Christopher Marlowe. The origins of Shakespeare's originality in the portrayal of men and women are to be found in the *Canterbury Tales* of Geoffrey Chaucer, insofar as they can be located anywhere before Shakespeare himself, Chaucer's savage and superb Pardoner overhears his own tale-telling, as well as his mocking rehearsal of his own spiel, and through this overhearing he is emboldened to forget himself, and enthusiastically urges all his fellow-pilgrims to come forward to be fleeced by him. His self-awareness, and apocalyptically rancid sense of spiritual fall, are preludes to the even grander abysses of the perverted will in Iago and in Edmund. What might be called the character trait of a negative charisma may be Chaucer's invention, but came to its perfection in Shakespearean mimesis.

The analysis of character is as much Shakespeare's invention as the representation of character is, since Iago and Edmund are adepts at analyzing both themselves and their victims. Hamlet, whose overwhelming charisma has many negative components, is certainly the most comprehensive of all literary characters, and so necessarily prophesies the labyrinthine complexities of the will in Iago and Edmund. Charisma, according to Max Weber, its first codifier, is primarily a natural endowment, and implies a primordial and idiosyncratic power over nature, and so finally over death. Hamlet's uncanniness is at its most suggestive in the scene of his long dying, where the audience, through the mediation of Horatio, itself is compelled to meditate upon suicide, if only because outliving the prince of Denmark scarcely seems an option.

Shakespearean representation has usurped not only our sense of literary character, but our sense of ourselves as characters, with Hamlet playing the part of the largest of these usurpations. Insofar as we have an idea of human disinterestedness, we tend to derive it from the Hamlet of Act V, whose quietism has about it a ghostly authority. Oscar Wilde, in his profound and profoundly witty dialogue, "The Decay of Lying," expressed a permanent insight when he insisted that art shaped every era, far more than any age formed art. Life imitates art, we imitate Shakespeare, because without Shakespeare we would perish for lack of images. Wilde's grandest audacity demystifies Shakespearean mimesis with a Shakespearean vivaciousness: "This unfortunate aphorism about art holding the mirror up to Nature is deliberately said by Hamlet in order to convince the bystanders of his absolute insanity in all art-matters." Of *Hamlet*'s influence upon the ages Wilde remarked that: "The world has grown sad because a puppet was once melancholy." "Puppet" is Wilde's own deconstruction, a brilliant reminder that Shakespeare's artistry of illusion has so mastered reality as to have changed reality, evidently forever.

The analysis of character, as a critical pursuit, seems to me as much a Shakespearean invention as literary character was, since much of what we know about how to analyze character necessarily follows Shakespearean procedures. His hero-villains, from Richard III through Iago, Edmund, and Macbeth, are shrewd and endless questers into their own self-motivations. If we could bear to see Hamlet, in his unwearied negations, as another hero-villain, then we would judge him the supreme analyst of the darker recalcitrances in the selfhood. Freud followed the pre-Socratic Empedocles, in arguing that character is fate, a frightening doctrine that maintains the fear that there are no accidents, that overdetermination rules us all of our lives. Hamlet assumes the same, yet adds to this argument the terrible passivity he manifests in Act V. Throughout Shakespeare's tragedies, the most interesting personages seem doom-eager, reminding us again that a Shakespearean reading of Freud would be more illuminating than a Freudian exegesis of

Shakespeare. We learn more when we discover Hamlet in the Freudian Death Drive, than when we read *Beyond the Pleasure Principle* into *Hamlet*.

In Shakespearean comedy, character achieves its true literary apotheosis, which is the representation of the inner freedom that can be created by great wit alone. Rosalind and Falstaff, perhaps alone among Shakespeare's personages, match Hamlet in wit, though hardly in the metaphysics of consciousness. Whether in the comic or the modern mode, Shakespeare has set the standard of measurement in the balance between character and passion.

In Shakespeare the self is more dramatized than theatricalized, which is why a Shakespearean reading of Freud works out so well. Character-formation after the passing of the Oedipal stage takes the place of fetishistic fragmentings of the self. Critics who now call literary character into question, and who proclaim also the death of the author, invariably also regard all notions, literary and human, of a stable character as being mere reductions of deeper pre-Oedipal desires. It becomes clear that the fortunes of literary character rise and fall with the prestige of normative conceptions of the ego. Shakespeare's Iago, who wars against being, may be the first deconstructionist of the self, with his proclamation of "I am not what I am." This constitutes the necessary prologue to any view that would regard a fixed ego as a virtual abnormality. But deconstructions of the self are no more modern than Modernism is. Like literary modernism, the decentered ego came out of the Hellenistic culture of ancient Alexandria. The Gnostic heretics believed that the psyche, like the body, was a fallen entity, mechanically fashioned by the Demiurge or false creator. They held however that each of us possessed also a spark or pneuma, which was a fragment of the original Abyss or true, alien God. The soul or psyche within every one of us was thus at war with the self or pneuma, and only that sparklike self could be saved.

Shakespeare, following after Chaucer in this respect, was the first and remains still the greatest master of representing character both as a stable soul and a wavering self. There is a substance that endures in Shakespeare's figures, and there is also a quicksilver rendition of the unsettling sparks. Racine and Tolstoy, Balzac and Dickens, follow in Shakespeare's wake by giving us some sense of pre-Oedipal sparks or drives, and considerably more sense of post-Oedipal character and personality, stabilizations or sublimations of the fetish-seeking drives. Critics like Leo Bersani and René Girard argue eloquently against our taking this mimesis as the only proper work of literature. I would suggest that strong fictions of the self, from the Bible through Samuel Beckett, necessarily participate in both modes, the sublimation of desire, and the persistence of a primordial desire. The mystery of Hamlet or of Lear is intimately invested in the tangled mixture of the two modes of representation.

Psychic mobility is proposed by Bersani as the ideal to which deconstructions of the literary self may yet guide us. The ideal has its pathos, but the realities of literary representation seem to me very different, perhaps destructively so. When a novelist like D. H. Lawrence sought to reduce his characters to Eros and the Death Drive, he still had to persuade us of his authority at mimesis by lavishing upon the figures of *The Rainbow* and *Women in Love* all of the vivid stigmata of normative personality. Birkin and Ursula may represent antithetical and uncanny drives, but they develop and change as characters pondering their own pronouncements and reactions to self and others. The cost of a non-Shakespearean representation is enormous. Pynchon, in *The Crying of Lot 49* and *Gravity's Rainbow*, evades the burden of the normative by resorting to something like Christopher Marlowe's art of caricature in *The Jew of Malta*. Marlowe's Barabas is a marvelous rhetorician, yet he is a cartoon alongside the troublingly equivocal Shylock. Pynchon's personages are deliberate cartoons also, as flat as comic strips. Marlowe's achievement, and Pynchon's, are beyond dispute, yet they are like the prelude and the postlude to Shakespearean reality. They do not wish to engage with our hunger for the empirical world and so they enter the problematic cosmos of literary fantasy.

No writer, not even Shakespeare or Proust, alters the available stock that we agree to call reality, but Shakespeare, more than any other, does show us how much of reality we could encounter if only we retained adequate desire. The strong literary representation of character is already an analysis of character, and is part of the healing work of a literary culture, which implicitly seeks to cure violence through a normative mimesis of ego, *as if it were stable*, whether in actuality it is or is not. I do not believe that this is a social quest taken on by literary culture, but rather that we confront here the aesthetic essence of what makes a culture *literary*, rather than metaphysical or ethical or religious. A culture becomes literary when its conceptual modes have failed it, which means when religion, philosophy, and science have begun to lose their authority. If they cannot heal violence, then literature attempts to do so, which may be only a turning inside out of the critical arguments of Girard and Bersani.

I conclude by offering a particular instance or special case as a paradigm for the healing enterprise that is at once the representation and the analysis of literary character. Let us call it the aesthetics of being outraged, or rather of successfully representing the state of being outraged. W. C. Fields was one modern master of such representation, and Nathanael West was another, as was Faulkner before him. Here also the greatest master remains Shakespeare, whose Macbeth, himself a bloody outrage, yet retains our imaginative sympathy precisely because he grows increasingly outraged as he experiences the equivocation of the fiend that lies like truth. The double-natured promises and the prophecies of the weird sisters finally induce in Macbeth an apocalyptic version of the stage actor's anxiety at missing cues, the horror of a phantasmagoric stage fright of missing one's time, of always reacting too late. Macbeth, a veritable monster of solipsistic inwardness but no intellectual, counters his dilemma by fresh murders, that prolong him in time yet provoke him only to a perpetually freshened sense of being outraged, as all his expectations become still worse confounded. We are moved by Macbeth, however estrangedly, because his terrible inwardness is a paradigm for our own solipsism, but also because none of us can resist a strong and successful representation of the human in a state of being outraged.

The ultimate outrage is the necessity of dying, an outrage concealed in a multitude of masks, including the tyrannical ambitions of Macbeth. I suspect that our outrage at being outraged is the most difficult of all our affects for us to represent to ourselves, which is why we are so inclined to imaginative sympathy for a character who strongly conveys that affect to us. The Shrike of West's *Miss Lonelyhearts* or Faulkner's Joe Christmas of *Light in August* are crucial modern instances, but such figures can be located in many other works, since the ability to represent this extreme emotion is one of the tests that strong writers are driven to set for themselves.

However a reader seeks to reduce literary character to a question of marks on a page, she will come at last to the impasse constituted by the thought of death, her death, and before that to all the stations of being outraged that memorialize her own drive towards death. In reading, she quests for evidences that are strong representations, whether of her desire or her despair. Such questings constitute the necessary basis for the analysis of literary character, an enterprise that always will survive every vagary of critical fashion.

Editor's Note

My "Introduction" expounds Mary Shelley's relation to the Romantic mythology of self and double, after which Percy Bysshe Shelley, Mary's husband and sublime lyric poet, emphasizes the pathos of Frankenstein's created Being.

Robert Kiely contextualizes *Frankenstein* in the tradition of the Romantic novel, while the classic feminist interpretation is rendered by Sandra Gilbert and Susan Gubar, after David Ketterer's Oedipal analysis of the novel's plot.

In Laura Claridge's exegesis, Mary Shelley's own "family romance" (in Freud's sense) is dominant, a judgment akin to William Veeder's Freudian account of "projection."

To Barbara Frey Waxman, Mary Shelley's book recreates "the world of motherhood," after which Matthew Brennan meditates upon the novel's landscapes.

Iain Crawford explores crucial literary allusions by Mary Shelley, while Paul Cantor investigates her "taming" of a characteristic Byronic hero.

Mary Lowe-Evans allegorizes the Creature as Coleridge's Albatross in *The Ancient Mariner*, after which Ludmilla Jordanova reminds us that, in the era of the Shelleys, science and medicine were fused.

Natural philosophy, then a mode of "natural magic," is seen as Dr. Frankenstein's quest for divine power by Crosbie Smith, while Debra Best unveils the domestic matrix of the novel in the final essay of this volume.

HAROLD BLOOM

Introduction

> there is a fire
> And motion of the soul which will not dwell
> In its own narrow being, but aspire
> Beyond the fitting medium of desire.
> —BYRON. *Childe Harold's Pilgrimage*, canto 3
>
> Ere Babylon was dust,
> The Magus Zoroaster, my dead child,
> Met his own image walking in the garden.
> That apparition, sole of men, he saw.
> For know there are two worlds of life and death:
> One that which thou beholdest; but the other
> Is underneath the grave, where do inhabit
> The shadows of all forms that think and live
> Till death unite them and they part no more
> —SHELLEY. *Prometheus Unbound*, act 1

The motion-picture viewer who carries his obscure but still authentic taste for the sublime to the neighborhood theater, there to see the latest in an unending series of *Frankensteins*, becomes a sharer in a romantic terror now nearly one hundred and fifty years old. Mary Shelley, barely nineteen years of age when she wrote the original Frankenstein, was the daughter of two great intellectual rebels, William Godwin and Mary Wollstonecraft, and the second wife of Percy Bysshe Shelley, another great rebel and an unmatched lyrical poet. Had she written nothing, Mary Shelley would be remembered today. She is remembered in her own right as the author of a novel valuable in itself but also prophetic of an intellectual world to come, a novel depicting a Prometheanism that is with us still.

"Frankenstein," to most of us, is the name of a monster rather than of a monster's creator, for the common reader and the common viewer have worked together, in their apparent confusion, to create a myth soundly based on a central duality in Mary Shelley's novel. A critical discussion of *Frankenstein* needs to begin from an insight first recorded by Richard Church and Muriel Spark: the monster and his creator are the antithetical halves of a single being. Spark states the antithesis too cleanly; for her Victor Frankenstein represents the feelings, and his nameless creature the intellect. In her view the monster has no emotion, and "what passes for emotion ... are really intellectual passions arrived at through rational channels." Spark carries this argument far enough to insist that the monster is asexual and that he demands a bride from Frankenstein only for companionship, a conclusion evidently at variance with the novel's text.

The antithesis between the scientist and his creature in *Frankenstein* is a very complex one and can be described more fully in the larger context of Romantic literature and its characteristic mythology. The shadow or double of the self is a constant conceptual image in Blake and Shelley and a frequent image, more random and descriptive, in the other major Romantics, especially in Byron. In *Frankenstein* it is the dominant and recurrent image and accounts for much of the latent power the novel possesses.

Mary Shelley's husband was a divided being, as man and as poet, just as his friend Byron was, though in Shelley the split was more radical. *Frankenstein; or, The Modern Prometheus* is the full title of Mary Shelley's novel, and while Victor Frankenstein is *not* Shelley (Clerval is rather more like the poet), the Modern Prometheus is a very apt term for Shelley or for Byron. Prometheus is the mythic figure who best suits the uses of Romantic poetry, for no other traditional being has in him the full range of Romantic moral sensibility and the full Romantic capacity for creation and destruction.

No Romantic writer employed the Prometheus archetype without a full awareness of its equivocal potentialities. The Prometheus of the ancients had been for the most part a spiritually reprehensible figure, though frequently a sympathetic one, in terms both of his dramatic situation and in his close alliance with mankind against the gods. But this alliance had been ruinous for man in most versions of the myth, and the Titan's benevolence toward humanity was hardly sufficient recompense for the alienation of man from heaven that he had brought about. Both sides of Titanism are evident in earlier Christian references to the story. The same Prometheus who is taken as an analogue of the crucified Christ is regarded also as a type of Lucifer, a son of light justly cast, out by an offended heaven.

In the Romantic readings of Milton's *Paradise Lost* (and Frankenstein is implicitly one such reading) this double identity of Prometheus is a vital element. Blake, whose mythic revolutionary named Orc is another version of Prometheus, saw Milton's Satan as a Prometheus gone wrong, as desire restrained until it became only the shadow of desire, a diminished double of creative energy. Shelley went further in judging Milton's Satan as an imperfect Prometheus, inadequate because his mixture of heroic and base qualities engendered in the reader's mind a "pernicious casuistry" inimical to the spirit of art.

Blake, more systematic a poet than Shelley, worked out an antithesis between symbolic figures he named Spectre and Emanation, the shadow of desire and the total form of desire, respectively. A reader of *Frankenstein*, recalling the novel's extraordinary conclusion, with its scenes of obsessional pursuit through the Arctic wastes, can recognize the same imagery applied to a similar symbolic situation in Blake's lyric on the strife of Spectre and Emanation:

My Spectre around me night and day
Like a Wild beast guards my way.
My Emanation far within
Weeps incessantly for my Sin.

A Fathomless and boundless deep,
There we wander, there we weep;
On the hungry craving wind
My Spectre follows thee behind.

He scents thy footsteps in the snow,
Wheresoever thou dost go
Thro' the wintry hail and rain.

Frankenstein's monster, tempting his revengeful creator on through a world of ice, is another Emanation pursued by a Spectre, with the enormous difference that he is an Emanation flawed, a nightmare of actuality, rather than dream of desire. Though abhorred rather than loved, the monster is the total form of Frankenstein's creative power and is more imaginative than his creator. The monster is at once more intellectual and more emotional than his maker; indeed he excels Frankenstein as much (and in the same ways) as Milton's Adam excels Milton's God in *Paradise Lost*. The greatest paradox and most astonishing achievement of Mary Shelley's novel is that the monster is *more human* than his creator. This nameless being, as much a Modern Adam as his creator is a Modern Prometheus, is more lovable than his creator and more hateful, more to be pitied and more to be feared, and above all more able to give the attentive reader that shock of added consciousness in which aesthetic recognition compels a heightened realization of the self. For like Blake's Spectre and Emanation or Shelley's Alastor and Epipsyche, Frankenstein and his monster are the solipsistic and generous halves of the one self. Frankenstein is the mind and emotions turned in upon themselves, and his creature is the mind and emotions turned imaginatively outward, seeking a greater humanization through a confrontation of other selves.

I am suggesting that what makes *Frankenstein* an important book, though it is only a strong, flawed novel with frequent clumsiness in its narrative and characterization, is that it contains one of the most vivid versions we have of the Romantic mythology of the self, one that resembles Blake's *Book of Urizen*, Shelley's *Prometheus Unbound*, and Byron's *Manfred*, among other works. Because it lacks the sophistication and imaginative complexity of such works, *Frankenstein* affords a unique introduction to the archetypal world of the Romantics.

William Godwin, though a tendentious novelist, was a powerful one, and the prehistory of his daughter's novel begins with his best work of fiction, *Caleb Williams* (1794). Godwin summarized the climactic (and harrowing) final third of his novel as a pattern of flight and pursuit, "the fugitive in perpetual apprehension of being overwhelmed with the worst calamities, and the pursuer, by his ingenuity and resources, keeping his victim in a state of the most fearful alarm." Mary Shelley brilliantly reverses this pattern in the final sequence of her novel, and she takes from *Caleb Williams* also her destructive theme of the monster's war against "the whole machinery of human society," to quote the words of Caleb Williams while in prison. Muriel Spark argues that *Frankenstein* can be read as a reaction "against the rational-humanism of Godwin and Shelley," and she points to the equivocal preface that Shelley wrote to his wife's novel, in order to support this view. Certainly Shelley was worried lest the novel be taken as a warning against the inevitable moral consequences of an unchecked experimental Prometheanism and scientific materialism. The preface insists that:

> The opinions which naturally spring from the character and situation of the hero are by no means to be conceived as existing

always in my own conviction; nor is any inference justly to be drawn from the following pages as prejudicing any philosophical doctrine of whatever kind.

Shelley had, throughout his own work, a constant reaction against Godwin's rational humanism, but his reaction was systematically and consciously one of heart against head. In the same summer in the Swiss Alps that saw the conception of *Frankenstein*, Shelley composed two poems that lift the thematic conflict of the novel to the level of the true sublime. In the "Hymn to Intellectual Beauty" the poet's heart interprets an inconstant grace and loveliness, always just beyond the range of the human senses, as being the only beneficent force in life, and he prays to this force to be more constant in its attendance upon him and all mankind. In a greater sister-hymn, "Mont Blanc," an awesome meditation upon a frightening natural scene, the poet's head issues an allied but essentially contrary report. The force, or power, is there, behind or within the mountain, but its external workings upon us are either indifferent or malevolent, and this power is not to be prayed to. It can teach us, but what it teaches us is our own dangerous freedom from nature, the necessity for our will to become a significant part of materialistic necessity. Though "Mont Blanc" works its way to an almost heroic conclusion, it is also a poem of horror and reminds us that Frankenstein first confronts his conscious monster in the brooding presence of Mont Blanc, and to the restless music of one of Shelley's lyrics of Mutability.

In *Prometheus Unbound* the split between head and heart is not healed, but the heart is allowed dominance. The hero, Prometheus, like Frankenstein, has made a monster, but this monster is Jupiter, the God of all institutional and historical religions, including organized Christianity. Salvation from this conceptual error comes through love alone; but love in this poem, as elsewhere in Shelley, is always closely shadowed by ruin. Indeed, what choice spirits in Shelley perpetually encounter is ruin masquerading as love, pain presenting itself as pleasure. The tentative way out of this situation in Shelley's poetry is through the quest for a feeling mind and an understanding heart, which is symbolized by the sexual reunion of Prometheus and his Emanation, Asia. Frederick A. Pottle sums up *Prometheus Unbound* by observing its meaning to be that "the head must sincerely forgive, must willingly eschew hatred on purely experimental grounds," while "the affections must exorcize the demons of infancy, whether personal or of the race." In the light cast by these profound and precise summations, the reader can better understand both Shelley's lyrical drama and his wife's narrative of the Modern Prometheus.

There are two paradoxes at the center of Mary Shelley's novel, and each illuminates a dilemma of the Promethean imagination. The first is that Frankenstein *was* successful, in that he did create Natural Man, not as he was, but as the meliorists saw such a man; indeed, Frankenstein did better than this, since his creature was, as we have seen, more imaginative than himself. Frankenstein's tragedy stems not from his Promethean excess but from his own moral error, his failure to love; he *abhorred his creature*, became terrified, and fled his responsibilities.

The second paradox is the more ironic. This either would not have happened or would not have mattered anyway, if Frankenstein had been an aesthetically successful maker; a beautiful "monster," or even a passable one, would not have been a monster. As the creature bitterly observes in chapter 17,

> Shall I respect man when he condemns me? Let him live with me in the interchange of kindness, and instead of injury I would bestow every benefit upon him with tears of gratitude at his acceptance. But that cannot be; the human senses are insurmountable barriers to our union.

As the hideousness of his creature was no part of Victor Frankenstein's intention, it is worth noticing how this disastrous matter came to be.

It would not be unjust to characterize Victor Frankenstein, in his act of creation, as being momentarily a moral idiot, like so many who have done his work after him. There is an indeliberate humor in the contrast between the enormity of the scientist's discovery and the mundane emotions of the discoverer. Finding that "the minuteness of the parts" slows him down, he resolves to make his creature "about eight feet in height and proportionably large." As he works on, he allows himself to dream that "a new species would bless me as its creator and source; many happy and excellent natures would owe their being to me." Yet he knows his is a "workshop of filthy creation," and he fails the fundamental test of his own creativity. When the "dull yellow eye" of his creature opens, this creator falls from the autonomy of a supreme artificer to the terror of a child of earth: "breathless horror and disgust filled my heart." He flees his responsibility and sets in motion the events that will lead to his own Arctic immolation, a fit end for a being who has never achieved a full sense of another's existence.

Haunting Mary Shelley's novel is the demonic figure of the Ancient Mariner, Coleridge's major venture into Romantic mythology of the purgatorial self trapped in the isolation of a heightened self-consciousness. Walton, in Letter 2 introducing the novel, compares himself "to that production of the most imaginative of modern poets." As a seeker-out of an unknown passage, Walton is himself a Promethean quester, like Frankenstein, toward whom he is so compellingly drawn. Coleridge's Mariner is of the line of Cain, and the irony of Frankenstein's fate is that he too is a Cain, involuntarily murdering all his loved ones through the agency of his creature. The Ancient Mariner is punished by living under the curse of his consciousness of guilt, while the excruciating torment of Frankenstein is never to be able to forget his guilt in creating a lonely consciousness driven to crime by the rage of unwilling solitude.

It is part of Mary Shelley's insight into her mythological theme that all the monster's victims are innocents. The monster not only refuses actively to slay his guilty creator, he mourns for him, though with the equivocal tribute of terming the scientist a "generous and self-devoted being." Frankenstein, the modern Prometheus who has violated nature, receives his epitaph from the ruined second nature he has made, the God-abandoned, who consciously echoes the ruined Satan of *Paradise Lost* and proclaims, "Evil thenceforth became my good." It is imaginatively fitting that the greater and more interesting consciousness of the creature should survive his creator, for he alone in Mary Shelley's novel possesses character. Frankenstein, like Coleridge's Mariner, has no character in his own right; both figures win a claim to our attention only by their primordial crimes against original nature.

The monster is of course Mary Shelley's finest invention, and his narrative (chaps. 11–16) forms the highest achievement of the novel, more absorbing even than the magnificent and almost surrealistic pursuit of the climax. In an age so given to remarkable depictions of the dignity of natural man, an age including the shepherds and beggars of Wordsworth and what W. J. Bate has termed Keats's "polar ideal of disinterestedness"—even in such a literary time Frankenstein's hapless creature stands out as a sublime embodiment of heroic pathos. Though Frankenstein lacks the moral imagination to understand him, the daemon's appeal is to what is most compassionate in us:

Oh, Frankenstein, be not equitable to every other, and trample upon me alone, to whom thy justice, and even thy clemency and affection, is most due. Remember that I am thy creature; *I ought to be thy Adam, but I am rather the fallen angel, whom thou drivest from joy for no misdeed.* Everywhere I see bliss, from which I alone am irrevocably excluded. I was benevolent and good; misery made me a fiend. Make me happy, and I shall again be virtuous.

The passage I have italicized is the imaginative kernel of the novel and is meant to remind the reader of the novel's epigraph:

Did I request thee, Maker, from my clay
To mold me man? Did I solicit thee
From darkness to promote me?

That desperate plangency of the fallen Adam becomes the characteristic accent of the daemon's lamentations, with the influence of Milton cunningly built into the novel's narrative by the happy device of Frankenstein's creature receiving his education through reading *Paradise Lost* as "a true history." Already doomed because his standards are human, which makes him an outcast even to himself, his Miltonic education completes his fatal growth in self-consciousness. His story, as told to his maker, follows a familiar Romantic pattern "of the progress of my intellect," as he puts it. His first pleasure after the dawn of consciousness comes through his wonder at seeing the moon rise. Caliban-like, he responds wonderfully to music, both natural and human, and his sensitivity to the natural world has the responsiveness of an incipient poet. His awakening to a first love for other beings, the inmates of the cottage he haunts, awakens him also to the great desolation of love rejected when he attempts to reveal himself. His own duality of situation and character, caught between the states of Adam and Satan, Natural Man and his thwarted desire, is related by him directly to his reading of Milton's epic:

It moved every feeling of wonder and awe that the picture of an omnipotent God warring with his creatures was capable of exciting. I often referred the several situations, as their similarity struck me, to my own. Like Adam, I was apparently united by no link to any other being in existence, but his state was far different from mine in every other respect. He had come forth from the hands of God a perfect creature, happy and prosperous, guarded by the especial care of his Creator; he was allowed to converse with and acquire knowledge from beings of a superior nature; but I was wretched, helpless, and alone. Many times I considered Satan as the fitter emblem of my condition, for often, like him, when I viewed the bliss of my protectors, the bitter gall of envy rose within me.

From a despair this profound, no release is possible. Driven forth into an existence upon which "the cold stars shone in mockery," the daemon declares "everlasting war against the species" and enters upon a fallen existence more terrible than the expelled Adam's. Echoing Milton, he asks the ironic question "And now, with the world before me, whither should I bend my steps?" to which the only possible answer is, toward his wretched Promethean creator.

If we stand back from Mary Shelley's novel in order better to view its archetypal shape, we see it as the quest of a solitary and ravaged consciousness first for consolation, then for revenge, and finally for a self-destruction that will be apocalyptic, that will bring down the creator with his creature. Though Mary Shelley may not have intended it, her novel's prime theme is a necessary counterpoise to Prometheanism, for Prometheanism exalts the increase in consciousness despite all cost. Frankenstein breaks through the barrier that separates man from God and gives apparent life, but in doing so he gives only death-in-life. The profound dejection endemic in Mary Shelley's novel is fundamental to the Romantic mythology of the self, for all Romantic horrors are diseases of excessive consciousness, of the self unable to bear the self. Kierkegaard remarks that Satan's despair is absolute because Satan, as pure spirit, is pure consciousness, and for Satan (and all men in his predicament) every increase in consciousness is an increase in despair. Frankenstein's desperate creature attains the state of pure spirit through his extraordinary situation and is racked by a consciousness in which every thought is a fresh disease.

A Romantic poet fought against self-consciousness through the strength of what he called imagination, a more than rational energy by which thought could seek to heal itself. But Frankenstein's daemon, though he is in the archetypal situation of the Romantic Wanderer or Solitary, who sometimes was a poet, can win no release from his own story by telling it. His desperate desire for a mate is clearly an attempt to find a Shelleyan Epipsyche or Blakean Emanation for himself, a self within the self. But as he is the nightmare actualization of Frankenstein's desire, he is himself an emanation of Promethean yearnings, and his only double is his creator and denier.

When Coleridge's Ancient Mariner progressed from the purgatory of consciousness to his very minimal control of imagination, he failed to save himself, since he remained in a cycle of remorse, but he at least became a salutary warning to others and made of the Wedding Guest a wiser and a better man. Frankenstein's creature can help neither himself nor others, for he has no natural ground to which he can return. Romantic poets liked to return to the imagery of the ocean of life and immortality, for in the eddying to and fro of the healing waters they could picture a hoped-for process of restoration, of a survival of consciousness despite all its agonies. Mary Shelley, with marvelous appropriateness, brings her Romantic novel to a demonic conclusion in a world of ice. The frozen sea is the inevitable emblem for both the wretched daemon and his obsessed creator, but the daemon is allowed a final image of reversed Prometheanism. There is a heroism fully earned in the being who cries farewell in a claim of sad triumph: "I shall ascend my funeral pile triumphantly and exult in the agony of the torturing flames." Mary Shelley could not have known how dark a prophecy this consummation of consciousness would prove to be for the two great Promethean poets who were at her side during the summer of 1816, when her novel was conceived. Byron, writing his own epitaph at Missolonghi in 1824, and perhaps thinking back to having stood at Shelley's funeral pile two years before, found an image similar to the daemon's to sum up an exhausted existence:

> The fire that on my bosom preys
>   Is lone as some volcanic isle;
> No torch is kindled at its blaze—
>   A funeral pile.

The fire of increased consciousness stolen from heaven ends as an isolated volcano cut off from other selves by an estranging sea. "The light of that conflagration will fade away; my ashes will be swept into the sea by the winds" is the exultant cry of Frankenstein's. creature. A blaze at which no torch is kindled is Byron's self-image, but he ends his death poem on another note, the hope for a soldier's grave, which he found. There is no Promethean release, but release is perhaps not the burden of the literature of Romantic aspiration. There is something both Godwinian and Shelleyan about the final utterance of Victor Frankenstein, which is properly made to Walton, the failed Promethean whose ship has just turned back. Though chastened, the Modern Prometheus ends with a last word true, not to his accomplishment, but to his desire:

> Farewell, Walton! Seek happiness in tranquillity and avoid ambition, even if it be only the apparently innocent one of distinguishing yourself in science and discoveries. Yet why do I say this? I have myself been blasted in these hopes, yet another may succeed.

Shelley's Prometheus, crucified on his icy precipice, found his ultimate torment in a Fury's taunt: "And all best things are thus confused to ill." It seems a fitting summation for all the work done by modern Prometheanism and might have served as an alternate epigraph for Mary Shelley's disturbing novel.

PERCY BYSSHE SHELLEY

On Frankenstein*

The novel of 'Frankenstein; or, the Modern Prometheus,' is undoubtedly, as a mere story, one of the most original and complete productions of the day. We debate with ourselves in wonder, as we read it, what could have been the series of thoughts—what could have been the peculiar experiences that awakened them—which conduced, in the author's mind, to the astonishing combinations of motives and incidents, and the startling catastrophe, which compose this tale. There are, perhaps, some points of subordinate importance, which prove that it is the author's first attempt. But in this judgment, which requires a very nice discrimination, we may be mistaken; for it is conducted throughout with a firm and steady hand. The interest gradually, accumulates and advances towards the conclusion with the accelerated rapidity of a rock rolled down a mountain. We are led breathless with suspense and sympathy, and the heaping up of incident on incident, and the working of passion out of passion. We cry "hold, hold! enough!"—but there is yet something to come; and, like the victim whose history it relates, we think we can bear no more, and yet more is to be borne. Pelion is heaped on Ossa, and Ossa on Olympus. We climb Alp after Alp, until the horizon is seen blank, vacant, and limitless; and the head turns giddy, and the ground seems to fail under our feet.

This novel rests its claim on being a source of powerful and profound

From *Frankenstein: The 1818 Text Contexts, Nineteenth-Century Responses, Modern Criticism* (A Norton Critical Edition). © 1996 by W.W. Norton & Company, Inc.

emotion. The elementary feelings of the human mind are exposed to view; and those who are accustomed to reason deeply on their origin and tendency will, perhaps, be the only persons who can sympathize, to the full extent, in the interest of the actions which are their result. But, founded on nature as they are, there is perhaps no reader who can endure anything beside a new love story, who will not feel a responsive string touched in his inmost soul. The sentiments are so affectionate and so innocent—the characters of the subordinate agents in this strange drama are clothed in the light of such a mild and gentle mind—the pictures of domestic manners are of the most simple and attaching character: the father's is irresistible and deep. Nor are the crimes and malevolence of the single Being, though indeed withering and tremendous, the offspring of any unaccountable propensity to evil, but flow irresistibly from certain causes fully adequate to their production. They are the children, as it were, of Necessity and Human Nature. In this the direct moral of the book consists; and it is perhaps the most important, and of the most universal application, of any moral that can be enforced by example. Treat a person ill, and he will become wicked. Requite affection with scorn;—let one being be selected, for whatever cause, as the refuse of his kind—divide him, a social being, from society, and you impose upon him the irresistible obligations—malevolence and selfishness. It is thus that, too often in society, those who are best qualified to be its benefactors and its ornaments, are branded by some accident with scorn, and changed, by neglect and solitude of heart, into a scourge and a curse.

The Being in 'Frankenstein' is, no doubt, a tremendous creature. It was impossible that he should not have received among men that treatment which led to the consequences of his being a social nature. He was an abortion and an anomaly; and though his mind was such as its first impressions framed it, affectionate and full of moral sensibility, yet the circumstances of his existence are so monstrous and uncommon, that, when the consequences of them became developed in action, his original goodness was gradually turned into inextinguishable misanthropy and revenge. The scene between the Being and the blind De Lacey in the cottage, is one of the most profound and extraordinary instances of pathos that we ever recollect. It is impossible to read this dialogue,—and indeed many others of a somewhat similar character,—without feeling the heart suspend its pulsations with wonder, and the "tears stream down the cheeks." The encounter and argument between Frankenstein and the Being on the sea of ice, almost approaches, in effect, to the expostulations of Caleb Williams with Falkland. It reminds us, indeed, somewhat of the style and character of that admirable writer, to whom the author has dedicated his work, and whose productions he seems to have studied.

There is only one instance, however, in which we detect the least approach to imitation; and that is the conduct of the incident of Frankenstein's landing in Ireland. The general character of the tale, indeed, resembles nothing that ever preceded it. After the death of Elizabeth, the story, like a stream which grows at once more rapid and profound as it proceeds, assumes an irresistible solemnity, and the magnificent energy and swiftness of a tempest.

The churchyard scene, in which Frankenstein visits the tombs of his family, his quitting Geneva, and his journey through Tartary to the shores of the Frozen Ocean, resemble at once the terrible reanimation of a corpse and the supernatural career of a spirit. The scene in the cabin of Walton's ship—the more than mortal enthusiasm and grandeur of the Being's speech over the dead body of his victim—is an exhibition of intellectual and imaginative power, which we think the reader will acknowledge has seldom been surpassed.

NOTE

*Written in 1817; published (posthumously) in *The Athenaeum Journal of Literature, Science and the Fine Arts*, Nov. 10, 1832.

ROBERT KIELY

Frankenstein

MARY WOLLSTONECRAFT SHELLEY
1818

It is something of a miracle that *Frankenstein*, originally published in 1818, has survived its admirers and critics. Although Scott had admired the Germanic flavor of *The Monk*, he praised the author of *Frankenstein* for writing in "plain and forcible English, without exhibiting that mixture of hyperbolical Germanisms with which tales of wonder are usually told."[1] On the other hand, Beckford, who had little use for earnest horror, noted on the flyleaf of his first edition copy of *Frankenstein*: "This is, perhaps, the foulest Toadstool that has yet sprung up from the reeking dunghill of the present times."[2]

Opinion about *Frankenstein* was strong from the beginning, but no critical thinking on the subject was more elaborate and self-conscious than that of Mary Shelley herself. The genesis of this novel was—even for a work of romantic fiction—uncommonly bookish and artificial. It was supposedly begun as part of a literary contest among Shelley, Mary, Byron, and Polidori to write a ghost story in a vein popular in Germany and France.[3] During the first year of her marriage to Shelley, Mary had set herself a formidable and exotic reading assignment which included *Clarissa*, *The Sorrows of Young Werter*, *Lara*, *The Arabian Nights*, *Wieland*, *St. Leon*, *La Nouvelle Héloïse*,

From *The Romantic Novel in England*. © 1972 by the President and Fellows of Harvard College.

Vathek, Waverley, The Mysteries of Udolpho, The Italian, The Monk, and *Edgar Huntley.*[4] She repeatedly acknowledged the influence of Milton and Coleridge during this period of her life and, of course, Godwin and Shelley were major forces in shaping her mind.

Frankenstein seems a little book to have borne up under such a mixed and mighty company of sponsors, midwives, and ancestors. Mary Shelley did not set out, like her father, to write a philosophical novel, yet her most famous work, written at Shelley's suggestion and dedicated to Godwin, is, to a large extent, an expression of her reaction to the philosophy and character of these two men. In places the narrative seems chiefly to provide the occasion for Mary to write a tribute to her father's idealism and a love poem to her husband. The hero of her novel, the young Genevese student of natural science, is a magnetic character, described by one admiring friend as possessing attributes which seem almost divine:

> Sometimes I have endeavoured to discover what quality it is which he possesses that elevates him so immeasurably above any other person I ever knew. I believe it to be an intuitive discernment; a quick but never-failing power of judgment; a penetration into the causes of things, unequalled for clearness and precision; add to this a facility of expression, and a voice whose varied intonations are soul-subduing music.[5]

Yet despite such expressions of love and veneration for the nobility of Frankenstein, Mary expresses through her characters certain reservations about him which have led some readers to interpret the novel as an unconscious repudiation of Shelley. As M. K. Joseph puts it, "With unassuming originality, [Mary's] 'modern Prometheus' challenges the whole myth of Romantic titanism, of Shelley's neo-Platonic apocalypse in *Prometheus Unbound,* and of the artist as Promethean creator."[6] Frankenstein is brilliant, passionate, sensitive, and capable of arousing feelings of profound sympathy in others, yet he is the creator of a monster which causes great suffering and finally destroys his maker. Signs of impatience and outright disgust with the obsessive ambitions of the hero are certainly present in the narrative.

Still, Frankenstein remains the hero throughout; he is the "divine wanderer," his face lighted up by "a beam of benevolence and sweetness," his spirit enlivened by a "supernatural enthusiasm." He is compared not with Faustus but with Prometheus in his desire to grasp "the secrets of heaven and earth." No one suffers more than he from his failure, and, indeed, there is a strong hint that the fault is more nature's than his that his godlike ambitions result in a monstrosity. For Mary, as for Shelley, nature's imperfect character only confirmed a belief in the superiority of mind over matter. After her husband's death, Mary referred to him as a "spirit caged, an elemental being, enshrined in a frail image,"[7] and confessed her reverence for the artist who would rather destroy his health than accept the limitations imposed by the body, whose "delicately attuned [mind] shatters the material frame, and whose thoughts are strong enough to throw down and dilapidate the walls of sense and dikes of flesh that the unimaginative contrive to keep in such good repair."[8]

In her novel *The Last Man*, published eight years after *Frankenstein*, Mary's narrator takes it as a universal truth "that man's mind alone was the creator of all that was good or great to man, and that Nature herself was only his first minister."[9] And in that same novel there is a character named Adrian, even more obviously patterned after Shelley than is Frankenstein, whose "slight frame was overinformed by the soul that dwelt within."[10] The fact that he is "all mind" does eventually make him behave strangely, but the implication is that the fault is the world's or society's, not his.

Applying the same logic to Frankenstein's attempt to manufacture a man, one might argue that the structural faultiness, the grotesqueness of the result, is another example of nature's failure to live up to man's expectations. Even the fact that the monster becomes a murderer and brings about the destruction of his master does not necessarily detract from the grandeur of Frankenstein's dreams. If he has not been able to create human life, he has been able to create a sublime facsimile. To some, a destructive force was still better than no force at all and the creation of a new menace better than a copy of a worn-out consolation. The Shelleys, like their friends Byron and M. G. Lewis, were fascinated by the correspondence between the terrifying and the magnificent, the proximity of ruinous and constructive forces at the highest levels of experience. "Nothing should shake the truly great spirit which is not sufficiently mighty to destroy it," said Shelley in reference to the personal relationships of geniuses.[11] The risk of calamity becomes the measure of all endeavor, and a great catastrophe is preferable to a small success. Viewed in this way the catastrophic abomination represented by Frankenstein's creature is not proof of its creator's folly, but an inverse indication of his potential greatness.

Potentiality is a key concept in the delineation of Frankenstein's character because, like so many romantic heroes, much of his allure derives from what he might have been, what he almost was, rather than from what he is. "What a glorious creature must he have been in the days of his prosperity," says his friend Walton, "when he is thus noble and godlike in ruin! He seems to feel his own worth and the greatness of his fall." The days of Frankenstein's prosperity do not occupy much of the narrative, but it is nonetheless clear that Walton is not altogether right. Though a good and gifted person before his "ruin," it is really afterward, by means of the uniqueness and depth of his suffering, that Frankenstein achieves superiority over her men. Having made a botch of his experiment, he may fail to impress any but the most loyal advocates in the days of his prosperity. But where actual achievement falters, the guilty and disappointed spirit can sketch the dimensions of its unfulfilled intention by describing the magnitude of its torment. We are reminded of Macaulay's remark about Byron: "He continued to repeat that to be wretched is the destiny of all; that to be eminently wretched, is the destiny of the eminent."[12]

2

Superiority through suffering is a major theme of Mary Shelley's novel, a romantic half-tragedy in which the fall from greatness is nearly all fall or, more accurately, where greatness is defined in terms of the personal pain which results from the consciousness of loss which cannot be recalled or comprehended by other men. In unique regret, Frankenstein discovers his true distinction: "I was seized by remorse and the sense of guilt which hurried me away to a hell of intense tortures, such as no language can describe." The failure of language, as always in romantic fiction, is meant to be a sign not of vacuity or of an imaginative limitation of the character or author, but of the singular noncommunicable nature of great experience.

It is unfortunate (though psychologically fitting) that in the popular mind the monster has assumed the name of his creator, because Mary Shelley considered it of some importance that the creature remain unnamed. As Elizabeth Nitchie points out, it was the custom in dramatic performances of *Frankenstein* to represent the monster's part on the playbill with "____." On first remarking this, Mary Shelley was pleased: "This nameless mode of naming the unnameable is rather good."[13] If the phenomenon itself cannot be named, neither can the feelings it evokes in its maker. No one can know what it is like to be the monster or its "parent."

What cannot be described cannot be imitated, and the pain it causes cannot be relieved. The following lines are Frankenstein's, but they might as easily have been spoken by the creature as by its creator:

> "Not the tenderness of friendship, nor the beauty of earth, nor of heaven, could redeem my soul from woe: the very accents of love were ineffectual. I was encompassed by a cloud which no beneficial influence could penetrate. The wounded deer dragging

its fainting limbs to some untrodden brake, there to gaze upon the arrow which had pierced it, and to die—was but a type of me."

"Gazing upon the arrow" can be a fairly protracted occupation even when no use is expected to come of it. Mary Shelley spends a great part of her narrative confronting her hero with images which evoke the sublimity of his mental state where ordinary words fail. Frankenstein journeys to Chamonix, where the mountain views elevate him from all "littleness of feeling" and "subdue and tranquilize" his grief though they cannot remove it. Mont Blanc provides him with a moment of "something like joy," but the Alps, though briefly impressive, are not in the end any more able than words to express or alleviate what Frankenstein feels. Trips up the Rhine, across the sea, even into the Arctic, hint at his unrest, but "imperial Nature," in all her "awful majesty," can no more provide truly adequate images of his misery than she can provide the fulfillment of his ambitious dreams.

At the end of the narrative, Frankenstein accuses himself of overreaching, but even in doing this, he immodestly compares himself with the prince of overreachers: "Like the archangel who aspired to omnipotence, I am chained in an eternal hell." Rather than looking back on his ambition with disgust, he remembers it with pleasure: "Even now I cannot recollect without passion my reveries while the work was incomplete. I trod heaven in my thoughts, now exulting in my powers, now burning with the idea of their effects." Despite the conventional speeches about the dangers of pride, it becomes more and more evident in the last pages of the novel that Frankenstein, though regretting the *result* of his extraordinary efforts, is not ashamed of having made the effort in the first place. He repeatedly warns Walton, who is engaged in an expedition into the Polar Sea, to content himself with modest ambitions and a quiet life, but when Walton's men threaten to turn the ship back, the dying Frankenstein rallies to urge them on:

"Did you not call this a glorious expedition? And wherefore was it glorious? Not because the way was smooth and placid as a southern sea, but because it was full of dangers and terror ... You were hereafter to be hailed as the benefactors of your species; your names adored as belonging to brave men who encountered death for honor and the benefit of mankind."

In his last breath, he begins to warn Walton once more not to make the same mistake he did, but then changes his mind:

"Seek happiness in tranquility and avoid ambition, even if it be only the apparently innocent one of distinguishing yourself in science and discoveries. Yet why do I say this? I have myself been blasted in these hopes, but another may succeed."

That Frankenstein does not die absolutely repentant once again raises the possibility that the monstrous result of his experiment was not the inevitable issue of pride but an accident of circumstance, the result of insufficient knowledge, or an imperfection in nature itself. If one wishes to accept Walton's reverent appraisal of his new friend, it can be said that Frankenstein has the immunity of all scientific and artistic genius from conventional morality, that he is somehow apart from and superior to material circumstances even when he himself seems to have brought them about. Just as Mary saw Shelley "caged" in a "frail image" and surrounded by misfortunes from which his superiority of mind detached and elevated him, so Walton sees Frankenstein as a man with a "double existence." "He may suffer misery and be overwhelmed by disappointments; yet, when he has retired into himself, he will be like a celestial spirit that has a halo around him, within whose circle no grief or folly ventures."

3

Mary learned her lessons in idealism well, and there is in her narrative a level on which her hero is above reproach. But it must be admitted that here is a mundane side to this fantastic tale. If genius can escape or withdraw from the material universe, ordinary mortals cannot. And however great their admiration for genius may be, they cannot fully separate it from the lesser objects of their perception.

Mary Shelley was a young and impetuous woman when she ran off with the poet; she was also an intelligent woman, but her journals and letters reveal that despite her efforts to form herself after her husband's image, common sense often intruded and made the task difficult. She was never intellectually disloyal to Shelley, yet she admitted that her mind could not follow his to the heights. Her novel, like almost everything else about her life, is an instance of genius observed and admired but not shared. In making her hero the creator of a monster, she does not necessarily mock idealistic ambition, but in making that monster a poor grotesque patchwork, a physical mess of seams and wrinkles, she introduces a consideration of the material universe which challenges and undermines the purity of ideal. In short, the sheer concreteness of the ugly thing which Frankenstein has created often makes his ambitions and his character—however sympathetically described—seem ridiculous and even insane. The arguments on behalf of idealism and unworldly genius are seriously presented, but the controlling perspective is that of an earthbound woman.

In making her hero a scientist rather than a poet or philosopher, Mary could hardly have avoided treating the material consequences of his theoretical projects. But, in almost all important respects, Frankenstein's scientific ambitions are at the level where they coincide with the highest desires of artists and metaphysicians, to investigate the deepest mysteries of life, to determine causes and first principles. The early descriptions of Frankenstein's youthful dreams are filled, like more recent forms of "science fiction," with outlandish schemes which combine the highest fancies of the imagination with an elaborate application of technical ingenuity. Though Frankenstein himself scorns the notion, his "scientific" method has a large dose of hocus-pocus in it and comes a good deal closer to alchemy than it does to physiology. The professor whom he most admires disclaims the inflated schemes of ancient pseudo-scientists, but then proceeds to claim for modern scientists the godlike ambitions previously invoked by poets and prophets:

> "Modern masters promise very little; they know that metals cannot be transmuted, and that the elixir of life is a chimera. But these philosophers, whose hands seem only to dabble in dirt, and their eyes to pore over the microscope or crucible, have indeed performed miracles. They penetrate into the recesses of nature, and show how she works in her hiding places. They ascend into the heavens ... They have acquired new and almost unlimited powers; they can command the thunders of heaven, mimic the earthquake, and even mock the invisible world with its own shadows."

The passage sounds like an answer to the Lord's questions about knowledge and power in the Book of Job. The obvious echoes of Biblical language show, among other things, that science is making religion (or, more particularly, the fear of God) obsolete. But, beyond this, the speech might be passed over as a conventional piece of hyperbole if Mary did not undercut it sharply by proceeding to show her hero trying literally to put his professor's words into practice by penetrating the "recesses of nature." Frankenstein digging about ran graveyards and charnel houses, matching eyeballs and sawing bones, is not an inspiring sight. Even less so is the bungled construct of muscles, arteries, and shriveled skin which he had intended as a perfectly proportioned and beautiful being. The gap between the ideal and the real, the ambition and the accomplishment, produces a result as gruesome and absurd as any pseudo-science of the Middle Ages. Still, Mary is not criticizing exalted ambition, but the misapplication of it, the consequence of what Frankenstein himself describes as "unrelaxed and breathless eagerness," a "frantic impulse," a trance-like pursuit of one idea. Through the mouth of her hero, she raises a question which in life she could probably never bring herself to ask her husband: "Is genius forever separate from the reasonable, the reflective, and the probable?"

The question is, one which troubled a great many romantic artists and critics. Hazlitt, for one, did not accept such a division as inevitable, and he criticized Shelley in words which parallel almost exactly Frankenstein's own terms of self-criticism after the failure of his experiment:

> Shelley's style is to poetry what astrology is to natural science—a passionate dream, a striving after impossibilities, a record of fond conjectures, a confused embodying of vague abstractions—a fever of the soul, thirsting and craving over what it cannot have, indulging its love of power and novelty at the expense of truth and nature, associating ideas by contraries, and wasting great powers by their application to unattainable objects.[14]

Hazlitt's impatience with Shelley, as expressed in the opening analogy, is based, to a large degree, on the poet's departure from the natural. Shelley himself was deeply aware of the problem, and *Alastor, or the Spirit of Solitude*, was, in part, a criticism of the pursuit of truth under unnatural conditions of isolation. The poet's invocation to Mother Nature could have been spoken by Frankenstein during the research which led to the creation of the monster:

> ... I have made my bed
> In charnels and on coffins, where black Death
> Keeps record of the trophies won from thee;
> Hoping to still these obstinate questionings
> Of thee and thine by forcing some lone ghost,
> Thy messenger to render up the tale
> Of what we are. In lone and silent hours,
> When night makes a weird sound of its own stillness,
> Like an inspired and desperate alchemist
> Staking his very life on some dark hope,
> Have I mixed awful talk and asking looks
> With my most innocent love; until strange tears,
> Uniting with those breathless kisses, made

Such magic as compels the charméd night
To render up thy charge.

The passage describes a kind of necrophilia, an unnatural probing into the secrets of nature; and yet, despite his disapproving moral, the poet appears to luxuriate in the contemplation of the forbidden and fruitless act. It is, after all, the poet-narrator, not Alastor, who is speaking in this passage. As the image of the "inspired and desperate alchemist" suggests, the question remains as to whether a poet of sufficient genius can transform inert and unlikely objects into "gold"; or, to extend the sexual metaphor of the lines, whether the intercourse of mind with dead matter can produce new and vital images of nature. Shelley seems to be reasoning in the negative and rhyming in the affirmative. He argues in the preface to *Alastor*, that no truly great human effort can succeed if it is removed from the nourishing warmth of "human sympathy." Yet neither his poetry nor his life provides consoling solutions to the solitude genius so often creates for itself. Even an early and, for Shelley, relatively simple definition of love must have given Mary uneasy moments.

> Love ... is ... the universal thirst for a communion not merely of the senses, but of our whole nature, intellectual, imaginative, and sensitive; and which, when individualized, becomes an imperious necessity ... The sexual impulse, which is only one, and often a small party of (its) claims, serves, from its obvious and external nature, as a kind of type or expression of the rest, a common basis, an acknowledged and visible link.[15]

It is not the kind of statement D. H. Lawrence would have admired, nor can its Platonism have been altogether comforting to a companion for whom the "visible link" of sex was the one claim not rivaled by Byron, Peacock, Hogg, Hunt, or Trelawny.

4

In describing the way in which Frankenstein's experiment seems most "unnatural," Mary Shelley implies a definition of the natural which is peculiarly feminine in bias. For her, Frankenstein's presumption is not in his attempt to usurp the power of the gods—she quite willingly grants him his "divine" attributes—but in his attempt to usurp the power of women. "A new species would bless me as its creator and source," says Frankenstein in the enthusiasm of his first experiments. "No father could claim the gratitude of his child so completely as I should deserve theirs." He seeks to combine the role of both parents in one, to eliminate the need for woman in the creative act, to make sex unnecessary. At least that would be the net result of his experiment if it were successful, despite the fact that he himself tends to see its consequences in grander and vaguer terms. Thus, while Mary grants her hero the nobility and even the innocence of his intentions, she cannot help but undercut them with her own womanly sense of how things are.

Stripped of rhetoric and ideological decoration, the situation presented is that of a handsome young scientist, engaged to a beautiful woman, who goes off to the mountains alone to create a new human life. When he confesses to Walton that he has "worked hard for nearly two years" to achieve his aim, we may wonder why he does not marry Elizabeth and, with her cooperation, finish the job more quickly and pleasurably. But one must be careful not to imply that Mary's irony is flippant or altogether conscious. Quite to the contrary, her reservations about her hero's presumptuous idealism are so deeply and seriously felt that they produce a symbolic nightmare far more disturbing and gruesome than the monster itself. As soon as the creature begins to show animation and Frankenstein realizes that he has made an abomination, the scientist races to his bedroom, paces feverishly about, and finally falls into a troubled sleep:

> "I slept indeed, but I was disturbed by the wildest dreams. I thought I saw Elizabeth, in the bloom of health, walking in the streets of Ingolstadt. Delighted and surprised, I embraced her; but as I imprinted the first kiss on her lips, they became livid with the hue of death; her features appeared to change, and I thought that I beheld the corpse of my dead mother in my arms; a shroud enveloped her form, and I saw the grave-worms crawling in the folds of the flannel. I started from my sleep with horror ... (and) beheld the wretch—the miserable monster whom I had, created."

In this extraordinary rendition of an Oedipal nightmare, Mary shows, without moral comment, the regressive depths of her hero's mind. Frankenstein's crime against nature is a crime against womanhood, an attempt—however unconscious—to circumvent mature sex. For Mary, this is the supreme symbol of egotism, the ultimate turning away from human society and into the self which must result in desolation. Having moved away from family, friends, and fiancée to perform his "creative" act in isolation, Frankenstein later beholds the monster, in a grotesquely exaggerated reenactment of his own behavior, "eliminate" his younger brother, his dearest friend, and his beloved Elizabeth.

All the crimes are sins against life in the bloom of youth and beauty, but the murder of the woman is the most effectively presented and, in a way, the most carefully prepared. Frankenstein's fears on his wedding night are presumably due to the monster's threat to pursue him even to his marriage chamber. But the immediate situation and the ambiguity of the language contribute to the impression that the young groom's dread of the monster is mixed with his fear of sexual union as a physical struggle which poses a threat to his independence, integrity, and delicacy of character. "Frankenstein describes the event in the following manner:

> "I had been calm during the day: but so soon as night obscured the shapes of objects, a thousand fears arose in my mind. I was anxious and watchful, while my right hand grasped a pistol which was hidden in my bosom; every sound terrified me; but I resolved that I would sell my life dearly, and note shrink from the conflict, until my own life, or that of my adversary, was extinguished.
>
> "Elizabeth observed my agitation for some time in timid and fearful silence; but there was something in my glance which communicated terror to her, and trembling she asked, 'What is it that agitates you, my dear Victor? What is it you fear?'
>
> "'Oh! peace, peace, my love,' replied I; 'this night and all will be safe; but this night is dreadful, very dreadful.'
>
> "... I reflected how fearful the combat which I momentarily expected would be to my wife, and I earnestly entreated her to retire, resolving not to join her until I had obtained some knowledge as to the situation of my enemy."

Frankenstein leaves the room, and it is while he is away that his bride is murdered by the monster on her untried marriage bed. The passage is filled with the language of anxiety, phallic inference, and imagery of conflict, yet it is in Frankenstein's absence—not in an eager assertion of his physical presence—that harm comes to Elizabeth. If we take the monster to be one side of Frankenstein's nature an alter-ego, then we see his physical potent self as brutish, ugly, and destructive, completely unintegrated with his gentle spirit. To depict a radical separation of mind from sexuality is one way to explore an unsatisfactory rapport between the imagination and the natural world. But what is important in the thematic terms of the novel is not the mere existence of the separation, but the fact that physical life is made ugly (indeed, is made to wither and die prematurely) because it is inadequately tended by the mind. The problem is not abuse but neglect.

The importance of the wedding night scene lies in its sexual connotation insofar as that provides the basic and concrete context in which, once again, to exemplify the hero's withdrawal from physical and emotional contact with living human beings. There are earlier instances of his separating himself from his family and from his friend Clerval, even while protesting, as he has with Elizabeth, that he continues to love them in spirit. The outrage dramatized in this novel is not restricted to a specifically sexual offense—nor is it directed against genius or ambition or idealism. The enemy is an egotism which, when carried to the extreme, annihilates all life around it and finally destroys itself.

5

While the main theme of the novel is the monstrous consequences of egotism, the counter-theme is the virtue of friendship. For, as Frankenstein's crime is seen as a sin against humankind more than against the heavens, it is through human sympathy, rather than divine grace, that it might have been avoided or redeemed. In her treatment of friendship, Mary shows the Coleridgean side of herself. She sees a friend as a balancing and completing agent, one who is sufficiently alike to be able to sympathize and understand, yet sufficiently different to be able to correct, and refine. Above all, the friend, in giving ear to one's dreams and sufferings, provides not only a temporary release from them, but the immediate excuse to order them by putting them into words.

The entire narrative of *Frankenstein* is in the form of three confessions to individuals with whom the speaker has unusually close ties. First, the young explorer Robert Walton writes to his sister in England as he journeys into the Arctic. There he rescues Frankenstein from a shipwreck and listens to his tale, which, in turn, contains a long narrative spoken by the monster to its creator. There is not a great deal of difference in the styles of the three narratives, though the emphasis in each is determined to a large extent by the speaker's relation to the listener. Walton's sister is an affectionate English lady who needs to be reassured that her brother is not in too much danger. He is lonely and he writes to her in detail about everything, trying usually to maintain an air of competence and calm. Frankenstein is a genius on the verge of despair and death, brought to glow again by the admiration of his rescuer. He tells his story to dissuade Walton from ruining himself similarly through excessive ambition, spares no emotion or rhetoric, and condescends to him from the superiority of his suffering. The monster wants pity from his creator; his narrative is the most sentimental of the three and the most pathetically modest in its claims.

Each narrator speaks of the importance of friendship—Walton and the monster because they feel the lack of it, Frankenstein because he has had friends and lost them. In Walton's second letter to his sister, he reports that he has hired a ship and is ready to set sail on his dangerous journey. The one thing that troubles him is that, though he has a well-trained crew, he has no soul companion:

> I have one want which I have never yet been able to satisfy ... I have no friend ... When I am glowing with the enthusiasm of success, there will be none to participate in my joy; if I am assailed by disappointment, no one will endeavour to sustain me in dejection ... I desire the company of a man who could sympathize with me; whose eyes would reply to mine. You may deem me romantic, my dear sister, but I bitterly feel the want of a friend. I have no one near me, gentle yet courageous, possessed of a cultivated as well as of a capacious mind, whose tastes are like my own, to approve or amend my plans. How would such a friend repair the faults of your poor brother!

When Walton's ship picks up the nearly frozen body of Frankenstein, the explorer hopes that at last he has found the ideal friend. He nurses, consoles, and entertains the survivor, but when he approaches the subject of friendship, Frankenstein, as always, agrees in theory, but finds a reason not to become involved in the situation at hand:

> "I agree with you ... we are unfashioned creatures, but half made up, if one wiser, better, dearer, than ourselves—such a friend ought to be—do not lend his aid to perfectionate our weak and faulty natures. I once had a friend, the most noble of human creatures, and, am entitled, therefore, to judge respecting friendship."

Frankenstein condescends to poor Walton even on the subject of friendship. It is too late for him to take up any new ties in life, he explains, because no man could ever be more to him than Clerval was and no woman more than Elizabeth. Of course, as Walton and the reader soon discover, despite Frankenstein's avowals of mutual influence and attachment, neither Clerval nor Elizabeth had any effect on him at all after his childhood and early youth. In fact, it is precisely the qualities which each of them personifies which might have saved Frankenstein from proceeding in his mad experiment. Clerval, though refined and cultivated, is essentially the outgoing, energetic, and enterprising friend who would counsel Frankenstein to climb the mountain rather than brood over it. Elizabeth was the "saintly soul," whose love softened and attracted, and who, whenever with Frankenstein, subdued him "to a semblance of her own gentleness."

Mary was sufficiently her mother's daughter to assume that a woman, as easily as another man, could be the soul companion, the ideal friend, of a man. She did not regard sexual love as an impediment to ideal friendship, nor, it would seem, as a "small party" of the claims of true love. Elizabeth and Frankenstein almost always address one another as "dear friend," and she and Clerval simply complement different sides of Frankenstein's nature. If it were to come to a choice of one or the other, the novel leaves little doubt that the feminine companion is the more valuable since she can provide both spiritual sympathy and physical affection. It is a great and painful loss for Frankenstein when Clerval is killed, but the death of Elizabeth is the end of everything for him. He dedicates himself to the pursuit and destruction of the monster, follows him to "the everlasting ices of the north" where, surrounded by blankness and waste, he confronts the sterility and uselessness of his life in a setting which anticipates that of the conclusions of Poe's *A. Gordon Pym* and Lawrence's *Women in Love*, and which was itself inspired by *The Ancient Mariner*.[16] Walton writes to his sister that he goes to "the land of mist and snow" partly because Coleridge's poem has instilled in him "a love for the marvelous." But in *Frankenstein*, unlike *The Ancient Mariner*, the icy region is not an early stage of a long and redemptive journey, but an end point, a cold blank, an image of sterility and failure.

An earlier scene of frozen desolation associated with isolation from human—especially feminine—companionship takes place between Frankenstein and the monster on a glacier at the base of Mont Blanc. The monster begs his maker to listen to him and proceeds to explain in detail how he has observed and imitated the ways of man, but is shunned because of his ugliness and is forced to wander over glaciers and hide in caves of ice because these are the only dwellings "man does not grudge." In other words, despite the bizarre details associated with his creation, the monster's lament is much the same as that of the physically presentable Caleb Williams: the world does not see him as he really is. His narrative is punctuated by outcries of loneliness:

"Everywhere I see bliss, from which I alone am irrevocably excluded."

"When I looked around, I saw and heard of none like me."

"I had never yet seen a being resembling me, or who claimed any intercourse with me. What was I?"

"I am an unfortunate and deserted creature ... I have no relation or friend upon earth."

The repetition of this theme, with slight variations, continues throughout the monster's narrative. However ludicrous or grotesque it may seem in the concrete, it is nonetheless in keeping with one of the central arguments of the novel that the monster should ask Frankenstein to make him a wife. This, in fact, is the object of his narration:

> "If I have no ties and no affections, hatred and vice must be my portion; the love of another will destroy the cause of my crimes ... My vices are the children of a forced solitude that I abhor; and my virtues will necessarily arise when I live in communion with an equal. I shall feel the affections of a sensitive being, and become linked to the chain of existence and events, from which I am now excluded."

The irony of the situation, though heavy-handed, is effective. Having removed himself from human companionship and the sexual means of procreation, Frankenstein brings into being a creature who, though not innately evil, is a torment to himself and to others precisely because he is without companionship and a sexual counterpart. In this respect the monster may well be taken as Frankenstein's alter-ego, his strange and destructive self, which finds no adequate means of communication, with others, no true resemblances, no reciprocation, a repressed and hidden beast for whom all acceptable forms of human commerce are unavailable and therefore hateful. Frankenstein himself calls the unnameable creature "my own spirit let loose from the grave ... forced to destroy all that was dear to me."

6

Mary saw, as did her father, the duality in human nature which is capable of bringing misery and ruin to the most gifted of beings. Her novel is not so pessimistic as *Caleb Williams* nor are the solutions implied in it so optimistic as those outlined in *Political Justice*. Neither her father's trust in system nor her husband's unworldliness seemed satisfactory to her. On the contrary, judging from the events of her novel, both alternatives were too likely to lead to that single-mindedness which, when carried to the extreme, was a kind of insanity. It would seem, in fact, that of all the romantic influences on her mind and work, Shelley's undoubtedly stimulated, but Coleridge's comforted; Shelley's provided confusion and enchantment, Coleridge's provided psychological and moral consolation. The ethereal reveries of her hero are loyal attempts to imitate Shelley, but they are among the most strained and unconvincing passages of the novel. Mary's natural inclination was toward synthesis, integration, a constant effort to find balance, relationship, correspondence, to root all ideals in natural process, and to find in nature the external signs of an ideal region. Her heart is with those, described by Coleridge, "who measuring and sounding the rivers of the vale at the feet of their furthest inaccessible falls have learned, that the sources must be far higher and far inward."[17] Despite his supposedly scientific approach to things, Frankenstein's error is to circumvent an elementary principle of nature in trying to achieve his rather vaguely conceived ambition.

In stressing friendship, and especially heterosexual love, as her "river of the vale," the natural symbol of a higher necessity, Mary presents her own concrete version of the theory of correspondence. We must give her more credit than to think that she supposed the problems of all men—including geniuses—would be solved by marriage to a good woman. What she does mean is that no being truly exists—except in an insane wilderness of its own creation—unless it finds and *accepts* a relationship of mutual dependence with another. The rapport with otherness is both the link with the objective world and the condition for self-delineation.

In his tenth essay from *The Friend*, Coleridge says, "In a self-conscious and thence reflecting being, no instinct can exist without engendering the belief of an object corresponding to it, either present or future, real or capable of being realized."[18] Mary Shelley's definition of a monster is precisely that being to which nothing corresponds, the product of a genius who tried to exercise its will without reference to other beings. Even Caleb Williams, at least until Falkland's death, is better off than the monster in that he can draw energy to shape some identity for himself from his strange bond with his master. Godwin wrote in his preface that he amused himself with the parallels between his story and that of Bluebeard: "Caleb Williams was the wife, who in spite of warning, persisted in his attempts to discover the forbidden secret; and, when he had succeeded, struggled as fruitlessly to escape the consequences, as the wife of Bluebeard in washing the key of the ensanguined chamber."

Frankenstein's first act after creating a new life is to disown it. The problem is not, as in *Caleb Williams*, an ambiguous fascination leading to abuse and immediate and obsessive pursuit. As soon as his dream is realized in concrete form, Frankenstein wants nothing to do with it. Despite his claims to scientific interest, he demonstrates no wish whatever to observe and analyze the imperfect results of his experiment. When he does finally pursue the monster, it is not in order to possess, dominate, or torment it, but to annihilate it. Though there is something ludicrous in the way the monster stumbles upon books and learns to read during his lonely wandering, the thematic consistency of the episode is unmistakable. The monster is most impressed by *Paradise Lost*; he compares himself with Adam before the creation of Eve, but, like a good Romantic, he finds Satan an even "fitter emblem" of his condition. Still, neither emblems, nor words can really help or define him any more than ordinary men can. He can find parallels but no connections and he concludes his encounter with books by envying Satan like all the others, for even he "had his companions."

The two dominant themes of *Frankenstein* never truly harmonize, nor does one succeed effectively in canceling out the other. Surely, the most explicit "moral" theme of the novel—expressed by the author with genuine conviction—is that man discovers and fulfills himself through others and destroys himself alone. Yet played against this, not so much as an argument but as an assumption, is the idea that the genius, even in his failures, is unique, noble, and isolated from other men by divine right.

Frankenstein is neither a pure hymn of praise to Godwin and Shelley nor a simple repudiation of them. Mary's uncertainties are not reflected in parody or burlesque, as Beckford's and Lewis's are in *Vathek* and *The Monk*. Her prose style is solemn, inflated, and imitative, an unhappy combination of Godwin's sentence structure and Shelley's abstract vocabulary. Whatever else she may have thought, Mary obviously did not regard her father or husband as silly. Her reservations about them were deep, complex, and mixed with genuine admiration.

After Shelley's death, Mary considered how best to educate her son, and a friend advised that she teach him to think for himself. Mary is said to have answered, "Oh my God, teach him to think like other people!"[19] If the young wife had been able to speak with the emphatic clarity of the widow, she probably would have had fewer nightmares and *Frankenstein* might never have been written. The book is a bad dream entwined with a moral essay. Like all romantic fiction, it resounds with the fascinating dissonance which usually results from intimate encounters between irrational symbols and reasonable statements.

NOTES

1. Sir Walter Scott, "Remarks on *Frankenstein*," *Blackwood's* (March 1818), reprinted in *Critical and Miscellaneous Essays of Sir Walter Scott*, I, 448.

2. Quoted in Howard B. Gotlieb, *William Beckford of Fonthill*, p. 61.

3. For a discussion of the genesis of *Frankenstein*, see James Rieger, *The Mutiny Within* (New York: G. Braziller, 1967), pp. 237–247.

4. *Mary Shelley's Journal*, ed. Frederick L. Jones (Norman: University of Oklahoma Press, 1947), pp. 32–33.

5. Quotations are taken from Mary W. Shelley, *Frankenstein, or The Modern*

Prometheus, ed. M. K. Joseph (London: Oxford University Press, 1969). The text is based on the third edition of 1831, Mary Shelley's revision of the 1818 first edition.

6. M. K. Joseph, Introduction to *Frankenstein*, p. xiv.

7. *Mary Shelley's Journal*, p. 183.

8. *The Letters of Mary W. Shelley*, ed. Frederick L. Jones, 2 vols. (Norman: University of Oklahoma Press, 1944), I, 281.

9. Mary Shelley, *The Last Man*, ed. Hugh J. Luke, Jr. (Lincoln: University of Nebraska Press, 1965), p. 5.

10. Ibid., p.18.

11. Quoted in *Mary Shelley's journal*, p. 20.

12. Thomas Macaulay, "Review of Thomas Moore's *Letters and Journals of Lord Byron*," *Edinburgh Review*, no. 53 (June 1831), 544.

13. Elizabeth Nitchie, *Mary Shelley* (New Brunswick, N.J.: Rutgers University Press, 1953); p. 219. For a fascinating account of the stage history of *Frankenstein*, see pp. 218–231.

14. William Hazlitt, "Review of Shelley's Posthumous *Poems*," *The Edinburgh Review*, no. 40 (July 1824), 494.

15. Percy Bysshe Shelley, "A Discourse on the Manners of the Ancients, relative to the Subject of Love," *Essays and Letters by Percy Bysshe Shelley*, ed. Ernest Rhys (London; 1886), p. 48.

16. For a discussion of the polar symbolism in *Frankenstein*, see James Rieger, *The Mutiny Within*, pp. 79–89.

17. *The Complete Works of Samuel Taylor Coleridge*, ed. W. G. T. Shedd, 7 vols. (New York, 1884), III, 326.

18. Ibid., II, 449.

19. Quoted in Ford K. Brown, *The Life of William Godwin* (London: J. M. Dent, 1926), p. 375.

DAVID KETTERER

Thematic Anatomy: Intrinsic Structures

The materials examined in the previous chapter might be described as centrifugal in orientation. An understanding of their significance involves a flight into areas outside the text of *Frankenstein*. Of course, within the text, not all that may be known about these materials is operational or of equal weight. There are centripetal or gravitational forces holding the text together which cause its component parts to assume certain lines of coherence. An identification of these lines of coherence will reveal the book's thematic anatomy. My terminology here makes the parallel with Frankenstein's construct self-evident. Once having decided on the creation of a human being, Frankenstein worked within a particular system of organization.

A distinction should be made between the idea content and the thematic content of a work. While an idea is essentially something static, a theme must involve process and development. Obviously enough, in the case of *Frankenstein*, the central idea presented itself in Mary's vision—the Lazarus-like raising to life of an artificially created man. The transition from idea to extended and successful narrative requires a "vertical" testing of exactly what the idea means in a number of different contexts and a "horizontal" exploration of its possible consequences in human action and response. What is of thematic interest will derive largely but not exclusively

From *Frankenstein's Creation: The Book, The Monster and Human Reality*. © 1979 by David Ketterer.

from the horizontal axis. The vertical potential should be considered as part of the idea context and will receive more emphasis in the next two chapters.

In considering the basic idea of *Frankenstein*, Mary Shelley saw two implications that allowed for thematic development. First of all, the subject raised the question of the "I" and the "not-I," the alien, the Other. From this point of view, Frankenstein's relationship with the monster becomes analogous with the other relationships in the book. The monster becomes an extreme instance of the Other. After all, the monster concept is a relative one and, since it is only meaningful from a human perspective, the human and the monstrous might be understood as enjoying a symbiotic existence. Perhaps some such reflection prompted the second implication, the logical step of treating the monster as Frankenstein's doppelgänger. These two secondary ideas, vertical elaborations, presented the major possibilities for the thematic lines of development traced in detail below. It will be immediately apparent that these lines of development combine either antagonistically or paradoxically. While the first emphasizes the reality of the Other, the second tends to validate nothing beyond the I.

(i) *Egotistic Perversion and Domestic Affection*

Frankenstein, like many artists and scientists, becomes involved in his work to the extent that the external world of nature and human relationships loses its influence. In his solitary cell "at the top of the house, and separated from all other apartments by a gallery and staircase"—an architectural analogue for the divorce of mind and body—he is oblivious to the processes of nature evident outside during an unusually prolific summer: "never did the fields bestow a more plentiful harvest or the vines yield a more luxuriant vintage" (p. 55). He ceases communication with his friends and family. At the same time, Frankenstein does appear to accept the reproach he attributes in imagination to his father: "If the study to which you apply yourself has a tendency to weaken your affections, and to destroy your taste for those simple pleasures in which no alloy can mix, then that study is certainly unlawful, that is to say, not befitting the human mind" (p. 56).

This moment of awareness and self-condemnation on Frankenstein's part is not without equivocation. He continues: "if no man allowed any pursuit whatsoever to interfere with the tranquility of his domestic affections, Greece had not been enslaved; Caesar would have spared his country; America would have been discovered more gradually; and the empires of Mexico and Peru had not been destroyed" (p. 56). The reader will observe that these instances include an odd-man-out. We have observed Mary's negative appraisal of the New World but the perhaps too rapid discovery of America is not an evil equal in magnitude to the other three examples, if it was indeed an evil at all (whether the discovery had been fast or slow it may be assumed that the Indian would have suffered). Here as elsewhere Mary is posing a question, not forcing a clear-cut conclusion.

At the tale's conclusion, after all the deaths and misery arising out of Frankenstein's creation, the same mixed judgement is upheld. When some of the sailors aboard the ice-locked ship seek to persuade Robert Walton, their captain and Frankenstein's rescuer, to return home, Frankenstein arouses in them a sense of the glory of their mission. In words that express his own ambitions, he reminds the sailors of their expectation "to be hailed as the benefactors of your species" (p. 214). And as part of a speech that echoes that of Dante's Ulysses, Frankenstein exhorts: "Do not return to your families with the stigma of disgrace marked on your brows. Return, as heroes who have fought and conquered and who know not what it is to turn their backs on the foe" (p. 215). But, as we have seen, the allusion is ironically employed; the voyage that Ulysses persuades his sailors to undertake is fatal. Hence his place amongst the flame-enveloped evil counsellors. Is Frankenstein condemning himself once again? His death-bed advice to Walton shortly afterwards would appear to indicate that this is so: "Seek happiness in tranquility and avoid ambition, even if it be only the innocent one of distinguishing yourself in science and discoveries." But immediately he reverses his position: "Yet why do I say this! I have myself been blasted in these hopes, yet another may succeed" (pp. 217–218).

One is left with a divided impression of Frankenstein exactly parallel to that provided by the conclusion of Marlowe's *Doctor Faustus*. The presentation of the final moments before Faustus's damnation has left commentators confused as to where Marlowe, the atheist, stands. The evidence for ambivalence and ironic undercutting here is a good deal more subtle than it is in Frankenstein's case and, indeed, some critics have denied its existence. But to my mind a convincing argument can be made that Marlowe is manipulating the traditional story in order to point up his admiration for Faustus and question the justice of his damnation. In the case of Mary's comparable sympathy for Frankenstein, it is likely, given the analogy between the book and the monster, that it has much to do with the fact that writing involves the same isolation and perhaps a similar twisting of the sexual impulse as Frankenstein's occupation. And like the writer, Frankenstein sees in his work the promise of immortality.

The relationship between creativity and sexual energy is something of a metaphoric if not a scientific cliché. Regarding the success of his initial experiments at animating dead matter, Frankenstein notes, "After so much time spent in painful *labour*, to arrive at once at the summit of my *desires*, was

the most gratifying *consummation* of my toils" (p. 52; my italics). The sexual
implications of the words emphasized are self-evident and surely intentional.
To the extent that creativity calls for isolation and self-absorption, it might
be regarded as a perversion of sexuality, specifically a form of masturbation
or incest.[1] When it comes to creating a monstrous mate, there are similar
hints that sexual energies are being improperly channelled: "I had an
insurmountable aversion to the idea of *engaging* myself in my loathsome task
in my father's house, while in habits of familiar *intercourse* with those I loved"
(p. 152; my italics). In *Frankenstein* the curse of sexual perversion is pervasive.
For example, the image of Frankenstein pursuing mother "nature to her
hiding places" has overtones both incestuous and necrophiliac: "I collected
bones from charnel-houses; and disturbed, with profane fingers, the
tremendous secrets of the human frame" (pp. 54–55). Such obsessions
cannot be adequately explained in terms of a gothic convention.

Imagistically, Frankenstein's ambitions amount to a desire to sexually
possess his dead mother. Following the successful animation of his monster,
Frankenstein takes to his bed (an unlikely sequence on any literal level, as
Irving Massey observes[2]) and experiences his Freudian fantasy in a dream.
Much like the allegorical conflict in *Dr. Faustus* between the Good and Bad
Angels, Frankenstein is presented with a choice between the healthy
extroverted sexuality held out to him by his fiancée Elizabeth and that
diseased, introverted, monstrous sexual passion he feels for his mother:

> I thought I saw Elizabeth, in the bloom of health, walking in the
> streets of Ingolstadt. Delighted and surprised, I embraced her;
> but as I imprinted the first kiss on her lips, they became livid with
> the hue of death; her features appeared to change, and I thought
> that I held the corpse of my dead mother in my arms; a shroud
> enveloped her form, and I saw the grave-worms crawling in the
> folds of the flannel. I started from my sleep with horror; a cold
> dew covered by forehead, my teeth chattered, and every limb
> became convulsed: when, by the dim and yellow light of the
> moon, as it forced its way through the window shutters, I beheld
> the wretch—the miserable monster whom I created. (p. 58)

Frankenstein's unnatural creation is introduced as a consequence of that
unnatural passion that causes Elizabeth to metamorphose into his mother's
corpse. The train of associations here suggests a pun, whether conscious or
not, in the next paragraph where a comparison is made with "A mummy
again endued with animation ..." (p. 58).

In the original version of *Frankenstein*, Elizabeth is less clearly opposed to the mother as a positive image of sexuality. Since she is there the daughter of Frankenstein's father's sister, Frankenstein's relationship with her is only some degrees less consanguineous than his relationship with his mother. However, one of the lengthier revisions in the 1831 version presents Elizabeth as related to the Frankenstein family only by adoption. Thus, and this I would deem a thematic improvement, a relatively clear opposition is initially established between destructive incest and true love. Subsequently, like other oppositions in the book, this one loses its apparent clarity.

While in the second edition most of the references to Elizabeth as "cousin" are routinely changed to "friend," "girl" or "Elizabeth" this does not always happen. In fact, increasingly, the term "cousin" is allowed to stand and imply a brother/sister element in the relationship that she and Frankenstein turn into that of husband and wife. Addressing Victor and Elizabeth from her death-bed as "My children," their mother had continued, "my firmest hopes of future happiness were placed on the prospect of your union" (p. 43). Later Frankenstein's father speaks to his son about his unquestionably ambiguous attitude towards Elizabeth. "You perhaps regard her as a sister, without any wish that she might become your wife. Nay, you may have met with another whom you may love; and considering yourself as bound in honour to Elizabeth, this struggle may occasion the poignant misery which you appear to feel." Frankenstein denies the charge but in echoing his mother's dying wish—"My future hopes and prospects are entirely bound up in the expectation of our union" (p. 151)—the spectre of Elizabeth's rival is invoked. In general terms, the spectre of incest is raised by Mary Shelley to suggest concerns which are enclosed, inturned and reflexive. Are we to intuit that the only love possible is that of Narcissus? If so what else in our environment is essentially a self-reflection? These are the questions that *Frankenstein* poses.

Other characters in the novel appear to be related in ways that amplify the motif of incest and perverted sexuality into a general condition. Following the murder of William, Frankenstein's younger brother, Clerval, Frankenstein's friend, intones: "dear lovely child, he now sleeps with his angel mother!" (p. 73). The exclamation mark at least allows for the possibility that some *double entendre* is being hinted at. Walton, the letter-writer of the outer narrative frame and the putative transcriber of the entire account, appears to enjoy an affectionate relationship with his sister Margaret. Since Walton's role largely mirrors Frankenstein's, it seems logical to impute an analogous incestuous attraction between the explorer and his "beloved Sister" (p. 212).

We have recently become attuned to the fact that literary works, to a greater or lesser degree, create roles for their readers.[3] In the case of

Frankenstein, the reader is required to put himself in the role of Margaret. Walton has prepared the narrative specifically for her eyes. By means of this narrative strategy, the reader is drawn into a construct of reflecting mirrors and forced to identify with what may be seen as the injured party. As Robert Kiely points out, Frankenstein usurps not only the power of God but also the power of woman.[4] He discovers a means of creating life which avoids the sexual means of procreation. The female function is distorted not only by the inturning motif of incest but also by the more radically solipsistic alternatives of homosexuality and masturbation.

The relationship between Frankenstein and his best friend Clerval is not exactly homosexual but Clerval does come across as a rather feminine character. Thus the qualities that attract Frankenstein to Elizabeth find their reflection in Clerval: "he might not have been so perfectly humane, so thoughtful in his generosity—so full of kindness and tenderness amidst his passion for adventurous exploit, had she not unfolded to him the real loveliness of beneficence and made the doing good, the end and aim of his soaring ambition" (p. 38). On the eve of Frankenstein's departure for university, his relationship with Clerval seems more passionate than friendly: "We sat late. We could not tear ourselves away from each other ..." (p. 44). When Frankenstein becomes ill Clerval nurses him: "He [Clerval] knew that I could not have a more kind and attentive nurse than himself" (p. 62).

One should be careful not to oversimplify. The relationship with Clerval appears to hold both the alternative possibilities of homosexuality and ideal friendship. In this respect his role reflects the negative and positive aspects of Elizabeth's and poses a similar question. If all love is incestuous, is all friendship in *Frankenstein* homosexual? The sexual nature of Frankenstein's feelings for Clerval is alluded to in this passage describing his revived spirits:

> Study had before secluded me from the intercourse of my fellow creatures, and rendered me unsocial; but Clerval called forth the better feelings of my heart; he again taught me to love the aspect of nature, and the cheerful faces of children. Excellent friend! How sincerely did you love me and endeavour to elevate my mind until it was on a level with your own! A selfish pursuit had cramped and narrowed me until your gentleness and affection warmed and opened my senses ... (p. 70)

If further evidence is required of Clerval's femininity there is the likelihood, as I have indicated in Chapter 1, that his name derives from that of Claire Clairmont. Mary has simply exchanged the French words "val" and "mont." The more feminine valley replaces the masculine mountain.

A link is established between Frankenstein's latent homosexuality and his scientific interests through Waldman, by far the more congenial of the two professors who influence him at university. He is described in terms which suggest a mixture of masculine and feminine traits: "His person was short, but remarkably erect; and his voice the sweetest I had ever heard." It is this hermaphroditical gentleman who speaks, as Frankenstein is to speak, of the need to "penetrate into the recesses of nature, and show how she works in her hiding places" (p. 47)

The ambivalent sexuality of Frankenstein's various relationships implies as much about relationships generally as it does about Frankenstein himself. And this ambivalence assumes a stark reality in the imperfect being that Frankenstein creates. Ironically, having removed himself from the sphere of domestic affection, he creates a being who craves companionship and a wife. Frankenstein's own impending marriage counterpoints and mocks the monster's desire for a mate. Repeatedly rebuffed, the monster comes to see that if he is to enjoy any kind of relationship it must be with someone who offers a reflection of himself: "I am alone, and miserable; man will not associate with me; but one as deformed and horrible as myself would not deny herself to me" (p. 144). He charges Frankenstein with making such a being and explains that his murderous career results from a denial of affection: "My vices are the children of a forced solitude ..." (p. 147). It was, of course, Frankenstein's enforced solitude that resulted in the begetting of the monster and, in murdering Frankenstein's friends and loved ones, the monster is essentially making manifest the consequences of that initial withdrawal.

A desire for friendship is initially voiced by Walton. In his second letter he writes: "But I have one want which I have never yet been able to satisfy; and the absence of the object of which I now feel as a most severe evil. I have no friend, Margaret." The friend for which he yearns, someone "gentle yet courageous, possessed of a cultivated as well as a capacious mind, whose tastes are like my own" (p. 19), is, of course, Frankenstein, who appears shortly, stranded on an ice floe. Frankenstein's reciprocal appreciation of Walton has an almost sexual quality causing Walton to record how "his lustrous eyes dwell on me with all their melancholy sweetness" (p. 31). Once again, the relationship desired and the relationship experienced is that of like for like. What is involved is not so much true feeling for another as self-love. But at the end of the book Walton is dissuaded from continuing his possibly suicidal and alienating quest for the North Pole in favour of returning to England and human community: "I may there find consolation" (p. 218). The question remains is there a real choice? The book's final impression is one of unrelieved loneliness. For a brief moment the three isolates, Walton,

Frankenstein and the monster, are together in the same room. However, Frankenstein is dead, the monster projects his self-immolation and soon Walton is left entirely alone.[5]

An ambiguous statement by the monster crystallizes the problem. He has been reading *The Sorrows of Werther* while eavesdropping on the lives of a family of poor cottage dwellers: "The gentle and domestic manners it described, combined with lofty sentiments and feelings, which had for their object something out of self, accorded well with my experience among my protectors, and with the wants which were forever alive in my own bosom" (p. 128). The ambiguous phrase is, of course, "something out of self." A reader's first reaction would be to gloss the phrase as "something other than the self." But Mary did not write "something other than the self." What she actually wrote has a quite other additional meaning. It might be more directly glossed as "something which comes out of the self." Love, as the relationships in *Frankenstein* appear to indicate, may be self-reflexive. I believe that the ambiguity here is deliberate, goes to the heart of the meaning of *Frankenstein* and is not to be resolved. Likewise is the case of the monster's later paradoxical apostrophe following his creator's death: "Oh Frankenstein! Generous and self-devoted being!" (p. 219). The contradictory qualities of generosity and self-love are presented as virtual synonyms.

The five interpolated stories variously probe the issues raised by the overall thematic pattern of egotistic perversion, friendship and human relationships. In the first such insert, Walton describes the master of his ship, "a mariner equally noted for his kindness of heart and the respect and obedience paid to him by his crew." This man, "having amassed a considerable sum in prize-money," had been engaged to marry a Russian lady whom he loved. However, she loved another, a poor man whom her father regards as beyond the pale in terms of marriage. Straightway, the sailor made over his wealth to his rival and left the country not returning until his former mistress and her lover were married. Is this the yardstick of selflessness by which events in *Frankenstein* should be measured? Is this mariner Mary Shelley's equivalent of Swift's Portuguese sailor in *Gulliver's Travels*? Walton's account continues: "'What a noble fellow!' you will exclaim. He is so; but then he is wholly uneducated: he is as silent as a Turk, and a kind of ignorant carelessness attends him, which, while it renders his conduct the more astonishing, detracts from the interest and sympathy which otherwise he would command" (p. 21). The monster is initially a similar prototype, a noble savage capable of intense feeling, but the account of the mariner clearly indicates that some modicum of intellectual accomplishment is a necessary part of human interaction. "[T]he interest and sympathy" the mariner presently fails to elicit is symptomatic of the love he failed to kindle in the heart of the Russian lady. Love and intellect may conflict but again they may not.

A second interpolation describes the circumstances of Frankenstein's father's marriage. His father's "most intimate" (p. 31) friend, Beaufort, a merchant, had fallen upon hard times and left Geneva with his daughter Caroline. When Frankenstein's father finally locates them, he finds Caroline in a distressed state after nursing Beaufort through a long illness from which he has just died. Two years later, Frankenstein's father married Caroline. Their love is rendered equivocal by the imagistic hint of incest. It is emphasized that, at the time, Frankenstein's father was already advanced in years. In marrying the daughter of a friend, he is marrying someone young enough to be his own daughter. Subsequently, Frankenstein draws attention to a picture of Caroline that combines possibilities of incest and necrophilia: "It was a historical subject, painted at my father's desire, and represented Caroline Beaufort in an agony of despair, kneeling by the coffin of her dead father" (p. 78).

The third interpolation concerns the introduction of Elizabeth to the family and sets up the ambiguous nature of her relationship with Frankenstein. As I have indicated, the version of this history in the 1831 edition constitutes a major revision of the 1818 version. In the earlier version, Elizabeth is Frankenstein's father's sister's daughter but in the lengthier revision she is not related. In the revision, Frankenstein's mother comes across Elizabeth while visiting the cottages of the poor near Lake Como. Elizabeth is one of a family of five children but, unlike the other four, she is thin and fair, "a distinct species, a being heaven-sent, and bearing a celestial stamp in all her features" (p. 34). The peasant mother explains that Elizabeth is not her child "but the daughter of a Milanese nobleman" (p. 35). Her German mother died on giving birth and Elizabeth was placed with this particular peasant family to be nursed. Following the death of her idealistic father, Elizabeth remained with her foster parents. Smitten, Frankenstein's mother arranges to adopt Elizabeth. As for Frankenstein's reaction, "We called each other familiarly by the name of cousin. No word, no expression could body forth the kind of relation in which she stood to me—my more than sister, since till death she was to be mine only" (p. 36). The intimations of immortality that she trails with her suggest a strong imagistic connection with Frankenstein's later metaphysical explorations. Like the monster, she appears to be "of a distinct species" (p. 34). To what extent, it must be asked, is Frankenstein's attachment to her contributive rather than opposed to the creation of his monster?

When Frankenstein's brother William is murdered, the family maid, Justine Moritz, is accused. Justine is rather awkwardly introduced, shortly before the discovery of William's body, in a fourth interpolation, this one in the context of a letter from Elizabeth to Frankenstein: "Do you remember on what occasion Justine Moritz entered our family? Probably you do not; I will relate her history, therefore, in a few words" (p. 64). Of itself, this ploy is a bit strained but the sense of dislocation is augmented by the information that she was a member of the household when Frankenstein was there, and present at his mother's death. She might have been referred to then rather than just before her presence becomes dramatically necessary. It is "flaws" such as this (perhaps deliberately contrived) that make the book, like the monster, seem something of a botched job. The same applies to the interpolations themselves; they suggest a patchwork effect. However, at the same time they are consistent with the enveloping patchwork structure of the entire narrative. The monster's story is inserted within Frankenstein's which, in turn, is inserted within Walton's communications to his sister.

Justine's story details the consequences of withheld affection. She was the disliked third child of a widow with four children. On seeing the situation, Frankenstein's mother had persuaded the widow to let her take in Justine, then aged twelve, as a servant. Justine formed a strong attachment to Frankenstein's mother and became ill following her death. Subsequently, her own brothers and sister died, leaving her mother isolated and feeling guilty about her neglected surviving daughter. Justine returned home at her mother's request. Their relationship was not altogether improved. Madame Moritz reverted to blaming Justine rather than herself for her misfortunes. However, Justine fulfilled her family obligations and remained at home until her mother's death "on the first approach of cold weather" (p. 66), whereupon Justine returned to the Frankenstein residence. Elizabeth notes that Justine's admiration for Frankenstein's mother led her "to imitate her phraseology and manners, so that even now she often reminds me of her" (p. 65). Elizabeth ends her account by referring again to this similarity and thus further emphasizing the extent to which a loving relationship depends upon or encourages a solipsistic likeness.

It is the monster's unlikeness that repeatedly frustrates his efforts at human contact. He gains an awareness of everything from which he is excluded during the period of education when he eavesdrops on a humble, affectionate family who live in a cottage. The arrival of Safie, the Arabian with whom the son Felix is in love, provides the monster with a somewhat contrived opportunity to benefit from her English lessons and, in the process, discover something about the complexities of human relationships. What the monster learns about Safie and her relationship with Felix forms the substance of the fifth, final and most extended interpolation accounting for the whole of Chapter 14. It is the book's central narrative unit.

The monster recounts how the poor cottagers, De Lacey, his son, ironically named Felix—"the saddest of the group" (p. 113)—and his daughter Agatha, had in more prosperous days lived in Paris. Also in Paris at that time was Safie's father, a Turkish merchant, who was, it seems, unjustly thrown in jail to await execution. It is at this point that the repeated motif of unjust trials connects with the successive interpolated accounts of human relationships. Felix, present at the trial, vows to engineer the Turk's escape. On visiting the Turk, he meets and falls in love with another visitor, the daughter Safie. To secure Felix's help, the Turk holds out the prospect of marriage to Safie. With the help of a translator, Safie writes Felix letters in French in which she describes how her Christian mother was captured and made a slave of the Turks, one of whom married her. Safie explains that her hopes of marrying a Christian and living an emancipated life derive from her mother. The information in Safie's letters amounts to an interpolation within an interpolation which may be seen as the innermost structural and, if Rubenstein is correct, psycho-biographical core of the narrative.

Thanks to Felix's help, the Turk escapes from prison the day before his expected execution and joins Felix and Safie in Italy to await a favourable opportunity to return to Turkey. He also awaits an opportunity to separate Safie from Felix since the idea of his daughter marrying a Christian is, in fact, abhorrent to him. Events favour the Turk's double-crossing intent. The French government, having discovered that Felix was responsible for the escape of their prisoner, throw his father and sister in jail. Felix returns to Paris and stands trial. The result of this trial—unjust by any human standards—is that the De Laceys are deprived of their wealth and exiled. While the De Laceys finally settle in the cottage in Germany where the monster comes across them, the Turk seizes the chance to flee to Constantinople with the idea that his daughter should follow. Instead, Safie seeks out Felix.

This prolonged account of true love and treachery bears more directly on the situation of the monster and Frankenstein than do the other interpolations. Safie in Germany, "alone, unacquainted with the language of the country, and utterly ignorant of the customs of the world" (p. 127), shares something of the monster's plight. The love she and Felix feel for one another is as genuine as the monster's collective love for the De Laceys. And just as the Turk acts treacherously towards Felix and Safie, so Frankenstein acts treacherously in failing to take responsibility for the well-being of his creation.

As nowhere else in the novel, the opposition between what appears positive—true love—and what appears negative—treachery—seems absolute. But Safie's attraction to Felix is based primarily on the element of likeness—he is a Christian—and the Turk's shabby intentions have to do with a lack of likeness—Felix is not a follower of Muhammed. Owing to her mother's influence, Safie had contemplated abandoning her birthplace and, in effect, denying her patrimony. And it should not be forgotten that the precipitating action of this interpolated history—the Turk's being thrown in jail—may be considered an act of treachery of which the Turk is the victim, not the perpetrator. The monster notes simply that the Turk's presence in Paris "became obnoxious to the government" "for some reason I could not learn." The logic of the history and of *Frankenstein* generally implies that what was at fault was simply the Turk's unlikeness. Indeed, "it was judged that his religion and wealth, rather than the crime alleged against him, had been the cause of his condemnation" (p. 122). At this point, the monster's own "obnoxious" unlikeness suggests an affinity with the Turk rather than with Safie. But this inextricable involvement of opposites is manifest in Safie's own person. Because of her mixed parentage, she is both Turkish and Arabian, Muhammadan and Christian. She epitomizes that thematic material in *Frankenstein* which organizes itself not so much in terms of egotistic perversion *or* domestic affection but rather egotistic perversion *and* domestic affection. The one thing appears to be the same as the other.

(ii) *The Doppelgänger Theme*

In considering the literary sources of *Frankenstein*, I alluded to the tradition of the doppelgänger.[6] However, this tradition is not a source in the specific sense that the other literary sources provided Mary with various spare parts. The doppelgänger motif constitutes an aspect of the book's thematic design and may not profitably be traced to any particular text or texts. *Frankenstein* simply takes its place in a literary tradition, the durability of which owes something to the nature of literature itself. To the extent that a writer peoples his pages with the creations of his own brain, his various characters may be regarded as alter egos. But the doppelgänger is most naturally suited to allegorical treatment as in the case of the medieval psychomachia. Although *Frankenstein* is far from being an overt allegory, there appears to be a growing consensus amongst critics that, from a certain point of view, the monster should be regarded as Frankenstein's double, "something out of self" (p. 128) in the monster's phrase. This insight was first directly recorded by Muriel Spark in 1951 and subsequently variously amplified by others.[7] A number of recent commentators, however, have denied the existence of any doppelgänger connection. Burton R. Pollin, for example, notes that Spark's *Child of Light* "offers the thesis—untenable in my eyes—that the monster constitutes Frankenstein's *Doppelgänger*."[8]

The problem, of course, is that Spark's interpretation makes manifest an allegorical dimension in a book the overriding tone of which is realistic. All manner of interpretative difficulties follow. If the monster is some kind of psychological projection, what of the other characters who either interact with him or are physically affected by his presence? Must they also be understood as aspects of Frankenstein's personality?[9] The answer, I believe, is both yes and no. The epistemological assumptions of realism coexist with the contradictory assumptions of allegory. The monster is both a psychological double and an independent character leading a realistic existence.

This dilemma exists in the context of the relationship between egotistic perversion and communal affection. From one point of view, the monster is different from Frankenstein, from another, he is the same person. From one point of view, egotistic perversion is very different from communal affection, from another, it amounts to the same thing. As my discussion has indicated, successful relationships with others in *Frankenstein* seem suspiciously close to relationships with mirror images, with doubles. At one point, Frankenstein observes that "in Clerval I saw the image of my former self" (p. 158). I avoided using the word "double" or "doppelgänger" in that previous section but the notion is clearly implicit in the affection/perversion business and, indeed, what I have distinguished as two thematic configurations should be regarded as one.

In this light, it is possible at least directly to face up to, if not exactly answer, the difficult question that most interpreters of the book have either sidestepped or simplified—exactly what aspect of Frankenstein does the monster represent? The usual conclusion, that the monster represents the destructive and diabolical nature of Frankenstein's overweaning intellectual ambition does not square with the actual presentation of the monster as a noble savage, an innocent more sinned against than sinning. What we have to do with here is a false splitting of the apparently good and the apparently evil. In a world where the concept of love is rendered ambiguously akin to incest, homosexuality and masturbation by the human tendency to transform the other into a replica of the self, the monster is, it would seem, that unalterable Other, and therefore the potential source and object of genuine love. But, at the same time, if human love is truly a matter of incest, homosexuality and masturbation then the monster represents the self that Frankenstein—and the reader—do not wish to recognize.

The ambiguities stated here in terms of love should also be understood in terms of the pursuit of scientific knowledge. Frankenstein's obsession with the secret of life cuts him off from the lives of friends and relations; does it also cut him off from an awareness of the possibility that what he takes to be the otherness of the life or reality that he is studying may be within himself? As with love, what appears to be outer directed may be egotistically inner directed. Both the nature of love and the nature of knowledge appear to be ambiguously self-reflective. The denial of this self-reflective element leads to the kind of schizophrenia evident in the relationship between Frankenstein and the monster. But this may not be the case and, thus again, the monster—the Other—is real. No one alternative should be chosen. Mary is dealing with the philosophical mysteries raised by all relationships between an I and an Other.

All of this paradoxical profundity will, of course, have no real bearing unless the reader of *Frankenstein* picks up the clues that establish the doppelgänger connection. And since, as I have indicated, some scholars have recently denied this connection, it may be worthwhile to trace the relevant evidence. A careful reader coming to the book, as surely virtually every reader does, with some knowledge of the basic plot idea may observe some calculation in Mary's early use of the words "animation" and "animated" in relation to Frankenstein. Frankenstein is near death when he boards Walton's ship: "as soon as he had quitted the fresh air, he fainted. We ... restored him to animation by rubbing him with brandy, and forcing him to swallow a small quantity" (p. 25). After hearing that Walton had previously observed the being that Frankenstein is pursuing, "a new spirit of life animated the decaying frame of the stranger." If this is not quite the same as the animation of Frankenstein's creation, it is certainly presented as a kind of resurrection. Frankenstein himself admits, "you have benevolently restored me to life" (p. 26).

By applying to Frankenstein the words "animation" and "animated" which also point to this monster, the result of his capability of "bestowing animation upon lifeless matter" (p. 52), Mary is implying an identity between the creator and his creation. Just before Frankenstein begins his narrative, Walton provides a retrospective image of the man with "his thin hand raised in animation, while the lineaments of his face are irradiated by the soul within" (p. 31). There is an element of tautology in this description which is worth stressing. It is Frankenstein's soul; spirit or anima that maintains his carcass in a state of animation. The relationship here between "soul" and "animation" suggests, as I shall subsequently argue in detail, that Frankenstein's ambitions are of a religious nature. However, at present it is only necessary to note that in the brief number of pages given to Walton's initial view of Frankenstein the word "animation" is used twice and the word "animated" once. To any reader aware of what is to come, the effect is to trigger an association between Frankenstein and the monster.

In fact, wherever someone is presented as being "animated" an attentive reader will think of the monster. There is no logical reason to limit the range of doppelgänger relationships. If the monster is actually some kind of psychological projection, who else or what else should be viewed similarly? Perhaps everybody if not everything. Following the death of Justine and with a sharpened sense of the fallen state of the world, Elizabeth claims that "men appear to me as monsters thirsting for each other's blood" (p. 92). I have already referred to the sense that Frankenstein and Walton, like Justine and Frankenstein's mother, are doubles. If the word "animated" is leant on in the way I suggest it should be, this doubling tendency multiplies. Frankenstein's parents, Clerval and Elizabeth all become hypothetical doubles of the monster or Frankenstein. Frankenstein speaks of his parents' conscientiousness towards himself as a child, "the being to which they had given life" and "the active spirit of tenderness that animated both" (p. 34) of them. Elizabeth's eyes "were ever there to bless and animate us" (p. 38). Clerval both benefits from these eyes and himself possesses an "animated glance" (p. 44). Subsequently, it is the monster who assumes the Frankenstein role when he rescues a drowning girl and attempts to "restore animation" (p. 141).

This last example brings us back to that narrower correspondence, the careful process whereby the reader comes to suspect that the name Frankenstein may apply to both the creator and his creation.[10] After all, in different ways either Frankenstein or his monster might be regarded as *The Modern Prometheus* of the subtitle. While Frankenstein mimics Prometheus' role as the creator of man, the monster rebels against his creator much as Prometheus rebelled against Zeus.[11] And as I have indicated in the previous chapter, it appears from the Miltonic analogies that both Frankenstein and the monster are akin to Adam and Satan.

There is real basis in the text for believing that the monster is Frankenstein in both name and substance. The fact that the creation and escape of the monster is barely described and, indeed, is deliberately denied the kind of empirical reality conveyed in cinematic adaptations, leaves the essential nature of the being open. The monster's first live entrance is presented as a consequence of Frankenstein's dream. Such circumstances certainly augment the sense that the monster is some kind of psychological projection and may even hint that much of the narrative is a dream or an hallucination—were it not, perhaps, for Walton's "framing" account. It should be further observed that the monster is introduced and takes his leave hovering over a prone Frankenstein; in the first case, Frankenstein is asleep in his bed, in the second, he is dead in his coffin; in the first case, Frankenstein (on "awakening") thinks of "A mummy again endued with animation" (p. 58), in the second, Walton (who, like Frankenstein earlier, is appreciating the horror of the creature for the first time) relates the texture and colour of the monster's "vast hand" to "that of a mummy" (p. 218).

This business of the monster hovering over Frankenstein is one of three occasions in the text where the elements of one scene are metamorphically reproduced in another. The situation where the scenery of Switzerland and the scenery of Germany come together was treated in the last chapter; the third case will be treated in the next. In general terms this reduplicative metamorphosis is a technical means of signalling the possibility that elements which appear to be distinct, separate and self-contained, may actually constitute an indivisible unity.

In the present case, it might be argued more specifically that the second tableau of the monster hanging over the horizontal figure of his creator makes manifest what is only metaphorical in the first tableau. If the life which Frankenstein bestows upon the monster is actually his own and the relationship between the differing qualities or natures they represent is antagonistic rather than symbiotic, then the animation of the one should bring about the inanimation or death of the other. The paradoxical terminology in Frankenstein's statement, "I conceived the idea, and executed the creation of a man" (p. 211), might be taken as expressing this involvement of life and death. And, in fact, following the monster's vivication, Frankenstein reveals, "I was lifeless and did not recover my senses for a long, long time." Were it not for the ministrations of his friend Clerval, "nothing ... could have restored me to life" (p. 62). Frankenstein is as much a Lazurus as his monster and twice the power of friendship, exercised first by Clerval and secondly by Walton, in the frozen Arctic wastes, brings about his resurrection. In retrospect, Frankenstein sees that he has been involved in a life–death struggle with this creation. The words of Professor Waldman, which initially inspired Frankenstein, were fatalistically "enounced to destroy me. As he went on, I felt as if my soul were grappling with a palpable enemy" (p. 48).

Soon after coming into contact with Frankenstein, Walton senses that "the man has a double existence: he may suffer misery, and be overwhelmed by disappointments; yet when he has retired into himself, he will be like a celestial spirit, that has a halo around him, within whose circle no grief or folly ventures" (p. 29). The monster is that celestial spirit. When he is not called a monster, a creature, a wretch, a fiend or a thing, he is referred to as a daemon (e.g., pp. 26, 76, 85, 165, 166, 203, 204, 219), a word which has been corrupted into demon but which originally meant simply spirit, whether good or bad.[12] It is Frankenstein himself who suggests that the monster be identified as his evil spirit: "I considered the being whom I had cast among mankind, and endowed with the will and power to effect purposes of horror ... nearly in the light of my own vampire, my own spirit let loose from the grave, and forced to destroy all that was dear to me" (p. 77). The monster is Jekyll to Frankenstein's Hyde. Or is it the reverse?

Following the death of William and the execution of Justine, Frankenstein "wandered like an evil spirit" (p. 90). Although Justine, persuaded for a while by her confession that she did actually kill young William, says, "I almost began to think that I was the monster that he [her confessor] said I was" (p. 87), the full force of this metaphorical recognition is reserved for Frankenstein as the creator of the *actual* monster who did murder William and caused Justine to be unjustly executed. The daemon is now clearly a demon, a fiend: "My abhorrence of this fiend cannot be conceived. When I thought of him, I gnashed my teeth, my eyes became inflamed, and I ardently wished to extinguish that life which I had so thoughtlessly bestowed" (p. 92). This expression of hatred puts Frankenstein in the monster role. He looks to Elizabeth "to chase away the fiend that lurked in my heart" (p. 93). But ultimately, Frankenstein sees himself as responsible for Elizabeth's death: "I am the cause of this—I murdered her. William, Justine, and Henry—they all died by my hands" (p. 185). "I am the assassin of those most innocent creatures; they died by my machinations" (p. 186).

I have no wish to transform likely defects into artistic virtues but, given this process of self-recognition, it is at least possible to argue that Frankenstein's failure to register surprise on first discovering that his creation can speak English is appropriate and revelatory since he is, in fact, speaking to himself. However this may be, as the narrative progresses, Mary makes increasing use of various kinds of reversals to further indicate that Frankenstein and the monster are ambiguously differentiated aspects of a single being. Although for the monster Frankenstein is equivalent to God, Frankenstein finds himself in a position where he must accede to his creation's wishes and manufacture a mate. "But," claims Frankenstein, "through the whole period during which I was the slave of my creature, I allowed myself to be governed by the impulses of the moment" (p. 153). This kind of ambiguous appositional syntax is frequently employed to reflect the book's thematic ambiguities. Here the question arises, is Frankenstein the "slave" of his inner "impulses" or is he "governed" by his "creature?" Once again, the distinction between what is external and what is internal is being conflated. According to the daemon's own account of his resolve to kill Elizabeth, "I was the slave, not the master, of an impulse, which I detested, yet could not disobey." After the death of Elizabeth, the monster declares with Milton's Satan[13] that "Evil thenceforth became my good" (p. 220). But in Mary Shelley's context, the phrase carries the implication that evil and good are in a sense synonymous.

On at least a couple of occasions a different kind of ironic reversal takes place when Frankenstein attributes to the monster qualities which might more appropriately be attributed to Frankenstein himself. While engaged in creating a mate, as agreed, Frankenstein observes the monster at his laboratory window: "As I looked on him, his countenance expressed the utmost extent of malice and treachery." Given that, in the next instant, Frankenstein "tore to pieces the thing on which [he] was engaged" (p. 166), it is he and not the monster who is guilty of treachery. He has gone back on his word. At a later point, a dying Frankenstein attempts to convince Walton of the need to destroy the monster: "He is eloquent and persuasive ... His soul is as hellish as his form, full of treachery and fiendlike malice" (p. 209). Once again, these qualities might more appropriately be applied to the man who is so compellingly advocating murder.[14]

The inextricable interinvolvement of Frankenstein and the monster is conveyed most concretely in terms of the ambiguous reversal of pursuer and pursued in the final quarter of the narrative. First it is the monster who follows Frankenstein but, after the murder of Elizabeth, Frankenstein proceeds to track his creation. For a moment, Frankenstein recognizes that the very creature he is tracking, fearing "that if I lost all trace of him I should despair and die, left some mark to guide me." But immediately Frankenstein rejects this attribution of benevolence to the monster and imagines "a spirit of good" which, in some paradoxical fashion, "followed and directed my steps" (p. 203). As Frankenstein sees things, it is the spirit of good and not the monster that places meals in his path.

If a reader is not ready at this point to entertain the possibility that Frankenstein and the monster are psychic doubles, further argumentation on my part will make little difference. But a couple of additional points should be made. The fact that one of Mary's best tales, "The Transformation" (1830), is undisputedly about a doppelgänger relationship between a dissolute young man and a misshapen dwarf who exchange identities does suggest that the evidence for a similar relationship in *Frankenstein* should be viewed in a positive light.[15] However, as a final piece of internal evidence we return to the monster's references to the "series of my being" (pp. 219, 222). I have already made the point that amongst the meanings that might be derived from this teasing phrase is the idea that the monster is co-existent with the series of incidents that make up the text itself. But the word "series" also serves as a point of identification with Frankenstein who earlier speaks of the "whole series of my life" (p. 178). In a sense, then, Frankenstein, the monster and the text constitute an identical reality. And what, after all, is a series but a sequence of separate yet connected elements moving towards wholeness or oneness?

By now it should be readily apparent that the doppelgänger theme and the thematic emphasis on patterns of sexual perversion—especially incest and homosexuality—are aspects of one another. If the relationship between Frankenstein and his monster is symptomatic of the self-reflective nature of all relationships then all relationships are self-involved. That self-involvement might forcibly be imaged as masturbatory but, given the exigencies of plot, what is actually masturbatory is presented more often as incestuous or homosexual. Irving Massey has realized that the monster's desire for a female mate is, in truth, only a pretext. The fact that "rape is the one crime he won't commit"[16]—even when presented with an unconscious Justine—suggests that his real desire is not directed towards women. Even allowing for the overt element of male chauvinism, there is truth in this remark. Frankenstein is clearly "the monster's only true love."[17] This love is finally acknowledged when the monster describes the dead Frankenstein as "the select specimen of all that is worthy of love and admiration among men" (p. 222).

So far I have explained the doppelgänger relationship as if Frankenstein were a representative man. His schizophrenia reflects the morally ambiguous nature of love and knowledge in our "fallen" world. But the book's impact depends upon the reader's intuition that while from one point of view, the mind of Frankenstein constitutes the entire narrative reality, from another, he is but a man among men. Between the extreme subjective and the extreme objective positions, the reader is faced with an infinity of choices as to what elements of seemingly external reality are to be understood as projections of Frankenstein's psyche. At one point on this spectrum the monster is as real as everybody else, at least as literal as the bug in Kafka's *The Metamorphosis*. After all, to Walton's perception the monster does survive Frankenstein's death. If, however, carefully sifting the evidence, the reader attempts to square the narrative with everyday reality and rest for a while with the notion that the monster is a projection of Frankenstein but most everything else is real, then some psychological explanation must be found for the pattern of murders, Frankenstein's apparent desire to murder those nearest and dearest to him. He presumably does not kill Clerval and Elizabeth for philosophical and epistemological reasons. Such reasons will only do if Clerval and Elizabeth are somehow aspects of Frankenstein's reality.

Given that the world of Frankenstein is basically familial, what is required on the level of psychological realism is some kind of proto-Freudian motivation. Mary Shelley has been careful to include the necessary evidence but, as is wise in such matters, she avoids drawing explicit conclusions. The reader should, however, understand Frankenstein's psychology as distinct from the kind of intimations, described in Chapter 2, that might be gleaned from the novel concerning Mary Shelley's own psychology. We have seen that the creation of the monster is intimately related to the dream in which Frankenstein embraces his mother's corpse. His mother died of scarlet fever. Elizabeth, who previously contracted the disease and recovered, was the source of the contagion. Consequently, as Martin Tropp astutely hypothesizes, at least subconsciously, Frankenstein must blame Elizabeth for causing his mother's death.[18] This would explain the necessity for Elizabeth's death and—although Tropp does not make the point—the death of Clerval since he shares many of Elizabeth's qualities. (Tropp rationalizes the death of Clerval somewhat differently as the destruction of Frankenstein's moral side.[19]) As Frankenstein's doppelgänger, the monster shares his love for his mother; hence it is the miniature of Frankenstein's mother which William is carrying that "softened and attracted" (p. 143) the monster. Tropp further supposes that Frankenstein would have subconsciously resented Elizabeth for ending his idyllic life as an only child.[20] Hence again, the death of Elizabeth and the deaths of William and Justine. Nor is it accidental that the biographical situation of Justine herself, described in the chapter following Frankenstein's dream, presents, as Tropp observes, an analogous case.[21] Her mother "accused her of having caused the death of her brothers and sister" (p. 66), presumably out of suppressed hatred.

If we follow Tropp's argument that Victor subconsciously wants to destroy all the rivals for his parents' love, we are provided with a possible explanation for the survival of his father—the only member of the household not killed directly by the monster (he dies "naturally" of grief). In view of the evidence concerning Frankenstein's intense feelings for his mother, we must assume a pronounced ambivalence in his feelings for his father. Something of the love/hate relationship between Frankenstein and his monster also exists between father and son here. We may intuit, then, that Victor's father and the monster are not killed for analogous reasons. The Oedipal complexities inherent in Victor's attitude towards his father are hinted at during the period in Ireland following Clerval's murder. Frankenstein finds himself in prison as the suspected murderer; Mr. Kirwin, a magistrate, tells him that a friend is to visit. Frankenstein's reaction is one of horror: "I know not by what chain of thought the idea presented itself, but it instantly darted into my mind that the murderer had come to mock at my misery and taunt me with the death of Clerval, as a new incitement for me to comply with his hellish desires." Mr. Kirwin is bewildered: "I should have thought, young man, that the presence of your father would have been welcome, instead of inspiring such violent repugnance." Immediately, Frankenstein's reaction changes from "anguish to pleasure" (p. 180). What is here bewildering to Mr.

Kirwin may be taken by the reader as revelatory of Frankenstein's psychology. The episode serves to identify Victor's father with the monster.

Little is to be gained by filling out and schematizing these psychological hints. It is enough to realize that events can be generally construed in a way that accords with Frankenstein's inner drives.[22] To turn the book into any kind of rigorous case history would be to inhibit that flexibility which enables the reader to move along the axis bounded at one end by Frankenstein as a man among men and at the other by Frankenstein as total reality. The interchangeable alignment of interior and exterior worlds, of psychology and mythology, allows for that metaphoric power which is at the heart of the book's vitality.

NOTES

1. Gordon D. Hirsch demonstrates that the creation of the monster is presented as a masturbatory activity. See "The Monster Was a Lady: On the Psychology of Mary Shelley's *Frankenstein*," 126.

2. *The Gaping Pig: Literature and Metamorphosis* (Berkeley: University of California Press, 1969), p. 126.

3. See, Wolfgang Iser, *The Implied Reader: Patterns of Communication in Prose from Bunyan to Beckett* (Baltimore: Johns Hopkins University Press, 1974); and Walter J. Ong, s.J., "The Writer's Audience Is Always a Fiction," *PMLA*, 90 (January 1975), 9–21.

4. *The Romantic Novel in England* (Cambridge, Mass.: Harvard University Press, 1972), p. 164.

5. Richard J. Dunn observes that the novel's structure reinforces the aloneness of the three narrators. See "Narrative Distance in *Frankenstein*," *Studies in the Novel*, 6 (Winter, 1974), 408–17.

6. See, in this connection, Masao Miyoshi, *The Divided Self: A Perspective on the Literature of the Double* (New York: New York University Press, 1970); and Carl F. Keppler, *The Literature of the Second Self* (Tucson: University of Arizona Press, 1972).

7. *Child of Light: A Reassessment of Mary Wollstonecraft Shelley* (Hadleigh, Essex: Tower Bridge, 1951), pp. 134–37. Muriel Spark sees the monster as Frankenstein's isolated reason. Irving Massey, on the other hand, interprets the monster as Frankenstein's physicality. See *The Gaping Pig*, p. 127. Harold Bloom's formulation suggests a way in which these divergent positions might be combined. He believes that the monster represents the mind and emotions turned outwards not inwards as in his creator's case. The monster is, therefore, more human than Frankenstein although eventually he develops into a daemon of pure consciousness. See the Afterword to the Signet *Frankenstein*, pp. 215–23.

8. "Philosophical and Literary Sources of *Frankenstein*," 105, n. 27. See also Charles Schug, "The Romantic Form of Mary Shelley's *Frankenstein*," *Studies in English Literature*, 17 (Autumn, 1977), 613–14.

9. For example, Lowry Nelson, Jr., calls *Frankenstein* "a significant fictional model of the mind." See "Night Thoughts on the Gothic Novel," *Yale Review*, 52 (Winter, 1963), 247.

10. Glynn R. Grylls speculates that John Trelawny was the first to call the monster Frankenstein in a letter to Claire dated November 27, 1869. See *Mary Shelley: A Biography*, p. 319, n. 2; and *The Letters of Edward John Trelawny*, ed. H. Buxton Forman (London:

Oxford University Press, 1910), p. 222. However, Grylls is wrong. There are at least two earlier instances. In Chapter 15 of Elizabeth Gaskell's *Mary Barton*, first published in 1847, this sentence occurs: "The actions of the uneducated seem to me typified in those of Frankenstein, that monster of many human qualities, ungifted with a soul, a knowledge of the difference between good and evil." See *Mary Barton* (London: John Lehmann Ltd., 1947), p. 167. *A Supplement to the Oxford English Dictionary* (1972) fails to note the examples from Trelawny and Gaskell but supplies a still earlier case. The entry reads: "**1838** Gladstone in *Murrays Handbk. Sicily* (1864) p. xlvi, 'They [*sc.* mules] really seem like Frankensteins of the animal creation.'" I am grateful to Patrick Parrinder for drawing my attention to the Gaskell and Gladstone references.

11. Masao Miyoshi makes this point in *The Divided Self*, pp. 82–83.

12. In view of the generic ambivalence of Frankenstein and its quasi-allegorical character, Angus Fletcher's study of daemonic figures in allegorical literature may be illuminatingly related to the monster. See his *Allegory: The Theory of a Symbolic Mode* (Ithaca: Cornell University Press, 1964).

13. *Paradise Lost*, IV, 110.

14. Small makes something like this point in *Ariel Like a Harpy*, p. 187.

15. Mary derived this story from Byron's unfinished drama, *The Deformed Transformed* (1824).

16. *The Gaping Pig*, p. 129.

17. *Ibid.*, p. 130.

18. *Mary Shelley's Monster*, p. 22.

19. *Ibid.*, p. 27.

20. *Ibid.*, p. 21.

21. *Ibid.*, p. 25.

22. For alternative analyses of most of the details which Tropp considers, see Morton Kaplan and Robert Kloss, "Fantasy of Paternity and the Doppelgänger: Mary Shelley's *Frankenstein*," *The Unspoken Motive: A Guide to Psychoanalytic Literary Criticism* (New York: The Free Press, 1973), pp. 119–45; and Joseph Gerhard, "Frankenstein's Dream: The Child as Father of the Monster," *Hartford Studies in Literature*, 7 (number 3, 1975), 97–115.

SANDRA M. GILBERT AND SUSAN GUBAR

Horror's Twin:
Mary Shelley's Monstrous Eve

W alton and his new friend Victor Frankenstein have considerably more in common than a Byronic (or Monk Lewis-ish) Satanism. For one thing, both are orphans, as Frankenstein's monster is and as it turns out all the major and almost all the minor characters in *Frankenstein* are, from Caroline Beaufort and Elizabeth Lavenza to Justine, Felix, Agatha, and Safe. Victor Frankenstein has not always been an orphan, though, and Shelley devotes much space to an account of his family history. Family histories, in fact, especially those of orphans, appear to fascinate her, and wherever she can include one in the narrative she does so with an obsessiveness suggesting that through the disastrous tale of the child who becomes "an orphan and a beggar" she is once more recounting the story of the fall, the expulsion from paradise, and the confrontation of hell. For Milton's Adam and Eve, after all, began as motherless orphans reared (like Shelley herself) by a stern but kindly father-god, and ended as beggars rejected by God (as she was by *God*win when she eloped). Thus Caroline Beaufort's father dies leaving her "an orphan and a beggar," and Elizabeth Lavenza also becomes "an orphan and a beggar"—the phrase is repeated (18, 20, chap. 1)—with the disappearance of her father into an Austrian dungeon. And though both girls are rescued by Alphonse Frankenstein, Victor's father, the early alienation from the patriarchal chain-of-being signalled by their orphanhood prefigures

From *The Madwoman in the Attic: The Woman Writer and the Nineteenth-Century Literary Imagination.* © 1979 by Sandra M. Gilbert and Susan Gubar.

the hellish fate in store for them and their family. Later, motherless Safie and fatherless Justine enact similarly ominous anxiety fantasies about the fall of woman into orphanhood and beggary.

Beyond their orphanhood, however, a universal sense of guilt links such diverse figures as Justine, Felix, and Elizabeth, just as it will eventually link Victor, Walton, and the monster. Justine, for instance, irrationally confesses to the murder of little William, though she knows perfectly well she is innocent. Even more irrationally, Elizabeth is reported by Alphonse Frankenstein to have exclaimed "Oh, God! I have murdered my darling child!" after her first sight of the corpse of little William (57, chap. 7). Victor, too, long before he knows that the monster is actually his brother's killer, decides that his "creature" has killed William and that therefore he, the creator, is the "true murderer": "the mere presence of the idea," he notes, is "an irresistable proof of the fact" (60, chap. 7). Complicity in the murder of the child William is, it seems, another crucial component of the Original Sin shared by prominent members of the Frankenstein family.

At the same time, the likenesses among all these characters—the common alienation, the shared guilt, the orphanhood and beggary—imply relationships of redundance between them like the solipsistic relationships among artfully placed mirrors. What reinforces our sense of this hellish solipsism is the barely disguised incest at the heart of a number of the marriages and romances the novel describes. Most notably, Victor Frankenstein is slated to marry his "more than sister" Elizabeth Lavenza, whom he confesses to having always considered "a possession of my own" (21, chap. 1). But the mysterious Mrs. Saville, to whom Walton's letters are addressed, is apparently in some sense *his* more than sister, just as Caroline Beaufort was clearly a "more than" wife, in fact a daughter, to her father's friend Alphonse Frankenstein. Even relationless Justine appears to have a metaphorically incestuous relationship with the Frankensteins, since as their servant she becomes their possession and more than sister, while the female monster Victor half-constructs in Scotland will be a more than sister as well as a mate to the monster, since both have the same parent/creator.

Certainly at least some of this incest-obsession in *Frankenstein* is, as Ellen Moers remarks, the "standard" sensational matter of Romantic novels.[24] Some of it, too, even without the conventions of the gothic thriller, would be a natural subject for an impressionable young woman who had just spent several months in the company of the famously incestuous author of *Manfred*.[25] Nevertheless, the streak of incest that darkens *Frankenstein* probably owes as much to the book's Miltonic framework as it does to Mary Shelley's own life and times. In the Edenic cosiness of their childhood, for instance, Victor and Elizabeth are incestuous as Adam and Eve are, literally incestuous because they have the same creator, and figuratively so because Elizabeth is Victor's pretty plaything, the image of an angelic soul or "epipsyche" created from his own soul just as Eve is created from Adam's rib. Similarly, the incestuous relationships of Satan and Sin, and by implication of Satan and Eve, are mirrored in the incest fantasies of *Frankenstein*, including the disguised but intensely sexual waking dream in which Victor Frankenstein in effect couples with his monster by applying "the instruments of life" to its body and inducing a shudder of response (42, chap. 5). For Milton, and therefore for Mary Shelley, who was trying to understand Milton, incest was an inescapable metaphor for the solipsistic fever of self-awareness that Matthew Arnold was later to call "the dialogue of the mind with itself."[26]

If Victor Frankenstein can be likened to both Adam and Satan, however, who or what is he *really*? Here we are obliged to confront both the moral ambiguity and the symbolic slipperiness which are at the heart of all the characterizations in *Frankenstein*. In fact, it is probably these continual and complex reallocations of meaning, among characters whose histories echo and re-echo each other, that have been so bewildering to critics. Like figures in a dream, all the people in *Frankenstein* have different bodies and somehow, horribly, the same face, or worse—the same two faces. For this reason, as Muriel Spark notes, even the book's subtitle "The Modern Prometheus" is ambiguous, "for though at first Frankenstein is himself the Prometheus, the vital fire-endowing protagonist, the Monster, as soon as he is created, takes on [a different aspect of] the role."[27] Moreover, if we postulate that Mary Shelley is more concerned with Milton than she is with Aeschylus, the intertwining of meanings grows even more confusing, as the monster himself several times points out to Frankenstein, noting "I ought to be thy Adam, but I am rather the fallen angel," (84, chap. 10), then adding elsewhere that "God, in pity, made man beautiful ... after His own image; but my form is a filthy type of yours.... Satan had his companions ... but I am solitary and abhorred" (115, chap. 15). In other words, not only do Frankenstein and his monster both in one way or another enact the story of Prometheus, each is at one time or another like God (Victor as creator, the monster as his creator's "Master"), like Adam (Victor as innocent child, the monster as primordial "creature"), and like Satan (Victor as tormented overreacher, the monster as vengeful fiend).

What is the reason for this continual duplication and reduplication of roles? Most obviously, perhaps, the dreamlike shifting of fantasy figures from part to part, costume to costume, tells us that we are in fact dealing with the psychodrama or waking dream that Shelley herself suspected she had written. Beyond this, however, we would argue that the fluidity of the narrative's symbolic scheme reinforces in another way the crucial significance of the Miltonic skeleton around which Mary Shelley's hideous progeny took shape. For it becomes increasingly clear as one reads *Frankenstein* with *Paradise Lost* in mind that because the novel's author is such an inveterate student of literature, families, and sexuality, and because she is using her novel as a tool to help her make sense of her reading, *Frankenstein* is ultimately a mock *Paradise Lost* in which both Victor and his monster, together with a number of secondary characters, play all the neo-biblical parts over and over again—all except, it seems at first, the part of Eve. Not just the striking omission of any obvious Eve-figure from this "woman's book" about Milton, but also the barely concealed sexual components of the story as well as our earlier analysis of Milton's bogey should tell us, however, that for Mary Shelley the part of Eve is all the parts.

On the surface, Victor seems at first more Adamic than Satanic or Eve-like. His Edenic childhood is an interlude of prelapsarian innocence in which, like Adam, he is sheltered by his benevolent father as a sensitive plant might be "sheltered by the gardener, from every rougher wind" (19–20, chap. 1). When cherubic Elizabeth Lavenza joins the family, she seems as "heaven-sent" as Milton's Eve, as much Victor's "possession" as Adam's rib is Adam's. Moreover, though he is evidently forbidden almost nothing ("My parents [were not] tyrants ... but the agents and creators of many delights"), Victor hints to Walton that his deific father, like Adam's and Walton's, did on one occasion arbitrarily forbid him to pursue his interest in arcane knowledge. Indeed, like Eve and Satan, Victor blames his own fall at least in part on his father's apparent arbitrariness. "If ... my father had taken the pains to explain to me that the principles of Agrippa had been entirely exploded.... It is even possible that the train of my ideas would never have received the fatal impulse that led to my ruin" (24–25, chap. 2). And soon after asserting this he even associates an incident in which a tree is struck by Jovian thunder bolts with his feelings about his forbidden studies.

As his researches into the "secrets of nature" become more feverish, however, and as his ambition "to explore unknown powers" grows more intense, Victor begins to metamorphose from Adam to Satan, becoming "as Gods" in his capacity of "bestowing animation upon lifeless matter," laboring like a guilty artist to complete his false creation. Finally, in his conversations with Walton he echoes Milton's fallen angel, and Marlowe's, in his frequently reiterated confession that "I bore a hell within me which nothing could extinguish" (72, chap. 8). Indeed, as the "true murderer" of innocence, here cast in the form of the child William, Victor perceives himself as a diabolical creator whose mind has involuntarily "let loose" a monstrous and "filthy demon" in much the same way that Milton's Satan's swelled head produced Sin, the disgusting monster he "let loose" upon the world. Watching a "noble war in the sky" that seems almost like an intentional reminder that we are participating in a critical rearrangement of most of the elements of *Paradise Lost*, he explains that "I considered the being whom I had cast among mankind ... nearly in the light of my own vampire, my own spirit let loose from the grave and forced to destroy all that was dear to me" (61, chap. 7).

Even while it is the final sign and seal of Victor's transformation from Adam to Satan, however, it is perhaps the Sin-ful murder of the child William that is our first overt clue to the real nature of the bewilderingly disguised set of identity shifts and parallels Mary Shelley incorporated into *Frankenstein*. For as we saw earlier, not just Victor and the monster but also Elizabeth and Justine insist upon responsibility for the monster's misdeed. Feeling "as if I had been guilty of a crime" (41, chap. 4) even before one had been committed, Victor responds to the news of William's death with the same self-accusations that torment the two orphans. And, significantly, for all three—as well as for the monster and little William himself—one focal point of both crime and guilt is an image of that other beautiful orphan, Caroline Beaufort Frankenstein. Passing from hand to hand, pocket to pocket, the smiling miniature of Victor's "angel mother" seems a token of some secret fellowship in sin, as does Victor's post-creation nightmare of transforming a lovely, living Elizabeth, with a single magical kiss, into "the corpse of my dead mother" enveloped in a shroud made more horrible by "grave-worms crawling in the folds of the flannel" (42, chap. 5). Though it has been disguised, buried, or miniaturized, femaleness—the gender definition of mothers and daughters, orphans and beggars, monsters and false creators— is at the heart of this apparently masculine book.

Because this is so, it eventually becomes clear that though Victor Frankenstein enacts the roles of Adam and Satan like a child trying on costumes, his single most self-defining act transforms him definitively into Eve. For as both Ellen Moers and Marc Rubenstein have pointed out, after much study of the "cause of generation and life," after locking himself away from ordinary society in the tradition of such agonized mothers as Wollstonecraft's Maria, Eliot's Hetty Sorel, and Hardy's Tess, Victor Frankenstein has a baby.[28] His "pregnancy" and childbirth are obviously manifested by the existence of the paradoxically huge being who emerges from his "workshop of filthy creation," but even the descriptive language of his creation myth is suggestive: "incredible labours," "emaciated with confinement," "a passing trance," "oppressed by a slow fever," "nervous to a painful degree," "exercise and amusement would ... drive away incipient disease," "the instruments of life" (39–41, chap. 4), etc. And, like Eve's fall into guilty knowledge and painful maternity, Victor's entrance into what Blake would call the realm of "generation" is marked by a recognition of the necessary interdependence of those complementary opposites, sex and death: "To examine the causes of life, we must first have recourse to death," he observes (36, chap. 4), and in his isolated workshop of filthy creation—filthy because obscenely sexual[29]—he collects and arranges materials furnished by "the dissecting room and the slaughterhouse." Pursuing "nature to her hiding places" as Eve does in eating the apple, he learns that "the tremendous secrets of the human frame" are the interlocked secrets of sex and death, although, again like Eve, in his first mad pursuit of knowledge he knows not "eating death." But that his actual orgasmic animation of his monster-child takes place "on a dreary night in November," month of All Souls, short days, and the year's last slide toward death, merely reinforces the Miltonic and Blakean nature of his act of generation.

Even while Victor Frankenstein's self-defining procreation dramatically transforms him into an Eve-figure, however, our recognition of its implications reflects backward upon our sense of Victor-as-Satan and our earlier vision of Victor-as-Adam. Victor as Satan, we now realize, was never really the masculine, Byronic Satan of the first book of *Paradise Lost*, but always, instead, the curiously female, outcast Satan who gave birth to Sin. In his Eve-like pride ("I was surprised ... that I alone should be reserved to discover so astonishing a secret" [37, chap. 4]), this Victor-Satan becomes "dizzy" with his creative powers, so that his monstrous pregnancy, bookishly and solipsistically conceived, reenacts as a terrible bibliogenesis the moment when, in Milton's version, Satan "dizzy swum / In darkness, while [his] head flames thick and fast / Threw forth, till on the left side op'ning wide" and Sin, Death's mother-to-be, appeared like "a Sign / Portentous" (*PL* 2. 753–61). Because he has conceived—or, rather, misconceived—his monstrous offspring by brooding upon the *wrong* books, moreover, this Victor-Satan is paradigmatic, like the falsely creative fallen angel, of the female artist, whose anxiety about her own aesthetic activity is expressed, for instance, in Mary Shelley's deferential introductory phrase about her "hideous progeny," with its plain implication that in her alienated attic workshop of filthy creation she has given birth to a deformed book, a literary abortion or miscarriage. "How [did] I, then a young girl, [come] to think of and to *dilate* upon so very hideous an idea?" is a key (if disingenuous) question she records. But we should not overlook her word play upon *dilate*, just as we should not ignore the anxious pun on the word *author* that is so deeply embedded in *Frankenstein*.

If the adult, Satanic Victor is Eve-like both in his procreation and his anxious creation, even the young, prelapsarian, and Adamic Victor is to risk a pun—*curiously* female, that is, Eve-like. Innocent and guided by silken threads like a Blakeian lamb in a Godwinian garden, he is consumed by "a fervent longing to penetrate the secrets of nature," a longing which—expressed in his explorations of "vaults and charnelhouses," his guilty observations of "the unhallowed damps of the grave," and his passion to understand "the structure of the human frame"—recalls the criminal female curiosity that led Psyche to lose love by gazing upon its secret face, Eve to insist upon consuming "intellectual food," and Prometheus's sister-in-law Pandora to open the forbidden box of fleshly ills. But if Victor-Adam is also Victor-Eve, what is the real significance of the episode in which, away at school and cut off from his family, he locks himself into his workshop of filthy creation and gives birth by intellectual parturition to a giant monster? Isn't it precisely at this point in the novel that he discovers he is not Adam but Eve, not Satan but Sin, not male but female? If so, it seems likely that what this crucial section of *Frankenstein* really enacts is the story of Eve's discovery not that she must fall but that, having been created female, she is fallen, femaleness and fallenness being essentially synonymous. For what Victor Frankenstein most importantly learns, we must remember, is that he is the "author" of the monster—for him alone is "reserved ... so astonishing a secret"—and thus it is he who is "the true murderer," he who unleashes Sin and Death upon the world, he who dreams the primal kiss that incestuously kills both "sister" and "mother." Doomed and filthy, is he not, then, Eve instead of Adam? In fact, may not the store of the fall be, for women, the story of the discovery that one is not innocent and Adam (as one had supposed) but Eve, and fallen? Perhaps this is what Freud's cruel but metaphorically accurate concept of penis-envy really means: the girl-child's surprised discovery that she is female, hence fallen, inadequate. Certainly the almost grotesquely anxious self-analysis implicit in Victor Frankenstein's (and Mary Shelley's) multiform relationships to Eve, Adam, God, and Satan suggest as much.

The discovery that one is fallen is in a sense a discovery that one is a monster, a murderer, a being gnawed by "the never-dying worm" (72, chap. 8) and therefore capable of any horror, including but not limited to sex, death, and filthy literary creation. More, the discovery that one is fallen—self-divided, murderous, material—is the discovery that one has released a "vampire" upon the world, "forced to destroy all that [is] dear" (61, chap. 7). For this reason—because *Frankenstein* is a story of woman's fall told by, as it were, an apparently docile daughter to a censorious "father"—the monster's narrative is embedded at the heart of the novel like the secret of the fall itself. Indeed, just as Frankenstein's workshop, with its maddening, riddling answers to cosmic questions is a hidden but commanding attic womb/room where the young artist-scientist murders to dissect and to recreate, so the murderous monster's single, carefully guarded narrative commands and controls Mary Shelley's novel. Delivered at the top of Mont Blanc-like the North Pole one of the Shelley family's metaphors for the indifferently powerful source of creation and destruction—it is the story of deformed Geraldine in "Christabel," the story of the dead-alive crew in "The Ancient Mariner," the story of Eve in *Paradise Lost*, and of her degraded double Sin— all secondary or female characters to whom male authors have imperiously denied any chance of self-explanation.[30] At the same time the monster's narrative is a philosophical meditation on what it means to be born without a "soul" or a history, as well as an exploration of what it feels like to be a "filthy mass that move[s] and talk[s]," a thing, an other, a creature of the second sex. In fact, though it tends to be ignored by critics (and film-makers), whose emphasis has always fallen upon Frankenstein himself as the archetypal mad scientist, the drastic shift in point of view that the nameless monster's monologue represents probably constitutes *Frankenstein's* most striking technical *tour de force*, just as the monster's bitter self-revelations are Mary Shelley's most impressive and original achievement.[31]

Like Victor Frankenstein, his author and superficially better self, the monster enacts in turn the roles of Adam and Satan, and even eventually hints at a sort of digression into the role of God. Like Adam, he recalls a time of primordial innocence, his days and nights in "the forest near Ingolstadt," where he ate berries, learned about heat and cold, and perceived "the boundaries of the radiant roof of fight which canopied me" (88, chap. 11). Almost too quickly, however, he metamorphoses into an outcast and Satanic figure, hiding in a shepherd's but which seems to him "as exquisite ... a retreat as Pandemonium ... after... the lake of fire" (90, chap. 11). Later, when he secretly sets up housekeeping behind the De Laceys' pigpen, his wistful observations of the loving though exiled family and their pastoral abode ("Happy, happy earth! Fit habitation for gods ..." [100, chap. 12]) recall Satan's mingled jealousy and admiration of that "happy rural seat of various view" where Adam and Eve are emparadised by God and Milton (*PL* 4. 247). Eventually, burning the cottage and murdering William in demonic rage, he seems to become entirely Satanic: "I, like the arch-fiend, bore a hell within me" (121, chap. 16); "Inflamed by pain, I vowed eternal hatred ... to all mankind" (126, chap. 16). At the same time, in his assertion of power over his "author," his mental conception of another creature (a female monster), and his implicit dream of founding a new, vegetarian race somewhere in "the vast wilds of South America," (131, chap. 17), he temporarily enacts the part of a God, a creator, a master, albeit a failed one.

As the monster himself points out, however, each of these Miltonic roles is a Procrustean bed into which he simply cannot fit. Where, for instance, Victor Frankenstein's childhood really was Edenic, the monster's anxious infancy is isolated and ignorant, rather than insulated or innocent, so that his groping arrival at self-consciousness—"I was a poor, helpless, miserable wretch; I knew and could distinguish nothing; but feeling pain invade me on all sides, I sat down and wept" (87–88, chap. 11)—is a fiercely subversive parody of Adam's exuberant "all things smil'd, / With fragrance and with joy my heart o'erflowed. / Myself I then perus'd, and Limb by Limb / Survey'd, and sometimes went, and sometimes ran / With supple joints, as lively vigor led" (*PL* 8. 265–69). Similarly, the monster's attempts at speech ("Sometimes I wished to express my sensations in my own mode, but the uncouth and inarticulate sounds which broke from me frightened me into silence again" (88, chap. 11) parody and subvert Adam's ("To speak I tri'd, and forthwith spake, / My Tongue obey'd and readily could name / Whate'er I saw" (*PL* 8. 271–72). And of course the monster's anxiety and confusion ("What was I? The question again recurred to be answered only with groans" [106, chap. 13]) are a dark version of Adam's wondering bliss ("who I was, or where, or from what cause, / [I] Knew not.... [But I] feel that I am happier than I know" (*PL* 8. 270–71, 282).

Similarly, though his uncontrollable rage, his alienation, even his enormous size and superhuman physical strength bring him closer to Satan than he was to Adam, the monster puzzles over discrepancies between his situation and the fallen angel's. Though he is, for example, "in bulk as huge / As whom the Fables name of monstrous size, / *Titanian*, or *Earth-born*, that warr'd on *Jove*," and though, indeed, he is fated to war like Prometheus on Jovean Frankenstein, this demon/monster has fallen from no heaven, exercised no power of choice, and been endowed with no companions in evil. "I found myself similar yet at the same time strangely unlike to the beings concerning whom I read and to whose conversation I was a listener," he tells Frankenstein, describing his schooldays in the De Lacey pigpen (113, chap. 15). And, interestingly, his remark might well have been made by Mary Shelley herself, that "devout but nearly silent listener" (xiv) to masculine conversations who, like her hideous progeny, "continually studied and exercised [her] mind upon" such "histories" as *Paradise Lost*, Plutarch's *Lives*, and *The Sorrows of Werter* [sic] "whilst [her] friends were employed in their ordinary occupations" (112, chap. 15).

In fact, it is his intellectual similarity to his authoress (rather than his "author") which first suggests that Victor Frankenstein's male monster may really be a female in disguise. Certainly the books which educate him— *Werter*, Plutarch's *Lives*, and *Paradise Lost*—are not only books Mary had herself read in 1815, the year before she wrote *Frankenstein*, but they also typify just the literary categories she thought it necessary to study: the contemporary novel of sensibility, the serious history of Western civilization, and the highly cultivated epic poem. As specific works, moreover, each must have seemed to her to embody lessons a female author (or monster) must learn about a male-dominated society. Werter's story, says the monster—and he seems to be speaking for Mary Shelley—taught him about "gentle and domestic manners," and about "lofty sentiments ... which had for their object something out of self." It functioned, in other words, as a sort of Romantic conduct book. In addition, it served as an introduction to the virtues of the proto-Byronic "Man of Feeling," for, admiring Werter and never mentioning Lotte, the monster explains to Victor that "I thought Werter himself a more divine being than I had ever ... imagined," adding, in a line whose female irony about male self-dramatization must surely have been intentional, "I wept [his extinction] without precisely understanding it" (113, chap. 15).

If *Werter* introduces the monster to female modes of domesticity and self-abnegation, as well as to the unattainable glamour of male heroism, Plutarch's *Lives* teaches him all the masculine intricacies of that history which his anomalous birth has denied him. Mary Shelley, excluding herself from the household of the second Mrs. Godwin and studying family as well as literary history on her mother's grave, must, again, have found in her own experience an appropriate model for the plight of a monster who, as James Rieger notes, is especially characterized by "his unique knowledge of what it is like to be born free of history."[32] In terms of the disguised story the novel tells, however, this monster is not unique at all, but representative, as Shelley may have suspected she herself was. For, as Jane Austen has Catherine Morland suggest in *Northanger Abbey*, what is woman but man without a history, at least without the sort of history related in Plutarch's *Lives*? "History, real solemn history, I cannot be interested in," Catherine declares "... the men all so good for nothing, and hardly any women at all—it is very tiresome" (*NA* 1, chap. 14).

But of course the third and most crucial book referred to in the miniature *Bildungsroman* of the monster's narrative is *Paradise Lost*, an epic myth of origins which is of major importance to him, as it is to Mary Shelley, precisely because, unlike Plutarch, it does provide him with what appears to be a personal history. And again, even the need for such a history draws Shelley's monster closer not only to the realistically ignorant female defined by Jane Austen but also to the archetypal female defined by John Milton. For, like the monster, like Catherine Morland, and like Mary Shelley herself, Eve is characterized by her "unique knowledge of what it is like to be born free of history," even though as the "Mother of Mankind" she is fated to "make" history. It is to Adam, after all, that God and His angels grant explanatory visions of past and future. At such moments of high historical colloquy Eve tends to excuse herself with "lowliness Majestic" (before the fall) or (after the fall) she is magically put to sleep, calmed like a frightened animal "with gentle Dreams ... and all her spirits compos'd / To meek submission" (*PL* 12. 595–96). Nevertheless, one of the most notable facts about the monster's ceaselessly anxious study of *Paradise Lost* is his failure even to mention Eve. As an insistently male monster, on the surface of his palimpsestic narrative he appears to be absorbed in Milton's epic only because, as Percy Shelley wrote in the preface to *Frankenstein* that he drafted for his wife, *Paradise Lost* "most especially" conveys "the truth of the elementary principles of human nature," and conveys a that truth in the dynamic tensions developed among its male characters, Adam, Satan, and God (xvii). Yet not only the monster's uniquely ahistorical birth, his literary anxieties, and the sense his readings (like Mary's) foster that he must have been parented, if at all, by *books*; not only all these facts and traits but also his shuddering sense of deformity, his nauseating size, his namelessness, and his orphaned, motherless isolation link him with Eve and with Eve's double, Sin. Indeed, at several points in his impassioned analysis of Milton's story he seems almost on the verge of saying so, as he examines the disjunctions among Adam, Satan, and himself:

> Like Adam, I was apparently united by no link to any other being in existence; but his state was far different from mine in every other respect. He had come forth from the hands of God a perfect creature, happy and prosperous, guided by the especial care of his Creator; he was allowed to converse with and acquire knowledge from beings of a superior nature, but I was wretched, helpless, and alone. Many times I considered Satan as the fitter emblem of my condition, for often, like him, when I viewed the bliss of my protectors, the bitter gall of envy rose within me.... Accursed creator! Why did you form a monster so hideous that even you turned from me in disgust? God, in pity, made man beautiful and alluring, after his own image; but my form is a filthy type of yours, more horrid even from the very resemblance. Satan had his companions, fellow devils, to admire and encourage him, but I am solitary and abhorred. [114–15, chap. 15]

It is Eve, after all, who languishes helpless and alone, while Adam converses with superior beings, and it is Eve in whom the Satanically bitter gall of envy rises, causing her to eat the apple in the hope of adding "what wants / In Female Sex." It is Eve, moreover, to whom deathly isolation is threatened should Adam reject her, an isolation more terrible even than Satan's alienation from heaven. And finally it is Eve whose body, like her mind, is said by Milton to resemble "less / His Image who made both, and less [to express] / The character of that Dominion giv'n / O'er other Creatures ..." (*PL* 8. 543–46). In fact, to a sexually anxious reader, Eve's body might, like Sin's, seem "horrid even from [its] very resemblance" to her husband's, a "filthy" or obscene version of the human form divine.[33]

As we argued earlier, women have seen themselves (because they have been seen) as monstrous, vile, degraded creatures, second-comers, and emblems of filthy materiality, even though they have also been traditionally defined as superior spiritual beings, angels, better halves. "Woman [is] a temple built over a sewer," said the Church father Tertullian, and Milton seems to see Eve as both temple and sewer, echoing that patristic misogyny.[34] Mary Shelley's conscious or unconscious awareness of the monster woman implicit in the angel woman is perhaps clearest in the revisionary scene where her monster, as if taking his cue from Eve in *Paradise Lost* book 4, first catches sight of his own image: "I had admired the perfect forms of my cottagers ... but how was I terrified when I viewed myself in a transparent pool. At first I started back, unable to believe that it was indeed I who was reflected in the mirror; and when I became fully convinced that I was in reality the monster that I am, I was filled with the bitterest sensations of despondence and mortification" (98–99, chap. 12). In one sense, this is a corrective to Milton's blindness about Eve. Having been created second, inferior, a mere rib, how could she possibly, this passage implies, have seemed anything but monstrous to herself? In another sense, however, the scene supplements Milton's description of Eve's introduction to herself, for ironically, though her reflection in "the clear / Smooth Lake" is as beautiful as the monster's is ugly, the self-absorption that Eve's confessed passion for her own image signals is plainly meant by Milton to seem morally ugly, a hint of her potential for spiritual deformity: "There I had fixt / Mine eyes till now, and pin'd with vain desire, / Had not a voice thus warn'd me, What thou seest, / What there thou seest fair Creature is thyself ..." (*PL* 4. 465–68).

The figurative monstrosity of female narcissism is a subtle deformity, however, in comparison with the literal monstrosity many women are taught to see as characteristic of their own bodies. Adrienne Rich's twentieth-century description of "a woman in the shape of a monster / A monster in the shape of a woman" is merely the latest in a long line of monstrous female self-definitions that includes the fearful images in Djuna Barnes's *Book of Repulsive Women*, Denise Levertov's "a white sweating bull of a poet told us / our cunts are ugly" and Sylvia Plath's "old yellow" self of the poem "In

Plaster."[35] Animal and misshapen, these emblems of self-loathing must have descended at least in part from the distended body of Mary Shelley's darkly parodic Eve/Sin/Monster, whose enormity betokens not only the enormity of Victor Frankenstein's crime and Satan's bulk but also the distentions or deformities of pregnancy and the Swiftian sexual nausea expressed in Lemuel Gulliver's horrified description of a Brobdignagian breast, a passage Mary Shelley no doubt studied along with the rest of *Gulliver's Travels* when she read the book in 1816, shortly before beginning *Frankenstein*.[36]

At the same time, just as surely as Eve's moral deformity is symbolized by the monster's physical malformation, the monster's physical ugliness represents his social illegitimacy, his bastardy, his namelessness. Bitchy and dastardly as Shakespeare's Edmund, whose association with filthy femaleness is established not only by his devotion to the material/maternal goddess Nature but also by his interlocking affairs with those filthy females Goneril and Regan, Mary Shelley's monster has also been "got" in a "dark and vicious place." Indeed, in his vile illegitimacy he seems to incarnate that bestial "unnameable" place. And significantly, he is himself as nameless as a woman is in patriarchal society, as nameless as unmarried, illegitimately pregnant Mary Wollstonecraft Godwin may have felt herself to be at the time she wrote *Frankenstein*.

"This nameless mode of naming the unnameable is rather good," Mary commented when she learned that it was the custom at early dramatizations of *Frankenstein* to place a blank line next to the name of the actor who played the part of the monster.[37] But her pleased surprise was disingenuous, for the problem of names and their connection with social legitimacy had been forced into her consciousness all her life. As the sister of illegitimate and therefore nameless Fanny Imlay, for instance, she knew what bastardy meant, and she knew it too as the mother of a premature and illegitimate baby girl who died at the age of two weeks without ever having been given a name. Of course, when Fanny dramatically excised her name from her suicide note Mary learned more about the significance even of insignificant names. And as the stepsister of Mary Jane Clairmont, who defined herself as the "creature" of Lord Byron and changed her name for a while with astonishing frequency (from Mary Jane to Jane to Clara to Claire), Mary knew about the importance of names too. Perhaps most of all, though, Mary's sense of the fearful significance of legitimate and illegitimate names must have been formed by her awareness that her own name, Mary Wollstonecraft Godwin, was absolutely identical with the name of the mother who had died in giving birth to *her*. Since this was so, she may have speculated, perhaps her own monstrosity, her murderous illegitimacy, consisted in her being—like Victor Frankenstein's creation—a reanimation of the dead, a sort of galvanized corpse ironically arisen from what should have been "the cradle of life."

This implicit fantasy of the reanimation of the dead in the monstrous and nameless body of the living returns us, however, to the matter of the monster's Satanic, Sinful and Eve-like moral deformity. For of course the crimes that the monster commits once he has accepted the world's definition of him as little more than a namelessly "filthy mass" all reinforce his connection with Milton's unholy trinity of Sin, Eve/Satan, and Death. The child of two authors (Victor Frankenstein and Mary Shelley) whose mothers have been stolen away by death, this motherless monster is after all made from dead bodies, from loathsome parts found around cemeteries, so that it seems only "natural" for him to continue the Blakeian cycle of despair his birth began, by bringing further death into the world. And of course he brings death, in the central actions of the novel: death to the childish innocence of little William (whose name is that of Mary Shelley's father, her half-brother, and her son, so that one can hardly decide to which male relative she may have been alluding); death to the faith and truth of allegorically named Justine; death to the legitimate artistry of the Shelleyan poet Clerval; and death to the ladylike selflessness of angelic Elizabeth. Is he acting, in his vile way, for Mary Shelley, whose elegant femininity seemed, in view of her books, so incongruous to the poet Beddoes and to literary Lord Dillon? "She has no business to be a woman by her books," noted Beddoes. And "your writing and your manners are not in accordance," Dillon told Mary herself. "I should have thought of you—if I had only read you—that you were a sort of ... Sybil, outpouringly enthusiastic ... but you are cool, quiet and feminine to the last degree.... Explain this to me."[38]

Could Mary's coolness have been made possible by the heat of her monster's rage, the strain of her decorous silence eased by the demonic abandon of her nameless monster's ritual fire dance around the cottage of his rejecting "Protectors"? Does Mary's cadaverous creature want to bring more death into the world because he has failed—like those other awful females, Eve and Sin—to win the compassion of that blind and curiously Miltonic old roan, the Godlike musical patriarch De Lacey? Significantly, he is clinging to the blind man's knees, begging for recognition and help—"Do not you desert me in the hour of trial!"—when Felix, the son of the house, appears like the felicitous hero he is, and, says the monster, "with supernatural force [he] tore me from his father ... in a transport of fury, he dashed me to the ground and struck me violently with a stick ... my heart sank within me as with bitter sickness" (119, chap. 15). Despite everything we have been told about the monster's physical vileness, Felix's rage seems excessive in terms of the novel's overt story. But as an action in the covert plot—the tale of the blind rejection of women by misogynistic/Miltonic patriarchy—it is inevitable and appropriate. Even more psychologically appropriate is the fact that having been so definitively rejected by a world of fathers, the monster takes his revenge, first by murdering William, a male child who invokes his father's name ("My papa is a syndic—he is M. Frankenstein—he will punish you") and then by beginning a doomed search for a maternal, female principle in the harsh society that has created him.

In this connection, it begins to be plain that Eve's—and the monster's—motherlessness must have had extraordinary cultural and personal significance for Mary Shelley. "We think back through our mothers if we are women," wrote Virginia Woolf in *A Room of One's Own*.[39] But of course one of the most dramatic emblems of Eve's alienation from the masculine garden in which she finds herself is her motherlessness. Because she is made in the image of a man who is himself made in the image of a male creator, her unprecedented femininity seems merely a defective masculinity, a deformity like the monster's inhuman body.[40] In fact, as we saw, the only maternal model in *Paradise Lost* is the terrifying figure of Sin. (That Eve's punishment for *her* sin is the doom of agonized maternity—the doom of painfully becoming no longer herself but "Mother of Human Race"— appears therefore to seal the grim parallel.) But all these powerful symbols would be bound to take on personal weight and darkness for Shelley, whose only real "mother" was a tombstone—or a shelf of books—and who, like all orphans, must have feared that she had been deliberately deserted by her dead parent, or that, if she was a monster, then her hidden, underground mother must have been one too.

For all these reasons, then, the monster's attitude toward the possibility (or impossibility) of finding a mother is unusually conflicted and complex. At first, horrified by what he knows of the only "mother" he has ever had— Victor Frankenstein—he regards his parentage with loathing. Characteristically, he learns the specific details of his "conception" and "birth" (as Mary Shelley may have learned of hers) through reading, for Victor has kept a journal which records "that series of disgusting circumstances" leading "to the production of [the monster's] ... loathsome person."[41] Later, however, the ill-fated miniature of Caroline Beaufort Frankenstein, Victor's "angel mother," momentarily "attract[s]" him. In fact, he claims it is because he is "forever deprived of the delights that such beautiful creatures could bestow" that he resolves to implicate Justine in the murder of William. His reproachful explanation is curious, though ("The crime had its source in her; be hers the punishment"), as is the sinister rape fantasy he enacts by the side of the sleeping orphan ("Awake, fairest, thy lover is near—he who would give his life but to obtain one look of affection from thine eyes" [127–28, chap. 16]). Clearly feelings of rage, terror, and sexual nausea, as well as idealizing sentiments, accrete for Mary and the monster around the maternal female image, a fact which explains the later climactic wedding-night murder of apparently innocent Elizabeth. In this fierce, Miltonic world, *Frankenstein* says, the angel woman and the monster woman alike must die, if they are not dead already. And what is to be feared above all else is the reanimation of the dead, specifically of the maternal dead. Perhaps that is why a significant pun is embedded in the crucial birth scene ("It was on a dreary night of November") that, according to Mary Shelley, rose "unbidden" from her imagination. Looking at the "demoniacal corpse to which I had so miserably given life," Victor remarks that "A *mummy* again endued with animation could not be so hideous as that wretch" (43, chap. 5). For a similarly horrific (and equally punning) statement of sexual nausea, one would have to go back to Donne's "Loves Alchymie" with its urgent, misogynistic imperative: "Hope not for minde in women; at their best / Sweetnesse and wit, they are but / *Mummy* possest."

Interestingly, the literary group at Villa Diodati received a packet of books containing, among other poems, Samuel Taylor Coleridge's recently published "Christabel," shortly before Mary had her monster-dream and began her ghost story. More influential than "Loves Alchymie"—a poem Mary may or may not have read—"Christabel"'s vision of femaleness must have been embodied for the author of *Frankenstein* not only in the witch Geraldine's withered side and consequent self-loathing ("Ah! What a stricken look was hers!") but also in her anxiety about the ghost of Christabel's dead mother ("Off, wandering mother! Peak and pine!") and in Christabel's "Woe is me / She died the hour that I was born." But even without Donne's puns or Coleridge's Romanticized male definition of deathly maternity, Mary Shelley would have absorbed a keen sense of the agony of female sexuality, and specifically of the perils of motherhood, not just from *Paradise Lost* and from her own mother's fearfully exemplary fate but also from Wollstonecraft's almost prophetically anxious writings.

Maria, or the Wrongs of Woman (1797), which Mary read in 1814 (and possibly in 1815) is about, among other "wrongs," Maria's search for her lost child, her fears that "she" (for the fantasied child is a daughter) may have been murdered by her unscrupulous father, and her attempts to reconcile herself to the child's death. In a suicide scene that Wollstonecraft drafted shortly before her own death, as her daughter must have known, Maria swallows laudanum: "her soul was calm ... nothing remained but an eager longing ... to fly ... from this hell of disappointment. Still her eyes closed not.... Her murdered child again appeared to her ... [But] 'Surely it is better to die with me, than to enter on life without a mother's care!'"[42] Plainly, *Frankenstein's* pained ambivalence toward mothers and mummies is in some sense a response to *Maria's* agonized reaching—from beyond the grave, it may have seemed—toward a daughter. Off, wandering mother! Peak and pine!" It is no wonder if Coleridge's poem gave Mary Wollstonecraft Godwin Shelley bad dreams, no wonder if she saw Milton's "Mother of Human Race" as a sorrowful monster.

Though *Frankenstein* itself began with a Coleridgean and Miltonic nightmare of filthy creation that reached its nadir in the monster's revelation of filthy femaleness, Mary Shelley, like Victor Frankenstein himself, evidently needed to distance such monstrous secrets. Sinful, motherless Eve and sinned-against, daughterless Maria, both paradigms of woman's helpless alienation in a male society, briefly emerge from the sea of male heroes and villains in which they have almost been lost, but the ice soon closes over their heads again, just as it closes around those two insane figure-skaters, Victor Frankenstein and his hideous offspring. Moving outward from the central "birth myth" to the icy perimeter on which the novel began, we find ourselves caught up once more in Walton's naive polar journey, where Frankenstein and his monster reappear as two embattled grotesques, distant and archetypal figures solipstically drifting away from each other on separate icebergs. In Walton's scheme of things; they look again like God and Adam, Satanically conceived. But now, with our more nearly complete understanding of the bewildered and bewildering perspective Mary Shelley adopted as "Milton's daughter," we see that they were Eve and Eve all along.

Nevertheless, though Shelley did manage to still the monster's suffering and Frankenstein's and her own by transporting all three from the fires of filthy creation back to the ice and silence of the Pole, she was never entirely to abandon the sublimated rage her monster-self enacted, and never to abandon, either, the metaphysical ambitions *Frankenstein* incarnated. In *The Last Man* she introduced, as Spark points out, "a new, inhuman protagonist," PLAGUE (the name is almost always spelled entirely in capitals), who is characterized as female and who sees to it that "disaster is no longer the property of the individual but of the entire human race."[43] And of course PLAGUE's story is the one that Mary claims to have found in the Sibyl's cave, a tale of a literally female monster that was merely foreshadowed by the more subdued narrative of "The Modern Prometheus."

Interestingly, PLAGUE's story ends with a vision of last things, a vision of judgment and of paradise nihilistically restored that balances *Frankenstein*'s vision of first things. With all of humanity wiped out by the monster PLAGUE, just as the entire Frankenstein family was destroyed by Victor's monster, Lionel Verney, the narrator, goes to Rome, that cradle of patriarchal civilization whose ruins had seemed so majestically emblematic to both Byron and Shelley. But where Mary's husband had written of the great city in a kind of ecstasy, his widow has her disinherited "last man" wander lawlessly about empty Rome until finally he resolves, finding "parts of a manuscript ... scattered about," that "I also will write a book ... [but] for whom to read?—to whom dedicated? And then with silly flourish (what so capricious and childish as despair?) I wrote,

DEDICATION

TO THE ILLUSTRIOUS DEAD

SHADOWS, ARISE, AND READ YOUR FALL!

BEHOLD THE HISTORY OF THE LAST MAN.[44]

His hostile, ironic, literary gesture illuminates not only his own career but his author's. For the annihilation of history may well be the final revenge of the monster who has been denied a true place in history: the moral is one that Mary Shelley's first hideous progeny, like Milton's Eve, seems to have understood from the beginning.

NOTES

Epigraphs: Milton, book 1, plate 10, lines 6–9; Hawthorne (on Fanny Fern), quoted in Caroline Ticknor, *Hawthorne and His Publishers* (Boston: Houghton Mifflin, 1913), p. 142; *Poems*, J. 532.

1. From Keats's annotations to *Paradise Lost*, quoted by Wittreich in *The Romantics on Milton*, p. 560.

2. George Eliot, *Middlemarch* (1871/1872; Cambridge, Mass.: Riverside Edition, 1956), book 1, chap. 7. All subsequent citations will be from this edition.

3. Letter to J. H. Reynolds, 17 April 1817, in *The Letters of John Keats*, ed. Hyder E. Rollins (Cambridge, Mass.: Harvard University Press, 1958), 1:130. See also Wittreich, p. 563, note 9.

4. *Middlemarch*, I, chap. 7.

5. Ibid.

6. Ibid., I, chap. 3.

7. Ibid.

8. Ibid.

9. Ibid. Interestingly; in deciding that Casaubon's work "would reconcile complex knowledge with devoted piety," Dorothea thinks at this point that "Here was something beyond the shallows of ladies'-school literature."

10. *A Room of One's Own*, p. 31.

11. Preface to *The World's Olio*, in *By a Woman writt*, ed. Joan Goulianos (Baltimore, Penguin Books, 1973), p. 60.

12. Anne Finch, "The Introduction," *Poems of Anne Countess of Winchilsea.*

13. From *Jane Anger her Protection for Women*, in Goulianos, p. 26.

14. See, for instance, Harold Bloom, "Afterword," *Frankenstein* (New York and Toronto: New American Library, 1965), p. 214.

15. Author's introduction to *Frankenstein* (1817; Toronto, New York, London: Bantam Pathfinder Edition, 1967), p. xi. Hereafter page references to this edition will follow

quotations, and we will also include chapter references for those using other editions. For a basic discussion of the "family romance" of literature, see Harold Bloom, *The Anxiety of Influence*.

16. Robert Kiely, *The Romantic Novel in England* (Cambridge, Mass.: Harvard University Press, 1972), p. 161.

17. Moers, *Literary Women*, pp. 95–97.

18. See Ralph Wardle, *Mary Wollstonecraft* (Lincoln, Neb.: University of Nebraska Press, 1951), p. 322, for more detailed discussion of these attacks on Wollstonecraft.

19. Muriel Spark, *Child of Light* (Hodleigh, Essex: Tower Bridge Publications, 1951), p. 21.

20. See *Mary Shelley's Journal*, ed. Frederick L. Jones (Norman, Okla.: University of Oklahoma Press, 1947), esp. pp. 32–33, 47–49, 71–73, and 88–90, for the reading lists themselves. Besides reading Wollstonecraft's *Maria*, her *A Vindication of the Rights of Woman*, and three or four other books, together with Godwin's *Political Justice* and his *Caleb Williams*, Mary Shelley also read parodies and criticisms of her parents' works in these years, including a book she calls *Anti-Jacobin Poetry*, which may well have included that periodical's vicious attack on Wollstonecraft. To read, for her, was not just to read her family, but to read *about* her family.

21. Marc A. Rubenstein suggests that throughout the novel "the act of observation, passive in one sense, becomes covertly and symbolically active in another: the observed scene becomes an enclosing, even womb-like container in which a story is variously developed, preserved, and passed on. Storytelling becomes a vicarious pregnancy." "'My Accursed Origin': The Search for the Mother in *Frankenstein*," *Studies in Romanticism* 15, no. 2 (Spring 1976): 173.

22. See Anne Finch, "The Introduction," in *The Poems of Anna Countess of Winchilsea*, pp. 4–6, and Sylvia Plath, "The Moon and the Yew Tree," in *Ariel*, p. 41.

23. Speaking of the hyperborean metaphor in *Frankenstein*, Rubenstein argues that Walton (and Mary Shelley) seek "the fantasied mother locked within the ice ... the maternal Paradise beyond the frozen north," and asks us to consider the pun implicit in the later meeting of Frankenstein and his monster on the *mer* (or *Mère*) de Glace at Chamonix (Rubenstein "'My Accursed Origin,'" pp. 175–76).

24. See Moers, *Literary Women*, pp. 99.

25. In that summer of 1816 Byron had in fact just fled England in an attempt to escape the repercussions of his scandalous affair with his half sister Augusta Leigh, the real-life "Astarte."

26. Matthew Arnold, "Preface" to *Poems*, 1853.

27. Spark, *Child of Light*, p. 134.

28. See Moers, *Literary Women*, "Female Gothic"; also Rubenstein, "'My Accursed Origin,'" pp. 165–166.

29. The *OED* gives "obscenity" and "moral defilement" among its definitions of "filth."

30. The monster's narrative also strikingly echoes Jemima's narrative in Mary Wollstonecraft's posthumously published novel, *Maria, or The Wrongs of Woman*. See *Maria* (1798; rpt. New York: Norton, 1975), pp. 52–69.

31. Harold Bloom does note that "the monster is ... Mary Shelley's finest invention, and his narrative ... forms the highest achievement of the novel." ("Afterword" to *Frankenstein*, p. 219.)

32. James Rieger, "Introduction" to *Frankenstein (the 1818 Text)* (Indianapolis: Bobbs-Merrill, 1974), p. xxx.

33. In Western culture the notion that femaleness is a deformity or obscenity can be traced back at least as far as Aristotle, who asserted that "we should look upon the female

state as being as it were a deformity, though one which occurs in the ordinary course of nature." (*The Generation of Animals*, trans. A. L. Peck [London Heinemann, 1943], p. 461.) For a brief but illuminating discussion of his theories see Katharine M. Rogers, *The Troublesome Helpmate.*

34. See de Beauvoir, *The Second Sex*, p. 156.

35. Adrienne Rich, "Planetarium," in *Poems: Selected and New* (New York: Norton, 1974), pp. 146–48; Djuna Barnes, *The Book of Repulsive Women* (1915; rpt. Berkeley, Calif., 1976); Denise Levertov, "Hypocrite Women," *O Taste & See* (New York: New Directions, 1965); Sylvia Plath, "In Plaster," *Crossing the Water* (New York: Harper & Row, 1971), p. 16.

36. See *Mary Shelley's Journal*, p. 73.

37. Elizabeth Nitchie, *Mary Shelly* (New Brunswick, N.J.: Rutgers University Press, 1953) p. 219.

38. See Spark, *Child of Light*, pp. 192–93.

39. Woolf, *A Room*, p. 79.

40. In "The Deluge at Norderney," Isak Dinesen tells the story of Calypso, niece of Count Seraphina Von Platen, philosopher who "disliked and mistrusted everything female" and whose "idea of paradise was ... a long row of lovely young boys ... singing his poems to his music." "Annihilated" by her uncle's misogyny, Calypso plans to chop off her own breasts with a "sharp hatchet." See *Seven Gothic Tales*, pp. 43–51.

41. Marc Rubenstein speculates that as a girl Shelley may actually have read (and been affected by) the correspondence that passed between her parents around the time that she was conceived.

42. *Maria*, p. 152.

43. Spark, *Child of Light*, p. 205.

44. *The Last Man*, p. 339.

LAURA P. CLARIDGE

Parent-Child Tensions in
Frankenstein: The Search for Communion

The rights of kings are deduced in a direct line from the king of Kings,
and that of parents from our first parent.
—Mary Wollstonecraft, *A Vindication of the Rights of Woman*

Everything must have a beginning.... And that beginning must be
linked to something that went before.
—Mary Shelley, *Frankenstein*

Surely no one needs to be reminded that *Frankenstein* is a book largely
reminiscent of Mary Shelley's own troubled family relationships; and in
support of the point, one need only turn to George Levin and U. C.
Knoepflmacher's excellent collection of essays, *The Endurance of Frankenstein*,
to find the matter well documented.[1] That an author's life becomes
translated into her fiction is hardly news on any account. But what has
somehow eluded proper treatment is the resultant real subject of this
"monster tale": the failure of human beings to "parent" their offspring in
such a way that they will be able to take part in society rather than retreat
into themselves.

An emphasis upon the proper assumption of parental responsibilities
was part of the age: Maria Edgeworth and Hannah More had, through their
educational treatises, influenced Walter Scott's Waverley themes, and Mary

From *Studies in the Novel*, vol. XVII, no. 1 (Spring 1985): 14–26. © 1985 by North Texas State
University.

Shelley in turn bowed in his direction by allowing her husband to send him presentation volumes of *Frankenstein* the month the novel was published anonymously. The romantic educators typically placed the blame for an adolescent's misconduct at the door of a negligent (though often well-meaning) parent. Shelley herself subtly indicts Victor's parents in exactly this way; and she suggests an even subtler subtext of family conflict in the letters Walton writes to Margaret. Previous commentators have, of course, noted Frankenstein's abuse of his monster; strangely enough, however, they have tended to ignore the precedent within his own family for Victor's later actions, as well as the familial tensions that Walton, Victor's shadow self, implies. Such critical shortsightedness has inevitable resulted in textual analyses that fail to account for the complexity of this novel.

Readers have quite correctly assumed the statement in Shelley's preface, "my chief concern has been to exhibit the amiableness of domestic affection and the excellence of universal virtues" to be a cover-up; but in ascribing to Mary Shelley a need to deny the ugliness of a nightmarish vision they have missed her real subterfuge.[2] She will indeed concern herself with "domestic affection"—but more precisely, the lack of it, and how such a lack *undermines* "universal virtue."[3] In Shelley's attention to parent–child relationships, she implies a far-ranging application to society at large: if we fail at this most primal unit of communication, what hope is there for compassionate interaction within the larger community? Shelley insists that man can live only through communion with others; solitude, for her, represents death.

Through his continual exaggerations of familial love, Victor Frankenstein reveals to us the inadequacy of the homelife that belies his oft-fevered protestations of attachment. Perhaps the inevitable ambivalence concerning our own childhood creates a suspension of critical acuity in our reading Victor's story, but a close study of the text undercuts severely his insistence upon the perfect home. Critics have generally fallen for his defenses: Kate Ellis basically accepts his myth of the happy home;[4] Gubar and Gilbert call his childhood, in Miltonic terms, Edenic.[5] Only Christopher Small suggests that in Victor's description there is a "strained emphasis on felicity."[6]

That Victor insists upon remembering "the best of all possible worlds" is the psychological defense of an only child (as he was for a long time) who maintains a love/hate relationship with his parents because he senses that they share an affection that in some way excludes him.[7] Victor is an object of their love, not a participant in it; he is "their plaything and their idol" (p. 33). In his recollections of his parents' relationship—recollections more fully developed in the 1831 edition—he emphasizes their devotion to each other, to the (implicit) detriment of their child. If, as Victor claims, everything was centered on fulfilling the mother's wishes, one must wonder at the son's extravagant account of the love left over for him: "they seemed to draw inexhaustible stores of affection from a very mine of love to bestow them upon me" (p. 33). The narrator strains his credibility too far when he assures us that "every hour of my infant life I received a lesson of patience, of charity, and of self-control" (p. 34)—precisely those virtues that the young adult scientist will lack. After being told that "for a long time I was their only care," we are to believe that the addition of Elizabeth to his little family effected nothing but unqualified joy. There is no mention of the inevitable sibling friction; instead, these siblings were "strangers to any species of disunion or disrepute. Harmony was the soul of companionship ..." (p. 36). Frankenstein early on models upon his parents as Elizabeth becomes his plaything. His mother tells him, "I have a pretty present for my Victor—tomorrow he shall have *it*" (p. 35, emphasis mine). The child subsequently accepts Elizabeth as his "promised gift" and makes her his own possession.

We misread the story (and many have) if we listen to Victor's hyperbolic descriptions of a family idyll without attuning our ears to the subtext. When, for instance, Henry Clerval asks Victor if they might talk "on an important subject" and Victor reacts with some anxiety, his friend quickly surmises that the scientist might be fearful to speak of his own home. Before proceeding, Clerval reassures his friend: "I will not mention it if it agitates you; but your father and cousin ... hardly know how ill you have been and are uneasy at your long silence" (p. 63). Victor responds: "How could you suppose that my first thought would not fly towards those dear, dear friends whom I love and who are so deserving of my love?" Both Clerval and the readers have some reason to doubt Victor's insistence. At this point in the narrative, he has not been home for five years; he will finally return home after yet another year passes, when he is summoned by his father upon William's death. Consequently, though he proclaims in frenzied terms that he loves his family "to adoration," we suspect that ambivalence, at the least, subverts his affection.

It is not only Victor who has troubled connections with his family; rather, we are in a world where parental irresponsibility and failure are the rule. Beaufort's pride puts his daughter in a difficult position; Safie's interests are betrayed by her father; Elizabeth is left an orphan; Justine's father dies and leaves his favorite at the mercy of a hard mother; and Henry Clerval's father attempts to keep him from the academic life he yearns to pursue. But more important than any family conflicts outside of the protagonist's is Walton's relationship to Margaret, that maternal sister who has apparently failed to be responsive to her younger brother's needs. He somewhat cynically reminds her, for instance, that of his efforts at poetry, she is "well acquainted with my failure and how heavily I bore the disappointment" (p. 17); and then, when discussing his latest venture, he implores: "And now, dear Margaret, do I not deserve to accomplish some great purpose? ... Oh, that some encouraging voice could answer in the affirmative!" (p. 17). Upon close reading we sense a compulsion on Walton's part to prove himself to Margaret; and if we ignore this underlying theme, as critics traditionally have done, we miss the emphasis in the novel on the murky undercurrents of what look at first glance to be straightforward parent–child relationships. In one sense, then, Victor's exaggerated (and therefore unmistakable) neglect of his progeny serves merely as a bolder-than-life projection of the novel's other, more oblique family conflicts.

The parental failures are emblematic for those people unwilling to fulfill their duties to society at large: just as the hunter, that mythical image of a strong and protective father, reacts incorrectly and injures his charge's rescuer, so even the priestly fathers respond insensitively to their children's needs.[8] Justine's callous mother follows her confessor's advice in removing her daughter from the surrogate family where she is happy (p. 66); and when Justine is accused of murdering William, her priest helps condemn this innocent by threatening her into a false confession of guilt (p. 87). Even the De Laceys, who represent the family most at ease with itself, fail; De Lacey, a parent who is treated with the greatest deference and respect, responds compassionately to Frankenstein's child because he is blind and therefore not prejudiced by appearances. It is, ironically, when his sighted children return that the old man excludes the monster from a chance of kinship; it is when his children enable their father to "see through their eyes" that he loses his own visionary powers.

If, as Ellen Moers has suggested, "most of the novel—two of the three volumes, can be said to deal with the retribution visited upon the monster and creator for deficient infant care,"[9] it is also true that inadequate parental guidance in later years leaves its mark on Victor Frankenstein. The young scientist is thirteen, on the threshold of adolescence, when the struggle to break free of his parents and to become his own man begins in earnest. Not all fathers welcome their child's ascendant power, with its accompanying suggestion that their own is on the wane. Mary Shelley implicates this tension through her fascination with "the tale of the sinful founder of his race whose miserable doom it was to bestow the kiss of death on all the younger sons of his fated house, just when they reached the age of promise" (p. 7). She revised the second version of her novel to emphasize Victor's lack of guidance at this important formative stage; the first version allows the elder

Frankenstein to share his son's interest in science, whereas in the second, Victor is left on his own.[10] In fact, when the exuberant youth tries to discuss his reading with his father, Alphonse Frankenstein carelessly glances at the title page and exclaims, "My dear Victor, do not waste your time upon this; it is sad trash" (p. 39). In one of Victor's rare insightful reflections, he explicitly criticizes his father's execution of his parental role: "If ... my father had taken the pains to explain to me [modern science] ... it is even possible that ... my ideas would never have received the fatal impulse that led to my ruin" (p. 39). Instead, he was abandoned "to struggle with a child's blindness ..." (p. 39). Finally, he is left mingling "a thousand contradictory theories and floundering desperately in a very slough of multifarious knowledge," guided by "childish reasoning" (p. 40).

John Dussinger has perceptively suggested that Frankenstein's academic pursuit is a rebellion against the moral obligations between father and son: "The center of evil is parental irresponsibility and selfishness, and the ideal of goodness is the father's bond to his son and the reciprocal bond of son to father.[11] Before there can be an interplay of love between father and child, the father has to fulfill his duties, a contract Mary Shelley well knew from her mother's writings. She also understood the pain of being rejected when her activities earned her father's disapproval, such as his refusal to see her after her marriage to Shelley or his callous warning not to grieve in excess for her dead child, lest she lose the love of those close to her.[12]

Just as William Godwin steamrolled over his daughter's sensibilities, so Alphonse Frankenstein too was insensitive to his son. Victor implies, for example, that his father insists that he depart for Ingolstadt soon after his mother's death, away from the sympathy of his native country and into new, strange surroundings with no one to guide him. There is the suggestion that Alphonse disapproves of his son's grief as a dilatory tactic. In fact, strong sense of parental disapproval informs the father/son reactions throughout the novel. Indeed, as Victor describes his father, we come to see a parent who loves only conditionally: his justice is a "virtue" which renders it necessary "that he should approve highly to love strongly" (p. 33).

The need to win approval from judgmental parents can at times compel the child toward excellence; but it can also be perverted into disastrous extremes, in which the child transforms his Promethean aspirations for success into those of overreaching and surpassing his parents at the cost of everything else. Victor has ambitiously planned that "a new species would bless me as its creator and source.... No father would claim the gratitude of his child so completely as I should deserve theirs." That after the "birth" he feels "guilty of a crime" comes, therefore, as no surprise to us—he has usurped his father's place in the hierarchy. No wonder then that he finds his interior self "in a state of insurrection and turmoil" (p. 48). His father had taken great precautions to ensure that his son disdain supernatural horrors (p. 55); yet, regardless of his disclaimer of responsibility for his creation, Frankenstein deliberately chose the form for his creature that was sure to provoke the most horror and dread in other mortals. Harold Bloom typifies those readers who gloss over Frankenstein's foreknowledge of his creature's ugliness, when he asserts: "the hideousness of his creature was no part of Victor Frankenstein's intention...."[13] Instead, we must read Victor's shock at his child's ugliness as mere repression of the truth, as he unwittingly admits: "I had gazed on him while unfinished; *he was ugly then* ..." (p. 58, emphasis mine).

Victor compensates for the sense of smallness his father has imparted by usurping his parents' powers as creators, but also by issuing forth a child whose physical nature will be inferior, in size, to no one. He acts out his anger at his family in an attempt to affirm his own selfhood. Just as he threw the door open to find "a spectre," so he exorcises the wolf under his bed, the parent as evil predator, by creating his own nightmare come true.[14] He recognizes from his progeny's first murderous act that the monster's destruction is his own: "I was the true murderer" (p. 89). By the end of the novel he has acknowledged that he is responsible for all the deaths. He admits: "I abhorred the face of man," a statement he fearfully retracts with "oh, not abhorred! ... I felt attracted even to the most repulsive among them ..." (pp. 184–85), a reflection we can hardly credit. Instead, his exclamation that he has turned a murderer loose upon society (p. 200) indicates the truer self-knowledge.

But Frankenstein is not alone in needing to dethrone his parents. Walton, that too often forgotten character who frames the novel subtly strikes out at Margaret, the sister who helped rear him. He reminds his sister again and again of his imminent destruction, and he presages pain for her whatever the outcome of his "voyage of discovery," as he continually alludes to his journey: "If I succeed, many years will pass before meeting again; if I fail, you will never see me again" (p. 18). In a sense he tries to "kill" his parent too, in tones redolent of the monster: "You will have visitings of despair, and yet be tortured by hope" (pp. 212–13).

Margaret, his mother substitute, has regarded his voyage with evil forebodings (p. 15), but Walton insists on his vision: "you cannot contest the inestimable benefits which I shall confer on all mankind, to the last generation ..." (p. 16). Since learning of his father's injunction against a seafaring life, the son has waited for his chance to disobey: "the favorite dream of my early years was this voyage" (p. 16). Walton's very uneasy relationship with his sister has been too often overlooked; his letters to her are usually thinly veiled threats to her power, attempts to assert his own autonomy.[15] Indeed, this "voyage of discovery" is, for him, a fight, in the Ericksonian schema,[16] between dependence and autonomy, an effort on his part to determine his relationship to the rest of society. If he, in the end, falls short of the godlike aspirations that, he emphasizes, "lift his soul to heaven," he will also turn back, however reluctantly, toward a finally integrated relationship between parent and child. Walton will "grow up," affirm himself, and return to his community, unlike his counterpart, that "soul mate" in whom he so rightly sees his own potential reflected.

II

Did I request thee, Maker, from my clay
To mould me Man, did I solicit thee
From darkness to promote me?
Paradise Lost, x, 743–45
            —(epigraph to *Frankenstein*)

Victor Frankenstein's role as father is intensified by that fulfillment of every parent's dream: he can deliberately, knowingly create his child; he can actually choose the parts. It is especially ironic, then, that he hates what he sees. Victor produces such a grotesque model for his procreation in part as a response to his own aggressive feelings toward his parents and the guilt these emotions provoke. He is anxious throughout the gestation period: "Every night I was oppressed by a slow fever, and I became nervous to a most painful degree" (p. 56). Consequently, he has geared himself to hate and fear his creature. In one sense, the ugliness affords him an escape from parental responsibilities; he can justify his immediate flight. After proving his godlike power to produce life, he is then able immediately to abandon it.

It is not, however, that Victor Frankenstein is unaware of familial connection to his monster; he feels what the duties of a "creator towards the creature" are, but he nonetheless makes no attempt to satisfy the monster's needs. He recognizes, "I ought to [have rendered] him happy before I complained of his wickedness" (p. 102). At one point the monster's tale of his life allows Frankenstein to offer his conditional concern, judging, in the manner of his father, his progeny worthy of attention: "His tale, and the feelings he now expressed, proved him to be a creature of fine sensations; and did I not as his maker, owe him, all the portion of happiness that it was in my power to bestow?" (p. 146). He continues to fail his creature, however, never gaining insight into the monster's tortured psyche, so that at the end of the novel he is able to exclaim without irony: "Let the cursed and hellish monster drink deep of agony; let him feel the despair that now torments me" (p. 202).

In noting Frankenstein's brutal disregard of any parental duties, we should recall his analysis of his parents' reaction to him as a child: "It was in their hands to direct to happiness or misery, according as they fulfilled their duties to me." They had a "deep consciousness of what they owed towards the being to which they had given life ..." (p. 34). In reality, however, his parents had regarded him as a plaything, a bauble (p. 33); and so Frankenstein views his creation as an object of his pleasure, until the "newborn" forces his way into his parent's consciousness.

It is also worth noting here that Mary Shelley began her writing with Chapter 4, wherein we see the father rejecting the monster's outstretched hand.[17] The monster labors under no delusion that he is loved: "You, my own creator, detest and spurn me ..." (p. 99). In response to the monster's pain, his father notices that "his countenance bespoke bitter anguish," but its "unearthly ugliness rendered it almost too horrible for human eyes" (p. 99). The monster's "deal"—"Do your duty towards me, and I will do mine towards you ..." (p. 99)—resonates with the sound of Mary Wollstonecraft's parental advice: "A right always includes a duty, and I think it may likewise fairly be inferred that they forfeit the right who do not fulfill the duty."[18] Since Frankenstein does not act out his proper role, his creature condemns him as "the author at once of my existence and its unspeakable torments" (p. 220). It is no coincidence that the portrait of Caroline kneeling, in agony, by her father's coffin is echoed at the novel's end, where the monster, in his own agony of despair, hangs over his dead father and utters exclamations of grief and horror. Caroline's beauty ensures that her portrait will elicit a strong sympathy from Frankenstein, but the monster has no such saving grace. Thus, with his arm extended yet again to his maker, he admits the impossibility of contact.

To substitute for the lack of human connection, the monster revels in self-education. He recognizes the wonders of speech, in which, unlike those around him, he locates mysterious powers. Viewing language as "a godlike science" (p. 112), he pays rapt attention to the lessons Felix offers to Safie. Through the De Laceys he learns that man is "at once so powerful, so virtuous, and magnificent, yet so vicious and base" (p. 119). Unlike his creator, who ponders meaning only insofar as its suggests power, the monster learns what life is about. He absorbs Felix's lessons. "I can hardly describe to you the effect of these books. They produced in me an infinity of new images and feelings ..." (p. 128). His lessons lead him, finally, to that question of intense psychological importance, without which the child never becomes the man; he tells his "father" that he finally asked himself "Who was I?" (p. 128). "The path of my departure was free; and there was none to lament my annihilation.... What was I? ... What was my destination?" (p. 128). It is worth quoting here at length from Bruno Bettelheim's analogous description of a child's self-discovery.

> The child asks himself: "Who am I? Where did I come from? ... He worries not whether there is justice for individual man, but whether *he* will be treated justly. He wonders who or what projects him into adversity, and what can prevent this from happening to him. Are there benevolent powers in addition to his parents? Are his parents benevolent powers? How should he form himself, and why? Is there hope for him though he may have done wrong? Why has all this happened to him?[19]

The tragedy is that for this introspective wanderer, the world will not support his answer; he will be answered only "with groans" (p. 121). Psychiatrist Selma Fraiberg, in *Every Child's Birthright*, writes that the unnurtured, unloved child grows into the aberrant adult—the criminal who seeks to negate his overwhelming sense of nothingness by inflicting pain on others—a scream that "I exist, I am."[20] It is not, then, the monster's nature that makes him so vengeful, as his creator deludes himself into thinking, but rather his overwhelming sense of isolation and despair at lacking human connections that in fact his father should have first provided. At the time of his first violent act, he is merely seeking fellowship with another human, and he assumes little William, the "beautiful child" so unlike himself, to be too young to have formed prejudices based on appearance. Enraged to the point of murder, he is motivated by a combination of being rejected by one so young and finding that the child, related to the monster's creator, is yet another agent of sorrow by the scientist's hand. Similarly, he strikes out at Justine because she represents to him the relationships he can never have: her condemnation will therefore be "just" because "the crime had its source in her; be hers the punishment" (p. 144). By issuing the ultimatum to Frankenstein, "On you it rests, whether I quit ... man and lead a harmless life, or become the scourge of your fellow creatures" (p. 101), the monster places the blame for his aggression where it properly lies. Frankenstein refuses the responsibility, and so, as U. C. Knoepflmacher observes in a different context, "The monster becomes father to the man and relentlessly imposes on its creator the same conditions of dependence and insecurity that it was made to suffer."[21]

In a last desperate attempt to evoke a one-to-one response, the monster forces his master into the Arctic race where he assures Frankenstein, "You will feel the misery of cold and frost, to which I am impassive" (p. 204). The cold serves as a metaphor for the comfortless, solitary life he has led, one he is bent on recreating for the agent of his pain. We become intensely, painfully aware of the monster's motivation for his aggression through the death scene of his father. Through the grief and horror at his successful patricidal act emerges the typical, unfathomable loyalty of the abused child: "Oh, Frankenstein! Generous and self-devoted being! I ... destroyed thee by destroying all thou lovedst." But the larger, more deadly truth about this "self-devoted being" is unwittingly echoed in his child's last suffocated observation: "Alas! He is cold, he cannot answer me" (p. 219).

III

In consequence of this primary mutual hostility of human beings, civilized society is perpetually threatened with disintegration. The interest of work in common would not hold it together; instinctual passions are stronger than reasonable interests. Civilization has to use its utmost efforts in order to set limits to man's aggressive instincts and to hold the manifestations of them in check by psychical reaction-formations.[22]

—Sigmund Freud, *Civilization and Its Discontents*

Of major significance in the struggle between Frankenstein and his monster are the efforts of the creator to escape his place in society, in contrast to the desperate attempts of the created to become situated within it. Frankenstein relates that his early life was passed in considerable seclusion; that it became his temper to avoid a crowd, a withdrawal making him "indifferent," therefore, to his "school-fellows in general" (p. 37). His apprehension at leaving his "amiable companions" of the hearth for the new territory of Ingolstadt is well founded, since he will be more alone here than ever. He creates his monster in solitude; and after the monster kills William, the scientist can justify his alienation from mankind by reason of his grief. He now shuns the face of man: "all sound of joy or complacency was torture to me; solitude was my only consolation—deep, dark, deathlike solitude" (p. 90). His father senses a hidden meaning to his son's withdrawal, ostensibly due to his mourning, and warns him that "excessive sorrow prevents improvement of enjoyment, or even the discharge of daily usefulness, without which no man is fit for society" (p. 91). The truth is the blunt reality previously noted: "I abhorred society." Victor wishes to pass his life on that "barren rock" (p. 169) where he will be uninterrupted by the pain of human contact; in contrast with Prometheus, whose bondage was a sacrificial act for the good of all mankind, Frankenstein wants to protect himself from the weariness of social intercourse.

In direct opposition to his maker, the monster longs for society and sympathy. He quickly becomes aware that there is no place for him, that he has been forbidden all that society holds dear: wealth and connections. If his own creator withholds from him human contact, he can expect nothing more from the rest of his world. He realizes: "No sympathy may I ever find." Though his vain efforts to assert his selfhood through aggressive acts have ruined him, he realizes his depravity is the fault of man: "the fallen angel becomes a malignant devil. Yet even that enemy of God and man had friends and associates in his desolation; I am alone." All humankind has sinned against him (p. 221). In the tradition of those who, regardless of their sins, know passion and thus know life, the monster will exult in self-destruction by fire. Frankenstein instead will die passively, "a fit end for a being who has never achieved a full sense of another's existence."[23]

If Mary Shelley offers us both Frankenstein and his monster as societal members who serve only to subvert civilization, she suggest in Robert Walton a resolution of the conflict between ambition and the need for intimacy which will result in a balanced world. Walton knows from the beginning of his trip that he is undergoing a rite of passage, a journey of discovery. We recognize a potential Frankenstein, another man ill at ease with family life, seeking out ultimate knowledge by conquering the world's uncharted regions. Indeed, Walton claims Frankenstein as his soul mate, and the scientist acts out the monster's role of deviant self, the other half, as he tempts Walton to continue his ill-fated voyage to the Pole. What distinguishes Walton from his counterpart, however, is his nascent sense of responsibility to his larger family aboard ship. In worrying about the difficulties of the voyage, he realizes he will need to be responsive to his men's fears; he "must raise the spirits of others" as well as sustain his own (p. 17). His description of his two favorite subordinates reflects the weaknesses they share with the novel's major characters: the lieutenant is "madly desirous of glory," and the ship's master has experienced a "youth passed in solitude" which by now we recognize to be a clear danger. Walton will, however, in fulfilling his "moral responsibility to the family," steer them clear of danger.

His sailors instinctively assume the protectorship of their captain; they approach him as a surrogate parent who will not fail them. They tell Frankenstein, "Here is our captain, and he will not allow you to perish in the open sea" (p. 24). Indeed, even as Walton carefully absorbs Frankenstein's story—a story that will help vicariously to redeem the captain's solipsistic quest—he ministers to the sick man. Although in a literal sense not true, Frankenstein's acclamation to Walton that "you have restored me to life" suggests the strange interchange whereby Walton fulfills properly Frankenstein's quest for knowledge as well as assuming a paternal role toward the progeny of that quest. In spite of his horror at the "appalling hideousness" of Frankenstein's creature, Walton takes the redemptive step that no one else in society has been willing to take, and, magically, calls on him *to stay* (p. 219, emphasis mine). The monster is transfixed; he looks on with wonder at the person who will finally acknowledge his outstretched hand.

Walton's voyage of discovery ends, then, in his assuming responsibilities of the mature adult, the man who turns back to society away from goals benefiting only the self, toward the goal of communion with others. He forswears his self-pity at having been a neglected child, a parentless boy, and takes on fully the role of parent himself—to the monster (he listens), and to his men (he turns back). As J. M. Hill remarks: "He chooses human connections."[24] In Walton, Mary Shelley has suggested the possibility of a successful, if subdued, modern Prometheus, stripped, through the expiations of Frankenstein and his monster, of Satanic aspirations. It is, perhaps, a domesticated Promethean vision that lacks the poetic grandeur of her spouse's ideal, but the novelist managed an understanding of basic human needs and limitations that, finally, may suggest less of a "dream story" than she modestly claimed as the basis for her novel.

NOTES

1. U. C. Knoepflmacher, "Thoughts on the Aggression of Daughters," in *The Endurance of Frankenstein*, ed. George Levine and U. C. Knoepflmacher (Berkeley: Univ. of California Press, 1979), pp. 88–119, offers the most extensive treatment of the biographical soundings. See also Kate Ellis, "Monsters in the Garden: Mary Shelley and the Bourgeois Family" and Ellen Moers, "Female Gothic" in the same volume.

2. Mary Shelley, *Frankenstein*, ed. M. K. Joseph (London: Oxford Univ. Press, 1969), p. 14. All future citations will refer to this text. I realize, of course, that Percy Shelley wrote this preface, but Mary apparently agreed to the authorial explanation.

3. As is by now well known, Shelley had much to exorcise from her own family relationships. Her mother had died soon after childbirth. Her father, according to Christopher Small, "regarded infants as mere parcels, to be handed from one person to another without adverse effect" (*Mary Shelley's Frankenstein* [Pittsburgh: Univ. of Pittsburgh Press, 1972], p. 70). And we can easily associate the solipsistic Victor, whose sense of responsibility toward his creation is severely limited, with the Shelley who will, as Mary acknowledges, appreciate his child most "when he has a nursery to himself and only comes to you, just dressed and in good humor" (Frederick L. Jones, ed. *Mary Shelley's Journal* [Norman: Univ. of Oklahoma Press, 1947], p. 205; the entry occurs on 21 Oct. 1838).

4. Ellis in *The Endurance of Frankenstein*, p. 136.

5. Sandra M. Gilbert and Susan Gubar, "Horror's Twin: Mary Shelley's Monstrous Eve," in *The Madwoman in the Attic* (New Haven: Yale Univ. Press, 1979), p. 230.

6. Small, p. 73.

7. J.M. Hill, "*Frankenstein* and the Physiognomy of Desire," *American Imago*, 32, (1975), 346.

8. Bruno Bettelheim, *The Uses of Enchantment* (New York: Vintage Books, 1977), p. 205.

9. Moers, in *The Endurance of Frankenstein*, p. 81.

10. Ellis, in *The Endurance of Frankenstein*, p. 142.

11. John A. Dussinger, "Kinship and Guilt in Mary Shelley's *Frankenstein*," *Studies in the Novel*, 7 (1976), 38.

12. Knoepflmacher discusses Shelley's relationship with her father, p. 113.

13. Harold Bloom, *The Ringers in the Tower* (Chicago: Univ. of Chicago Press, 1971), p. 124.

14. Whether, as Bruno Bettelheim shows, the "wolf" is embodied in the mean witch or the nasty stepmother—or, we might add, the ugly monster—is irrelevant.

15. A close reading of Mary Shelley's letters, with their two-edged sentiments, will illumine the nature of those she creates for Walton, Anticipating the arrival of Shelley's children by Harriet, Mary exclaims: "I long [for those children] whom I love so tenderly, then there will be a sweet brother and sister for my William who will lose his pre-eminence as eldest and be helped third at table ..." (Frederick L. Jones, ed., *The Letters of Mary W. Shelley* [Norman: Univ. of Oklahoma Press, 1944], p. 16). Or again: "[And did my love] think about our home, our babe and his poor Pecksie? But I'm sure you did ..." (*Letters*, p. 14). Nothing straightforward here.

16. See Erik Erikson, *Childhood and Society* (New York: Norton, 1950), p. 251.

17. Knoepflmacher, p. 100.

18. Mary Wollstonecraft, *A Vindication of the Rights of Woman* (London: Walter Scott, n.d.), p. 222.

19. Bettelheim, p. 47.

20. Selma Fraiberg, *Every Child's Birthright* (New York: Basic Books, 1977), p. 48.

21. Knoepflmacher, p. 103.

22. Dussinger, p. 49, quoting from Freud's *Civilization and Its Discontents*.

23. Bloom, p, 125.

24. Hill, p. 335.

WILLIAM VEEDER

Frankenstein:
Self-Division and Projection

T he war of Eros and Agape enters *Frankenstein*[1] IN THE OPENING frame as men manifest a potential for androgyny and a penchant for bifurcation. At their best, Robert Walton and Victor Frankenstein balance gender traits admirably. Their "manly" qualities—ambition, daring, scientific intelligence, physical hardihood—are tempered by a sympathetic love of neighbor which manifests itself publicly in concern for human welfare and privately in affection for Margaret and Elizabeth. Robert and Victor also tend, however, to Erotic extremism. Masculine and feminine traits in their psyches polarize into willfulness and weakness; love for woman and concern for society are seriously undermined. After establishing bifurcation in the opening frame of Frankenstein, Mary Shelley goes on to show how Victor's riven psyche attempts to heal itself through the creation of the monster.

ROBERT AND MARGARET

The first androgyne was FatherSky–MotherEarth. Their sundering in mythology[2] is reflected in the opposition of Eros and Agape. "Eros is the way by which man mounts up to the Divine, not the way [of Agape] by which the divine steps down to man.... this upward attraction of the soul is Eros" (Nygren 178, 172). Erotic males aspire skyward in *Frankenstein*. Robert's

From *Mary Shelley and Frankenstein:* The Fate of Androgyny. © 1986 by The University of Chicago.

"enthusiasm which elevates me to heaven" (10) resounds in Victor's admiration for scientists who "ascend into the heavens" (42) and his exultation at having "trod heaven in my thoughts" (209). Both men reflect Percy Shelley who insists, "I could not descend to common life" (*PSL* 1:228, 10 Jan. 1812). Shelley's *Queen Mab* contrasts "native" spirituality with "earthliness," our moribund physicality. The heroine Ianthe's spirit "reassumed / Its native dignity" when "Instinct with inexpressible beauty and grace, / Each stain of earthliness / Had passed away" (1:134–37). Even when transcendence is thwarted, Shelley insists upon the Erotic equation of native and celestial. "Woe had beaten to earth a mind [Wolfstein's in *St. Irvyne*] whose native and unconfined energies aspired to heaven" (*JS* 5:144).

For Mary Shelley, the native *is* the earthly. "Human affections are the native, luxuriant growth of a heart ... seek[ing] objects on whom to expend its yearnings" (*Perkin Warbeck* 3:351). *Frankenstein* presents nature in the form of "the mighty Jura opposing its dark side to the ambition that would quit its native country" (190). Ambitious males are forced to recognize, if not to accede to, the priority of the native. Walton in the opening frame laments that, unlike the "merchant-man now on its homeward voyage," he who has aspired beyond mundane commerce "may not see my native land, perhaps, for many years" (16). Victor soon admits "how much happier that man is who believes his native town to be the world, than he who aspires to become greater than his nature will allow" (48). (...)

VICTOR AND THE MONSTER

"The relation of the Monster to Frankenstein is constantly shifting and this raises an enormous critical problem because any discussion will run the risk of falsely stabilizing the connection between the two" (Seed 333). The surest proof of this "shifting" quality is the number of different critical interpretations of the monsters.[8] A critic today must seek not the false stability of any totalizing explanation but the legitimate coherence of a reading consistent with itself, a reading which consciously recognizes its partial quality as it follows a single thread or threads through the whole fabric. Victor's parthenogenetic creation of the monster can be seen as, among other things, an emblem and consequence of psychic bifurcation. Will informs the procreative urge. Victor determines to surpass his father, and indeed all men, as progenitor. "No father could claim the gratitude of his child so completely as I should deserve theirs" (49). As ejaculatory Prometheus, Victor "at the summit of my desires" enjoys "the most gratifying consummation.... pour[ing] a torrent of light into our dark world" (47, 49). Such presumption proves costly, however. The physical weakness

which increases with Victor's labors—"my person had become emaciated....
my voice became broken" (49, 51)—has a decidedly sexual aspect. "My
candle was nearly burnt out" (52). After the creation, "I was lifeless" (57).
The consequence of will is impotence.

With his Percy-like emaciation and broken voice, Victor becomes
Mary's first version of the "frail" male who recurs throughout her husband's
work. How differently the Shelleys view this "blighted ... withered" figure is
evident in their attitudes toward the cause of his "blasted" condition. Percy
finds indomitably heroic the blasted Ahasuerus. "Even as a giant oak ...
scathed ... A monument of fadeless ruin," Ahasuerus stands "like the scathed
pine tree's height ... majestic even in death" (*Queen Mab* 7:259–61;
"Fragment from the Wandering Jew" 2, 9). Shelley can, moreover, reward
the blasted sufferer with new life.

> ... slowly from his [Lionel's] mien there
> passed
> The desolation which it spoke;
> ... as when the lightning's blast
> Has parched some heaven-delighting oak,
> The next spring shows leaves pale and rare,
> But like flowers delicate and fair ...
>   (*Rosalind and Helen* 785–90)

Though Mary admires the passive determination to resist a cruel fate, her
subject in *Frankenstein* is the active will to godhead. She blasts sky-aspirers.
After lightning reduces the Ahasuerus-like oak to a "blasted stump" (35),
other forces of nature blast the parthenogenetic Promethean. "I [Victor] am
a blasted tree.... blasted and miserable" (158, 187). There is no Shelleyan
aura of indomitable manliness here, let alone any flowering delicate and fair.

The gender-role reversal implicit in Victor's statement that "the bolt
has entered my soul" (158) and in the monster's threat that "the bolt will ...
ravish from you your happiness" (165) has in fact occurred already. During
his emaciating labors on the creature, Frankenstein "became as timid as a
love-sick girl" (51). He is not just castrated, he is made feminine. Or rather,
effeminate. The truly feminine would be strengthened by the masculine
presence, whereas bifurcation has so thoroughly isolated female from male in
Victor that effeminacy is inevitable. He is love*sick*.

Parthenogenesis thus means more than creation from the self, it means
creation of a self. To signal that a new creator as well as a new creature is
emerging, Mary's language operates on two levels. Frankenstein in the
laboratory longs for the time "when my creation should be complete" (52);

later he defines the monster's awakening as the moment from which "I dated my creation" (72). Victor moves from male toward female during the creative act because the creature is absorbing his masculinity. Once alive, the creature is the expression of Victor's male self, the ego-centric Eros, as Victor is now the Dionysiac. The creature as male self is now both killer and lover. The killer expresses, as we will see in chapter 4, the antisocial aspect of Eros, which "despised man and recked so little of his personal worth that it would willingly dissolve him" (D'Arcy 39). Now we must focus on the *psychic* role of Eros and examine the amatory, as opposed to the homicidal, aspect of the monster's relationship with Victor. "Burning with love of his own body, he prays to escape from it in order to possess it; but death brings only the ironic retribution of transformation." What Kahn says here of Shakespeare's Adonis (32) is true of Erotic narcissists throughout nineteenth- and twentieth-century literature. Frankenstein desires himself because, as we shall see in detail in chapter 5, he imagines that through self-embrace and consequent self-generation he can achieve immortality.

His love object, a creature emphatically male in gender and prowess displays physical features conventional with the ravisher. "His hair was of a lustrous black, and flowing; his teeth of a pearly whiteness" (52). The monster's first conscious act is straight out of seduction stories. He enters the sleeper's chamber, draws aside the bed curtains, and, with a smile and murmured words, reaches out his hand. Horrified into the conventional flight, the sleeper reacts revealingly: "Sometimes my pulse beat so quickly and hardly, that I felt the palpitation of every artery; at others, I nearly sank to the ground through languor and extreme weakness" (54). By attributing to a male the "palpitation" and "languor" traditional with female passion and its aftermath, Mary Shelley is suggesting a complex reversal of roles. As the monster bodies forth Victor's male self, Frankenstein becomes the effeminate beloved who like "a love-sick girl" awaits the ravishing bolt. Victor is thus strikingly similar to Freud's Dr. Schreber, whose desire to produce a new race of beings required him, so he thought, to become female ("Psychoanalytic Notes upon an Autobiographical Account of a Case of Paranoia [Dementia Paranoides]," *SE* 12:9–82). A particularly intriguing link with Shelley surfaces in Schreber's belief that he was destined to be the "*Eternal Jew.*" "The Eternal Jew (in the sense described) had to be unmanned (transformed into a woman) to be able to bear children" (Chabot 15). O'Flaherty describes how in various myths the dismembered male is reassembled as female (294), and how the man transformed into woman becomes impotent (307). She even describes a male who, having bifurcated himself, attempts to make love to his female half (312). The god-aspiring aspect of self-copulation is traced by Singer from ancient Egyptian creation stories, through Christianity, and on to the Romantic period with William Blake (121–22).

My argument for role reversal in *Frankenstein* must address a basic objection to seeing Victor as the feminine, Dionysiac Eros. Why would Mary make him the effeminate half of the riven psyche when she could have dramatized self-projection more conventionally in terms of Pygmalion? Victor is male, so why not have him create a female? Mary patterns her narrative not upon Pygmalion but upon Percy. Shelley's narratives in both prose and verse feature obsessively the self-divided male pursuing himself. While these tales of self-division and self-pursuit make obvious the male's effeminization, they leave problematic Shelley's attitude toward it. In *St. Irvyne*, for example, Wolfstein, like Frankenstein, leaves his woman and pursues a huge male figure, "the gigantic form of Ginotti, who stalked onwards majestically.... a feeling of desperation urged Wolfstein onwards; he resolved to follow Ginotti, even to the extremity of the universe" (*JS* 5:140). As in *Frankenstein*, the extremity-directed pursuit is ultimately psychic.

> He [Wolfstein] sighed deeply when he reflected on the terrible connexion, dreadful though mysterious, which subsisted between himself and Ginotti. His soul sank within him at the idea of his own littleness, when a fellow mortal might be able to gain so strong, though sightless, an empire over him. (*JS* 5:141)

Like Frankenstein, whose recurrent professions of bafflement indicate limited self-knowledge, Wolfstein shows with the words "mysterious" and "sightless" that he cannot perceive the nature of his relationship with Ginotti. We see that Ginotti as a "power I feel within myself" (*JS* 5:141) is the projected male half of Wolfstein, the now dominant force controlling the once active protagonist.

Just as Frankenstein learns that every move of his polar pursuit is scrutinized by the monster, Wolfstein knows that Ginotti "watches my every action" (*JS* 5:141). As the monster in fact orchestrates Victor's pursuit, Ginotti boasts that "every event in your life has ... occurred under my particular machinations" (*JS* 5:170). In the process, Wolfstein like Frankenstein experiences emasculation ("his own littleness") and becomes effeminate:

> "Oh! do with me what thou wilt, strange, inexplicable being!— Do with me what thou wilt!" exclaimed Wolfstein, as an ecstasy of frenzied terror overpowered his astonished senses.... In a voice which was fascination itself, the being [Ginotti] addressed me, saying, "Wilt thou come with me? wilt thou be mine?" I felt a

decided wish never to be his.... My neck was grasped firmly......
Yes, yes, I am thine." (*JS* 5:166, 183–84)

The emergence of the feminine in *St. Irvyne* involves more than giving
to the protagonist lines conventional with women. Wolfstein's relation with
Ginotti is duplicated in his sister Eloise's relationship with Ginotti (in the
role of "Nempere"). Eloise too finds Ginotti-Nempere "gigantic" (*JS* 5:174).
As Wolfstein succumbed to the "empire" of Ginotti "within" him, Eloise
recognizes "the resist- / less empire which he possessed within her" (*JS*
5:175). Such verbal echoes equate Eloise with the effeminate Wolfstein and
thus emphasize how consistently feminine the perspective is in *St. Irvyne*.
Shelley's inclination toward passivity is embodied in the very point of view
adopted in his early fiction. Passive characters watch enthralled with or
paralyzed by the oncoming aggressors whom they cannot escape: Wolfstein-
Eloise with Ginotti-Nempere, and Verezzi-Julia with Zastrozzi-Matilda in
Zastrozzi. However aggressive Percy is at times, his passive, feminine
element is so evident that Mary knew in *Frankenstein* to make the passive
figure Victor rather than the monster.

Shelley's empathy with the feminine in his life and art is clear enough,[9]
but the meaning of role reversal in *St. Irvyne* is not. What does self-division
signify here? Granted that it reflects the terrible antagonism of Agape and
Eros in Shelley: to what extent does his sympathy with Wolfstein affect his
judgment upon, and our response to, male self-pursuit?

Unable to answer this question with the inchoate novel of Shelley's
adolescence, we can move on six years and ask it again of a poem which,
though not without difficulties, defines more clearly the sexual sources of
self-division and self-pursuit. *Alastor* is *Frankenstein* in miniature. Critics
have often linked Victor to Shelley's self-description early in the poem ("I
have made my bed / In charnels and on coffins.... Like an inspired and
desperate alchymist / Staking his very life on some dark hope" [23–24,
31–32]), but much more is involved. Percy's Poet-protagonist, like Mary's
scientist-protagonist, leaves behind a loving woman and confronts a self-
projection. "Her voice was like the voice of his own soul" (153). Victor's
revulsion at parthenogenesis is paralleled by the Poet's trauma at
autoeroticism. Confronted with the dream woman's "parted lips ... panting
bosom," the Poet "reared his shuddering limbs and quelled / His gasping
breath" (179, 182–84). The subsequent orgasm ("dissolving" [1871] is
traumatic.[10] "His strong heart sunk and sickened with excess / Of love....
blackness veiled his dizzy eyes, and night / Involved and swallowed up the
vision" (181–82, 188–89). Can this be what Holmes calls it, sexuality
"celebrated and indulged" (305)? That the "sickened with excess" clause ends

with "of love" does not make love an operative, redemptive force here. Too little and too late, "love" remains an afterthought which we experience as an attempt to defuse the real drama. We have this experience again when "spread his arms to meet / Her panting bosom" appears after we have already seen the protagonist's limbs "shuddering."

Autoeroticism in *Alastor* has the same consequences as parthenogenesis in *Frankenstein*, physically and psychologically. As Victor becomes physically "emaciated" and impotent (49, 51), the Poet's "limbs were lean.... his listless hand / Hung like dead bone within its withered skin" (248, 250–51). What apparently distinguishes the two protagonists psychologically—that the Poet seems to pursue his *female* half—is in fact their paramount similarity. Awakening after his first orgasm into a new world ("The cold white light of morning ... / Spread round him where he stood. Whither have fled / The hues of heaven that canopied his bower / Of yesternight?" [193, 196–98]), the Poet is in fact a new being. An adult caught now in the coils of passion, he like "an eagle grasped / In folds of the green serpent, feels her, breast ..." (227–28). Especially since the Poet was earlier grasped in the arms of the dream-beloved (187), we assume that the eagle grasped by the Lamia-like serpent is feeling "her" breast, the serpent's breast. We assume, in other words, that the eagle and thus the Poet is masculine like the eagle embraced by the serpent in Shelley's source, Ovid's tale of Hermaphroditus. But the *Alastor* clause ends, "...... feels her breast / Burn with the poison." Her breast is that of the eagle-Poet, who is penetrated by the now phallic beloved. The Poet, like Victor Frankenstein, has been made female by sexual experience, and sets forth in pursuit of his male half.

The outcome of the pursuit is identical in *Alastor* and *Frankenstein*. Poet, like scientist, remains locked within himself. During "daylight ... the Poet kept mute conference / With his soul" (223–24); afterwards "A Spirit seemed / To stand beside him.... as if he and it / Were all that was" (479–80, 487–88). The *Alastor* landscape indicates the Poet's narcissism no less than the Arctic wastes reflect Victor's self-obsession. "Yellow flowers / For ever gaze on their own drooping eyes, / Reflected in.... a well.... Hither the Poet came. His eyes beheld / Their own wan light" (406–8, 457, 469–70). Death awaits the Poet as inevitably as it does Victor. Both men eulogize home, but neither really prefers domesticity to his fatal pursuit of self.

What all this means is clearer in *Alastor* than in *St. Irvyne*. Shelley's preface to the poem includes a sentence criticizing "the Poet's self-centred seclusion [which] was avenged by the furies of an irresistible passion pursuing him to speedy ruin" (15). I say clearer because this one sentence of criticism does not make the preface or the poem clear, as the half century of controversy over *Alastor* attests.[11] The very fact that serious readers disagree whether the critical sentence is consistent with the rest of the preface and with the poem reflects deep division within Shelley himself. Agape again wars with Eros.

In the preface, the Percy of Agape who shares Mary's belief in sympathetic communion and thus criticizes the Poet for abandoning the Arab Maid is countered by the Erotic Percy who empathizes intensely with a Poet very much like himself (emaciated, balding, vegetarian, with "lofty hopes of divine liberty" [159], questing after "knowledge and truth and virtue" [158]). The result of Shelley's self-division is that the preface is self-contradictory, its critical sentence being the one unqualifiedly negative note in an otherwise fierce paean.

> The picture is not barren of instruction to actual men. The Poet's self-centred seclusion was avenged by the furies of an irresistible passion pursuing him to speedy ruin. But that Power which strikes the luminaries of the world with sudden darkness and extinction, by awakening them to too exquisite a perception of its influences, dooms to a slow and poisonous decay those meaner spirits that dare to abjure its dominion. Their destiny is more abject and inglorious as their delinquency is more contemptible and pernicious. They who, deluded by no generous error, instigated by no sacred thirst of doubtful knowledge, duped by no illustrious superstition, loving nothing on this earth, and cherishing no hopes beyond, yet keep aloof from sympathies with their kind, rejoicing neither in human joy nor mourning with human grief; these, and such as they, have their apportioned curse.... They are morally dead. They are neither friends, nor lovers, nor fathers, nor citizens of the world, nor benefactors of their country. Among those who attempt to exist without human sympathy, the pure and tender-hearted perish through the intensity and passion of their search after its communities, when the vacancy of their spirit suddenly makes itself felt. All else, selfish, blind, and torpid, are those unforeseeing multitudes who constitute, together with their own, the lasting misery and loneliness of the world. Those who love not their fellow-beings live unfruitful lives, and prepare for their old age a miserable grave.
>
> 'The good die first,
> And those whose hearts are dry as summer dust,
> Burn to the socket!'
>
> (*CP* 15)

The critical Shelley of Agape insists sincerely upon "error" and "superstition," but the persistence of readers' confusion is understandable. The Erotic Shelley counters the critical nouns with laudatory adjectives, "generous" and "illustrious." Moreover, "generous" takes back the very criticism made of the Poet. "Generous" (*genus, generis*, race, kind, family) posits that bond with humankind which the Poet's self-centered seclusion sunders. Just ask the Arab Maid whether his error is generous.

The Erotic Shelley also counters the critical thrust of the preface by deflecting it. Most of the paragraph is directed against solipsists *un*like the poet who are too "selfish, blind, and torpid" to ever "search after ... communities." Yet not one solipsist, let alone an "unfeeling multitude" of them, ever appears in *Alastor*. And communities appear only in the "alienated home" (76) of the Poet and in the cities abandoned by him (108–12). The poem thus denies us any experience of the two factors which justify the preface's praise for the protagonist. Since we do not experience his superiority to the multitudinous solipsists, we find inordinate the preface's extensive castigation of them. And where in the poem does the Poet actually seek after communities?

What seems slightly hysterical in the preface—Shelley's fierce castigation of the unfeeling multitude and his ardent espousal of the deep-feeling Poet—enters *Alastor* itself after the protagonist dies. Praise for him is rapturous ("ah! Thou hast fled! / The brave, the gentle, and the beautiful, / The child of grace and genius" [688–90]) and contempt for the multitude is intense ("many worms / And beasts and men live on" [691–92]). Neither emotion, however, seems warranted by our experience of a poem where the protagonist is at best flawed and the world is almost entirely absent.

Frankenstein too is about an egotist who escapes into solitude (his laboratory) in order to return to the community (as benefactor). He dies, as in *Alastor*, without achieving his goal, because both tales portray "self-centred seclusion ... avenged by the furies of an irresistable passion." The difference between the tales is that Mary's single-minded response to male self-division provides her novel with a unity of moral and aesthetic effect which is denied to Percy's self-divided poem. Mary forgoes the convenience of castigating the multitude and portrays movingly the community absent from *Alastor*. Unlike the Percy who loves his protagonist's self-love, Mary hates the self-absorption of men who abandon adoring women. *Frankenstein* is *Alastor* rewritten by the Arab Maid.

The anger felt by Mary Shelley as Arab Maid explains why she insists upon making Frankenstein's psychic projection male, not female. Destruction is both the consequence of such projection and the function of the projected self. To make this self female would be to subscribe to a long tradition which sees woman as lethal and which represents this lethality in the figure of the femme fatale. Though Mary Shelley recognizes destructive capacities in herself and in other women (as we shall see in chapter 6), she insists that the principal source of domestic and social ruin is male. Men reject complementarity for self-projection, domesticity for self-indulgence, marriage for self-union. The monster is masculine because chaos is.

Alastor helps Mary see not only the troubled psyche of Percy Shelley but also his inability to face those troubles squarely. He can present the Poet as failed androgyne—a male too restless to settle down yet too weak to quest successfully—but he cannot resist an overbalancing sense of his self-portrait's superiority. He can reveal the psyche bifurcated, with the feminine preponderant, but he will not indict self-pursuit decisively. Such self-deception is highlighted in *Frankenstein* by an allusion first noted by Leonard Wolf (25). Victor describes the monster as "one who fled from me" (21).

> They flee from me, that sometime did me seek,
> With naked foot stalking in my chamber.

Sir Thomas Wyatt's great love poem is parodied by Victor's situation. The monster first seeks Frankenstein in his bedchamber (presumably on naked feet, since where would the creature have gotten shoes large enough?), and then flees from his bedchamber on the wedding night. Genders are ludicrously reversed as the male monster replaces Wyatt's beloveds. Parody emphasizes the amatory nature of Victor's pursuit of the male, even as it provides a standard for criticizing his inversion of conventional roles.

Mary's parody reflects Frankenstein's own grotesque parody of complementarity. Instead of uniting with Elizabeth, Victor substitutes for her. He projects his male element outward in the monster, allows the female to become dominant in himself, and spends the rest of the novel seeking to make love to his self. What Victor has done, in effect, is to create not an androgyne but a hermaphrodite. "The hermaphrodite is an earthly and physical parody of that [androgynous] state" (Hoeveler 81). Traditionally the hermaphrodite unites in one body the genitals of the two genders, which is not the case with Victor's monster. But Victor's hermaphrodite is not the monster: it is the monster and himself as unnatural male-female. The difference between this "hermaphrodite" and a traditional one, the separation of masculine and feminine into two figures, captures better than any single figure the true essence of hermaphroditism. "In the hermaphrodite the sexual separation is exaggerated ... two separated parts, instead of their union, their fusion, in the androgyne."[12] Hoeveler shows that for Blake "the hermaphroditic self has existed [only] since the fall, since the separation of male and female" (84). As a blasphemous parody of the Incarnation (not the divine descending to redeem the flesh, but flesh aspiring to divinity), "the hermaphrodite ... symbolizes the attempts by the anti-christ figures of Satan, Rahab, and Tirzah to form a substitute androgyne" (Hoeveler 98).

Whether or not Mary Shelley comprehended Blake, she could find blasphemous parody in a more immediate source, *Paradise Lost*. Satan couples with Sin to produce Death. Particularly since Sin is a self-projection of Satan, his self-congress consititutes in effect both Victor's dream of immortality and Milton's parody of hermaphroditism as narcissistic self-union. The Satan-Sin coupling is Eros for Milton, and is contrasted by him with what follows in *Paradise Lost*—the Agape of the Son's love for the Father and marriage to the Church. As reader of Milton and as orthodox Christian, Mary Shelley believes that the only way for flesh to reunite with spirit is for parents to bring forth immortal souls in their children. Victor has this opportunity with Elizabeth, but instead pursues the satanic alternative of desiring his monster-self. Hermaphroditism is the true expression of Eros, as adrogyny is of Agape.

COMPLEMENTARITY OR SELF-SUFFICIENCY

The hermaphrodite is important for our understanding of the psyche in *Frankenstein* because it implicates Percy's alternative to Mary's ideals of androgyny and complementarity. Shelley, as we have seen, rejects complementarity. The alternative which he proposes at his best is a feminist equality which partakes of Agape because it assures the otherness of the beloved. "The doctrine of sympathy implied the dissolution of sex roles ... [and thus provided] a psychological alternative to the traditional polarization of the sexes into separate spheres and complementary identities.... love goes wrong only when couples are joined as opposites" (Brown 3, 221). We have seen, however, that Eros leads Shelley repeatedly to deny woman's equality by occluding her otherness. Particularly with the ego-centric Eros in ascendancy, Shelley sees the beloved as projection—which makes the male both lover and beloved, and thus self-sufficient.

Self-sufficient is just what the hermaphrodite aspires to be. "Recogniz[ing] that it was the concept of an all-sufficient self that was the most serious threat to reintegration," Blake shows his radical antagonism to institutional Christianity by choosing the Virgin Mary as emblem for the "type of hermaphrodite who claims sexual self-sufficiency" (Hoeveler 85, 90–91). Sexual self-sufficiency is also what the Erotic Shelley aspires to. It prompts his railings against gender distinctions ("I almost wish that Southey had not made the glendoveer a male—these detestable distinctions will surely be abolished in a future state of being" [*PSL* 1:195, 26 Nov. 1811]). And it prompts him to create his own emblem of self-sufficiency, the "sexless bee" of *The Witch of Atlas*. Is this bee a hermaphrodite in Blake's pejorative sense of the term, or a version of the true asexuality which Blake espoused? Is Shelley's Witch as sexless bee distinct from the hermaphrodite which she creates, or is the hermaphrodite a projection of herself? And in either case, how does Shelley mean us to react to the hermaphrodite? Such questions about *The Witch* have vexed scholars for decades. Readers of *Frankenstein* may more profitably focus on Mary's response to the sexless bee.

Her distaste for *The Witch* has always seemed to me inordinate. "This poem is peculiarly characteristic of his [Percy's] tastes ... discarding human interest and passion, to revel in the fantastic ideas that his imagination suggested" (*CP* 388). I now believe that what Mary actually hates is the ideal of self-sufficiency and the whole notion of self-projection which the sexless bee emblemizes. She senses in *The Witch of Atlas* (1820) another of Percy's responses to *Frankenstein*. Unlike the Shelley figure Victor Frankenstein, who creates a monstrous hermaphrodite out of fire and clay, Percy's benign Witch creates a harmless hermaphrodite out of "fire and snow" (321). *The Witch* asserts Shelley's purity and feminine creativity in the face of Mary's indictment of him as Promethean monster-botcher. Mary then counterattacks. Her later fiction targets self-projection, self-sufficiency, and the bee emblem in ways which illuminate retrospectively her initial indictment of hermaphroditism in *Frankenstein*.

Where Mary seems closest to characterizing woman as a projection of the male is where her divergence from Percy is most emphatic.

> Richard [Perkin Warbeck] had found in Lady Katherine a magic mirror, which gave him back himself arrayed with a thousand alien virtues. (*Perkin Warbeck* 2:236)

The key here is "alien." Lady Katherine is very different from Perkin: as a fiery Scot raised at her baronial father's court, she is any-thing but a mere reflection or projection of the gentle Perkin raised in Flemish poverty. Katherine in most conventional fashion can achieve the status of good wife only by being other, by remaining integral, because only then can she contribute the thousand virtues which are "alien" to her man and native to herself.

The complementary oneness which Perkin achieves with Katherine is denied to Falkner after his egotism causes Alithea's death and his subsequent "agony ... thenceforth she was not to be the half of his existence, as he had hoped" (2:234). Wild Falkner lacks that better half which derives its force precisely from not being a self-projection, but from being located far enough outside the man to guide him morally. "The better part of yourself will, when she speaks, appear to leap out, as if, for the first time, it found its other half" (2:211). Mary can, like Percy, imagine a better self within the flawed male, but she relates that self to the beloved very differently. For Percy, the beloved is excellent in proportion as she is not other. For Mary, the individual's better half is still only half; it needs the better half of another. Only together are two better halves good enough.

However much Mary in the fiercest throes of the Shelley legend may eulogize her marriage, she knows in her heart that Percy never found her complementary. He, like his look-alike Adrian, "seemed destined not to find the half of himself, which was to complete his happiness" (*The Last Man* 65). Why? As Mary sees it, Percy never accepted her ideal of complementarity. Medwin concurs in effect when he describes Shelley in terms of the antitype ideal: "he thirsted after his likeness—and he found it not" (139). Adrian, who like Shelley drowns without finding his better half, speaks for Percy and Victor and all too many men, in Mary's view—"I have consorted long with grief, entered the gloomy labyrinth of madness, and emerged, but half alive" (54). When Mary Godwin eloped with young Percy Shelley, she had in mind a different type of "consort." Her growing recognition of the Promethean as a man only "half alive" may be what prompts her to have Frankenstein admit in 1831, "we are unfashioned creatures, but half made up" (232).

Mary is thus striking back at a pretense to self-sufficiency which characterizes males throughout the Romantic period. Emerson contends that "a highly endowed man with good intellect and good conscience is a Man-woman and does not so much need the complement of woman to his being as another" (*Journals*, June 14, 1842). This Shelleyan view is opposed by Melville—"self-reciprocally efficient hermaphrodites being but a fable" (*Pierre* 259. Shelley delights in his fable of the "sexless bee" because his hermaphrodite means an escape from the impossible tensions of the corporeal, a benign castration. Mary hates the bee because she sees complementarity as the ultimate androgyny, the complete intercourse. Again using Percy against himself, Mary takes up the bee emblem and reverses its significance. "Bee-like" are the newly wedded Ethel and Villiers in *Lodore* who "sipped the honey of life, and, never cloyed, fed perpetually on sweets" (2:188). Instead of the ultimately neutering dream of sexless bee, Mary very conventionally defines emotional *and* physical intercourse as the proper mode for the Promethean. "He [Castruccio] forgot ambition, and the dreams of princely magnificence.... and seemed to bury himself, as a bee in the fragrant circle of a rose, in the softest and most humane emotions" (*Valperga* 1:121).

Notes

1. I use James Rieger's edition of *Frankenstein* so that I can draw upon all three versions of the novel: the 1818 original, the corrections made by Mary Shelley in the Thomas copy of *Frankenstein* in 1823, and her extensive rewriting for the Colburn and Bentley edition of 1831. These various revisions present no consistent pattern that I can discover. (For recent discussions of textual variants see Rieger [*F* xliv], Ketterer, and Poovey.) Some changes add grist to my mill, others show Mary making less in 1831 of what I make much of in the 1818 text. She both plays up and tones down radical criticisms, and sometimes she seems to have forgotten or to have still not recognized the force of an image or action. Rather than insisting upon what is manifestly untrue—that any one version of *Frankenstein* is the definitive edition—I will choose for the text of a particular scene the version which seems to me to contribute most to the overall coherence of the novel, recognizing full well how self-serving this could become. The 1818 edition is cited most frequently, largely because, I suppose, it reflects most directly the subversive forces which generated the project and which were dampened in Mary Shelley's later, more conservative years.

2. See Joseph Campbell (283), Eliade (115), O'Flaherty (310), and Singer (7, 51).

8. Among various explanations of Victor and the monster as "doubles" or components of a single psyche—Bloom, Cantor, Hirsch, Hogle, Kaplan and Kloss, Ketterer, Kiely, Levine (b), Massey, Masao Miyoshi (*The Divided Self* [New York: New York University Press, 1969], 79–89), Seed, Small, Spark, and Tropp—the one closest to mine is Knoepflmacher's. "The Monster now assumes Victor's phallic aggression; and Victor becomes as tremulous and 'timid as a love-sick girl'" (106). Excellent as this insight is, the "now" indicates the difference between Knoepflmacher's sense of the novel and mine. "Now ... and" makes the two events in the sentence seem causal, or at least sequential, when in fact the second event precedes the first by nearly one hundred pages. Victor becomes the love-sick girl on page 54, whereas the aggression referred to by Knoepflmacher occurs on page 149. In my view of causal sequence, Mary Shelley has Victor become effeminate *when the monster awakens*, because the creature embodies the creator's phallic drives. Victor, of course, does not *intend* to be rendered effeminate. He (at a deep level of the unconscious) expects to allow full expression to the feminine side of himself which he envisions joining with the projected masculine side. Effeminacy is Mary's work, her insistence that the halves of the psyche will polarize unless each finds complementarity in the two halves of an other.

Seeing the monster as Victor's male, passional side runs counter to two long-standing critical positions: that the creature is an intellectual force, and that he is feminine. Spark follows Church in viewing the "Monster firstly as representing reason in isolation.... a symbol of Mary's overstrained intellectual conscience" (137). That the monster has an intellectual side is as incontestable as that he has a feminine side; at issue is his specific function in relation to Victor. To equate the monster with intellect leaves Spark in the awkward position of having to account for such apparently passionate acts as his erotic killing of Elizabeth on the bridal bed and his pathological desire for revenge against Victor. "What passes for emotion .... are really intellectual passions arrived at through rational channels" (149). The monster knows better. "I was the slave, not the master of an impulse, which I detested, yet could not disobey.... an insatiable passion" (218). How can such a slave of passion represent intellect when Victor as the slave of this "slave" says, "through the whole period during which I was the slave of my creature, I allowed myself to be governed by the impulses of the moment" (151)? Seeing the creature as animal passion fits not only with the text but also with tradition, for, as Small notes, what Prometheus botched in his creation of the male was precisely his "animal" side (48–49).

Any claims for the monster as male must acknowledge the ways in which he is female, as an expression of Mary Shelley's inner life and as a potential androgyne with strong feminine traits. Critics who stress his feminine side are Gilbert and Gubar, Knoepflmacher, and Poovey. The unquestionable maleness of the creature physically is what allows him to express the male extreme of Victor's unconscious. The maleness of the creature is further confirmed by various elements of plot and characterization. Once Robert Walton, for example, has engaged in a Shelley-like quest for a male in the opening frame, Victor's pursuit of the monster continues that quest—unconsciously before Elizabeth's death, purposively (though without real self-knowledge) afterwards. Moreover, if Victor intuitively feels himself feminine, this answers the Kaplan–Kloss question of why he does not create the monstress and thus get rid of the monster. Victor wants not to be rid of him, but to forestall any female who might preempt Victor himself with the creature. Finally, the most sustained case for the monster's femininity is Hirsch's argument that the creature is suffering from penis envy. Although the proud possessor of a penis could, I feel, experience all the privations which Hirsch attributes to the monster, Hirsch is properly directing attention to one of the most basic issues of *Frankenstein*, incompleteness.

9. Shelley's inclination to the feminine is indicated in various ways in his art. As Moore notes, Shelley projects himself (though always with reservations) into that sympathetic father-killer, Beatrice Cenci (28), and into Rosalind, who is suspected unjustly of adultery and atheism in *Rosalind and Helen* (36–37). See also Carpenter (63). In *Epipsychidion*, Shelley's description of his interaction with the prostitute (if this is indeed who she is) makes *him* female, pierced and penetrated. "Flame / Out of her looks into my vitals came ... A killing air ... pierced like honey-dew / Into the core of my green heart" (259–60, 262–63). Soon the phallic one is Emily: "All other sounds were penetrated / By the small, still, sweet spirit of that sound [her respiration]" (330–31). Shelley again is female: "I stood, and felt the dawn of my long night / Was penetrating me with living light" (341–42).

10. Among the few critics who recognize the orgasmic quality of the moment are John C. Bean ("The Poet Borne Darkly: The Dream-Voyage Allegory in Shelley's *Alastor*," *KSJ* 23 [1974]: 60–76); and Brown (58).

11. For stages of the *Alastor* debate see Olwen Ward Campbell (187–96); Raymond A. Havens, "Shelley's *Alastor*," *PMLA* 45 (1930): 1098–1115; Marion Clyde Wier, "Shelley's 'Alastor' Again," *PMLA* 46 (1931): 947–50, and Havens' reply (950–51); Paul Mueschke and Earle Leslie Griggs, "Wordsworth as the Prototype of the Poet in Shelley's *Alastor*," *PMLA* 49 (1934): 229–45; Marcel Kessel, Paul Mueschke and Earle Leslie Griggs, "'The Poet in Shelley's *Alastor*': A Criticism and a Reply," *PMLA* 51 (1936): 302–12; Arthur E. Du Bois, "Alastor: The Spirit of Solitude," *JEGP* 35 (1936): 530–45; Evan K. Gibson, "'Alastor': A Reinterpretation," *PMLA* 62 (1947): 1022–45; Frederick L. Jones, "The Vision Theme in Shelley's *Alastor* and Related Works," *SP* 44 (1947): 108–25; Albert Gerard, "*Alastor*, or the Spirit of Solipsism," *PQ* 33 (1954): 164–77; Joseph Raben, "Coleridge as the Prototype of the Poet in Shelley's *Alastor*," *RES* 17 (1966): 278–92; Timothy Webb, "Coleridge and Shelley's *Alastor*: A Reply," *RES* 18 (1967): 402–11; W. H. Hildebrand, "Shelley's Early Vision Poems," *SJR* 8 (1969): 198–215; Luther L. Scales, Jr., "The Poet as Miltonic Adam in *Alastor*," *KSJ* 21–22 (1972–73): 126–44; Lloyd Abbey, "Shelley's Bridge to Maturity: From 'Alastor' to 'Mont Blanc,'" *Mosaic* 10 (1977): 69–84; Lisa M. Steinman, "Shelley's Skepticism: Allegory in 'Alastor,'" *ELH* 45 (1978): 255–69.

12. Hoeveler (82) quotes Franz von Baader from *La Notion D'Androgynie* by des Fontaines (Paris: Depot General, Le François, 1938), 139.

BARBARA FREY WAXMAN

Victor Frankenstein's Romantic Fate: The Tragedy of the Promethean Overreacher as Woman

> My temper was sometimes violent and my passions vehement; but by some law in my temperature they were turned not towards childish pursuits but to an eager desire to learn ... the secrets of heaven and earth ... my inquiries were directed to the metaphysical, or in its highest sense, the physical secrets of the world.[1]

With these words Mary Shelley establishes Victor Frankenstein as the modern Prometheus of her novel's subtitle, the presumptuous human being who wishes to probe new territory where human beings are forbidden by the deity. These words also suggest that Victor's driving desire for forbidden knowledge of the world and especially of human nature—"the mysterious soul of man ... occupied me" (37)—is the innate tragic flaw of his personality; he is the passionate Byronic man, his Byronic energies directed irrevocably from birth. and by temperament toward this pursuit of superhuman knowledge: "The world was to me a secret which I desired to divine. Curiosity, earnest research to learn the hidden laws of nature ... are among the earliest sensations I can remember" (36). Victor's innate, internally compelling thirst for knowledge about human nature summons his tragic destiny. The "immutable laws" of Victor's destiny are internal laws that decree his "utter and terrible destruction" (41).

From *Papers on Language and Literature*, vol. 23, no. 1 (Winter 1987): 14–26. © 1987 by The Board of Trustees, Southern Illinois University.

Mary Shelley depicts Victor's search for forbidden knowledge of "the mysterious soul of man" differently from many male Romantic authors who create the modern Promethean/Byronic soul; through Victor she lays bare not only the mysterious soul of man, but the mysterious soul of woman, pushing the boundaries of her readers' knowledge beyond what Carolyn Heilbrun has described as the predominating "male myths about women, interpreting women for male purposes."[2] Shelley speaks of Victor's pursuit of knowledge in female metaphors: metaphors of pregnancy and childbirth describe Victor's acquisition and use of forbidden knowledge concerning "natural philosophy," as well as the consequences of its use. When, for example, Victor briefly considers thwarting his destiny and giving up his pursuit of this knowledge, he uses these female metaphors: "I ... set down natural history and all its progeny as a deformed and abortive creation" (41). Yet his fate is to pursue this knowledge to fruition and to suffer its tragic consequences, as irrevocably as most women act out of their sexuality and experience the consequences, which up until this century were often dire—death in childbirth, a reality which Shelley learned about from the fate of her own mother, Mary Wollstonecraft.

Much has been said by critics, especially such feminist critics as Ellen Moers, Sandra Gilbert, and Susan Gubar, about this sexual metaphor and about Mary Shelley's use of the "female gothic" mode in her book. These critics try to connect Shelley's use of the sexual metaphor and the "birth myth" to the fact that she was "caught up in such a maelstrom of sexuality at the time she wrote the novel." As Gilbert and Gubar reasonably claim, "Mary Shelley explained her sexuality to herself in the context of her reading [hence her pursuit of knowledge] and its powerfully felt implications."[3] This biographical context works with literary convention's comparisons of the act of giving birth to a child to the act of creating a text; anyone who has read Shakespeare's sonnets knows about this comparison of the child to the text as a way of securing one's immortality. I too will explore this sexual metaphor and birth myth, demonstrating how Shelley enables Victor to analyze and reinterpret motherhood so that he and readers of the novel—men and women who are not mothers—may experience maternity intellectually and emotionally.

Shelley helps readers to understand motherhood in its often tragic context as—although she would hardly use these terms—a pair of dialectical relationships or binary oppositions which, in Robert Scholes's words, "organize the flow of value and power" in motherhood;[4] she suggests through Victor's experiences that most mothers alternately experience both poles of the two oppositional relationships, almost as a process of reversals. The first opposition is creative energy, or life, versus destructive energy, or death; the second is love versus hatred. Victor's experiencing of these two binary oppositions allows him to understand the profundity and tragic potential of maternity.

Interestingly, by having a male protagonist experience psychologically both pregnancy and the birth of his "creature," Shelley is breaking down the usual distinctions between the male and female psyche, the emotional perspectives that western culture has erected over the centuries. Victor uses his "phallogocentric" learning and masculine reasoning powers to bypass women's biological route to motherhood, thereby experiencing a blended sexuality which Hélène Cixous has called "the *other bisexuality*, ... multiple, variable and ever-changing, consisting as it does of the 'non-exclusion either of the difference or of one sex.'"[5] In fact, Shelley appears to be doing the kind of feminist writing that Cixous in "The Laugh of the Medusa" hails as "'working [in] the in-between, inspecting the process of the same and of the other without which nothing can live, undoing the work of death ...'"; through Victor, Shelley works with concepts of the "same," male, and the "other," female, bringing both Victor and the reader from the pole of life to the pole of death and back. While Cixous might praise such writing and glorify Victor's experiencing of bisexuality, Shelley, working in the (patriarchal) Romantic context, must phallocentrically curb any enthusiasm she might feel for Victor's androgynous experience and view it as belonging to the realm of forbidden experience because it tampers with nature, both nature as the protector of the secret sources of life, and as the biological essence of women. Hence, although Victor's maternal experience begins in hope and love, it ends in despair and hatred, and in death: the death of loved ones, the death of Victor's capacity for love, and the death of Victor—a tragedy of grand, Romantic proportions.

Before exploring Victor's "forbidden" and tragic experiences, we must consider what is implicit in the claim that Victor experiences maternity. Such a claim implies an essentialist or biologistic view that there *is* a pure, essential state of pregnancy and motherhood to be experienced and that women can experience physically and emotionally in the same way, cross-culturally, regardless of prior social experiences that an individual woman may have had. Many feminist critics have in recent years called this view untenable because it perpetuates a univocal and reductive notion of sexual difference that reinforces patriarchal society, or promotes what Toril Moi describes as "the metaphysical essentialism underlying patriarchal ideology, which hails God, the Father or the phallus as its transcendental signified."[6] Instead, these critics, including Moi and her role model, Julia Kristeva, advocate as a truly feminist stance or process a deconstruction of the opposition between masculinity and femininity. They challenge the very notion of sexual identity, opting for androgyny or a multiplicity of sexual differences. Simone de Beauvoir ushered in this anti-essentialist view with her sweeping claim, "One is not born a woman; one becomes one."[7] Ann Rosalind Jones similarly argues against the notions that sexual identity is innate and that sexuality can be experienced purely outside of social relationships and "damaging acculturation." Citing recent psychoanalytic theory, Jones claims that sexuality "is formed through the individual's encounters with the nuclear family and with the symbolic systems" that are activated as the mother and father relate to the child by acting out their own "socially imposed roles."[8] Where does Mary Shelley fit into this debate over the concept of femininity (culture) vs. femaleness (biology)?

On one level, Shelley seems to write in archetypes or pure essences in her novel, archetypes that go back through the Hebraic spirit of *Paradise Lost* to The Book of Genesis and through the Hellenic spirit of the Romantics (including Percy Shelley and Byron) to Aeschylus's *Prometheus Bound*. Even many of the landscapes of *Frankenstein* have an archetypal, metaphysical quality, from the snow-capped Alps to the lakes and oceans to the frozen Hell of the Arctic wastes where Victor and his creature end their deadly struggle. And if Shelley were indeed "caught up in a maelstrom of sexuality" when writing her book, she might, given this context, very plausibly be seen as also expressing herself in sexual archetypes or essences in order to describe Victor's experiences. Part of what makes Shelley's description of Victor's "pregnancy" powerful is that it seems to speak in the female Voice that Cixous describes, touching the pre-Oedipal Mother or the Lacanian Imaginary, "a space outside time" which Cixous claims is "the source of the song that resonates through all female writing." Although Cixous states that men may occasionally write in this space too, she says this is rare because they repress more libidinal drives than women;[9] thus, she reaches a biologistic conclusion in her designation of female writing, and her descriptions reflect Shelley's description of Victor's womb-like workshop of creation. On another level, however, into Victor's womb-space comes phallocentric thinking, a process that reasons out the sources of life and the way to build a creature. Patriarchal language also enters, particularly phallic objections to the "filthy" nature of the female creative process. Does this invasion break down the opposition between male and female, both undermining the biologistic impulse of the novel, and, as Moi says of Cixous, leading to Victor's bisexual experience or integration of "both penis and nipple"—of penis and womb?

It may not be possible or desirable to reconcile these readings of the oppositional forces of the novel (the desire for neat closure or unified meaning in a text is after all phallogocentric), but we can hold the conflict in abeyance and speak of the novel also in Kristevan terms as describing not a female essence, but the multiplicity and "marginality" of all feminine sexual experiences constructed by patriarchal society,[10] something which Victor learns of in the isolation of his laboratory. In her essay "Woman's Time," Kristeva speaks of pregnancy in terms that reject the notion of a pure female experience and that reach beyond male and female sexual identities. Pregnancy is the "redoubling up of the body, separation and coexistence of the self and of an other, of nature and consciousness, of physiology and speech," and it not only challenges the concept of identity but it also is "accompanied by a fantasy of totality—narcissistic completeness." These qualities characterize Victor as he labors to create the monster, and reflect Kristeva's view that "the very dichotomy man/woman as an opposition between two rival entities may be understood as belonging to *metaphysics*."[11] The feminist theories of Kristeva, Jones, Cixous, and Moi join with the metaphorics of creation described by Moers, Gilbert, and Gubar to provide the context for the following reading of Victor's experiences.

Victor's search for the creative energy necessary to reenact human life begins as a naive idealist's lofty ambition: "what glory would attend the discovery [of the elixir of life] if I could banish disease from the human frame and render man invulnerable to any but a violent death!" (40). He wants to use his considerable intellectual gifts not for self-aggrandizement, which Cixous would characterize as belonging to the (masculine) libidinal realm of the Proper, but rather for the benefit of humankind as a kind of nurturing mother, illustrating the (female) realm of the *Gift*,[12] Victor seems unaware that in his fantasy he is dangerously overstepping "natural" bounds and becoming a pretender to godlike powers. His ambition is not dissimilar to a first-time pregnant women's pride and grandiose hopes for her unborn child, as western culture frames those feelings; she is intimately linked to the creative process, and she may fantasize that she is carrying the next leader of the nation, the savior of a people. Yet even the first-time pregnant woman's rosy hopes are not unalloyed with fears: that she may miscarry, that she may not survive the labor and delivery, that the child will be stillborn, and that she is carrying a malformed child or even a non-human being, a "hideous progeny"—some pregnant women actually dream that they are carrying animals in their wombs. A pregnant woman usually intuits how close she is to death even as she is carrying life and feeling the pulses of the creative process in her own body; surely, when she became pregnant and wrote of pregnancy in her novel, Shelley must have had in mind her mother's death in childbirth. A man, denied the experience of pregnancy and childbirth, cannot so closely feel intimations of death in life-pulses, and Victor is ignorant of them in his first fantasies of creating life. He must gradually travel beyond the role of male and of ordinary human being after he vows to "pioneer a new way, explore unknown powers, and unfold to the world the deepest mysteries of creation" (47). Through his inspired intellect and sensitivity, he will gradually assume a woman's emotional outlook, sensing death in life both as he labors to give birth and after the birth.

The night after he vows to unfold the mysteries of creation, Victor begins to undergo internal emotional changes suggesting a feminizing of himself, a symbolic creation of a womb and preparation of that womb for the reception and gestation of the fetus: "I closed not my eyes that night. My internal being was in a state of insurrection and turmoil; I felt that order would thence arise, but I had no power to produce it" (47). As this passage suggests, Victor is already experiencing the vulnerability and turmoil of the newly pregnant woman as her body changes before her eyes. The passage also suggests that he feels the pregnant woman's incomparable sensation of being productive internally in a realm that is hers, yet beyond her conscious control, which is similar to Kristeva's description of pregnancy's impact on the individual.[13] In his commitment to unfold the mysteries of creation Victor is, moreover, about to experience an even more important aspect of motherhood: the merging of life and death energies. By embarking on the female experience, as Gilbert and Gubar point out, Victor "learns that 'the tremendous secrets of the human frame' are the interlocking secrets of sex and death."[14] Ultimately, both Victor and the reader will be made aware of "the horror of sexuality" as tied to death through the Monster's appearance on Victor and Elizabeth's wedding night and his murder of Elizabeth.[15]

In assuming a woman's outlook on birth, as he labors to create life, Victor must recognize and deny the binary opposition between the life force and the death force; they are really one and the same. Raising questions about the source of the life principle, which requires meddling with death and the dead, and in addition exchanging one accustomed sexual role for another, takes great courage and "almost superhuman enthusiasm" (50); Victor's larger-than-life grandeur is evident in the courage and enthusiasm he exhibits throughout his undertaking. Throughout his search for life, Victor bravely connects himself with death: "To examine the causes of life, we must first have recourse in death ... I must also observe the natural decay and corruption of the human body" (50). He comes to understand how life and death are parts of one whole or positions on one continuum: "I beheld the corruption of death succeed to the blooming cheek of life ... I paused, examining and analysing all the minutiae of causation, as exemplified in the change from life to death, and death to life" (51). Many critics have observed that Shelley uses the language of sexuality and maternity to describe Victor's arrival at the Godlike knowledge of the source of life and acquisition of the power "of bestowing animation upon lifeless matter" (51): this success has been achieved "after days and nights of incredible labour and fatigue" with "painful labour" leading to "gratifying consummation" (51). U.C. Knoepflmacher suggests that Victor's success is Shelley's playing out of her fantasy to restore her dead mother and her first dead child to life, again merging death with life.[16]

In analyzing the components of the life–death principle, Victor views the dazzling, empowering core of its truth, a prospect reserved for superhuman heroes, promethean seekers, God, Satan,[17] or women. With a woman's perspective shaped by experiencing pregnancy and childbirth, he understands how death "feeds" the creative process, and he feels the woman's exhaustion at and after conception. His new knowledge impregnates him with the being he is about to bring to life. He has already come a long way from the oppressive "phallogocentrism" of western culture that Kristeva and Cixous write against.[18]

Shelley expands Victor's consciousness of womanhood—and the reader's—by taking him inside a woman's womb, or rather by constructing a womb around him in the metaphor of his laboratory, "a solitary chamber, or ... cell, at the top of the house, ... my workshop of filthy creation" (53). Gilbert and Gubar observe that Shelley uses the word "filthy" to suggest "obscenely sexual,"[19] obscene perhaps because of sex's disconcerting juxtaposition of life and death, or obscene because Shelley has internalized a patriarchal view of female sexuality. In his cell/womb Victor handles the elements of death gathered from "the unhallowed damps of the grave" (53) and erases the "ideal bounds" between life and death in order to create life: "Life and death appeared to me ideal bounds, which I should first break through, and pour a torrent of light into our dark world" (52); grandly and like the "tarnished angel" Satan, Victor pretends to the Godlike here by discovering that death and life are one and by envisaging his central role in another Genesis story, replete with the creation of light and life and the gratitude of the race he will engender. The breakdown of the barrier between life and death is suggested by this unifying image of the liquid light (life) being poured into the dark vessel (death).

As he works, Godlike, in his laboratory, Victor also alludes to the sensations of a pregnant woman, her intimate involvement with the forces of light/life and darkness/death and the irreversible forward motion from sexual consummation to conception and from gestation to delivery "No one can conceive [a significant choice of verb] the variety of feelings which bore me onwards, like a hurricane, in the first enthusiasm of success" (52). In his irrevocable commitment to his project, once he experiences life-and-death energy, Victor understands the range, intensity, and movement of a pregnant woman's feelings in our culture. This is an "unnatural" understanding for men, or perhaps a bisexual feeling, just as it is "unnatural" for man to attempt to endow lifeless matter with life; Victor steps outside his masculine role and his human role in his workshop of creation, and Shelley wants us to recognize his separation from nature throughout the "creature's" gestation: "It was a most beautiful season ... but my eyes were insensible to the charms of nature" (53). He is as insensible to nature as his creature will, ironically, be sensible, "a genuine Wordsworthian child," says Knoepflmacher, who is able "to derive intense 'pleasure' in the natural world."[20] Victor is not only cut off from nature, but also from human nature in the form of his family and friend Clerval during this time of his travail. As he confesses, "I shunned my fellow creatures as if I had been guilty of a crime" (55).

Victor's neglect of his "domestic affections" and his unnatural "heart and soul" engagement with his task of creating a being has tragic consequences, an appropriate Romantic lesson of reverence for nature and human nature. Yet as unnatural and unloving as Victor's preoccupation with his labors may seem, it is not so different from the pregnant woman who may become absentmindedly detached from her environment, focussing instead on herself and the absorbing process occurring inside her body in a way that some might view as egocentric. Shelley is giving Victor the opportunity to experience this "natural" aspect of femaleness and may not entirely condemn Victor for his singlemindedness.

In addition to the breakdown of the life and death barrier, the weakening of the love–hatred opposition is increasingly evident during Victor's "pregnancy"; he neglects those he loves when he becomes absorbed in his fond hopes for the "child" he is about to bring forth. He even forgets his "more than sister" Elizabeth, who embodies "the living spirit of love" (37). Instead, he describes the "dreams that had been my food and pleasant rest for so long a space," "the beauty of the dream" (56–57), and the beauty he anticipates in the creature for whom he labors—"I had selected his features as beautiful" (56). Although he has been working with the horrors of death to bring forth life, Victor, unlike many pregnant women in western culture, seems wholly unprepared for the possibility that he may bring forth a deformed creature. The naive male mother is still emotionally unfamiliar with the gambles inherent in the birthing process and seems prepared only to love a pretty, lovable baby.

Clearly Victor is shocked at bringing forth a hideous monster, a loathsome abortion. This may be the ultimate insight emerging from Victor's breakdown of life and death: that one can give birth not only to glorious life but also to a monster. It is also the moment when anticipated love for a "child," which Kristeva characterizes as an otherwise rarely encountered experience, "love for an other ... forgetting oneself" (49) turns into intense and egocentric loathing; when Godlike love for a new race of "many happy and excellent creatures [who] would owe their being to me" (52) is transformed into satanic hatred and revulsion; when the desire to nurture becomes the compulsion to destroy in Victor. As Harold Bloom remarks, "Frankenstein's tragedy stems ... from his own moral error, his failure to love."[21] And Moers also notes that Shelley's novel is "most feminine" at this point, when Victor feels "revulsion against newborn life, and the drama of guilt, dread, and flight surrounding birth and its consequences."[22] This moment begins the playing out of his tragic "feminized" destiny, as Victor's loathing and rejection give the being he created the motivation to kill everyone Victor has ever loved.

At this moment, the distinctions between love and hatred become blurred as love-loyalties change: forgotten love for his family and Clerval is henceforth renewed, while anticipated love of the creature for whom he has labored painfully turns into a loathing that fuels Victor's mania to destroy the "'miserable monster'" after the monster's rampage begins. As George Levine points out, love and hate in *Frankenstein* "are seen as symbiotic."[23] Victor hates the creature whose ugliness has stifled his love and thwarted his hopes, making him feel "the bitterness of disappointment" (57) that many a loving parent especially a mother because of her initially deer bonding with the child—has felt, but on a blessedly short-term basis. The long-term hatred that Victor feels for his child is the hellish core of the tragedy of motherhood. He hates the creature whose demands he had expected to fulfill gladly, demands which henceforth he will perceive as horrible encroachments on his own life. Shelley herself had described "that 'strange perversity' a mother's hatred."[24]

There are moments in the rest of the narrative when Victor's loathing teeters on the verge of affection for the monster, and this painful blurring of love and hatred is played out appropriately against two archetypally primitive, Romantic, larger-than-life canvases: the Alpine forests of Switzerland and the frozen wastelands of the North Pole. Shelley removes the love–hatred struggle far from England, where she must have struggled between her own yearning and resentment toward the mother who abandoned her by dying in childbirth. The monster eloquently persuades Victor to suspend his loathing and thirst for revenge and listen to his tale: "Will no entreaties cause thee to turn a favourable eye upon thy creature? ... Believe me, Frankenstein, I was benevolent; my soul glowed with love and humanity; but am I not ... miserably alone? ... Let your compassion be moved ... Listen to my tale" (96). Victor is moved by this plea and feels the stirrings of parental sympathy and obligation, if not love: "... compassion confirmed my resolution [to hear the tale].... For the first time, also, I felt what the duties of a creator towards his creature were, and that I ought to render him happy before I complained of his wickedness" (97). Victor the androgynous parent agrees to hear his creature's tale of growing up.

Victor continues to fluctuate between rage—especially after the monster describes his murder of brother William, "an analogue" for Shelley's second child William who died in infancy, according to Knoepflmacher[25]— and a maternal, nurturing compassion which prompts him to honor the monster's request for a companion: "His tale and the feelings he now expressed proved him to be a creature of fine sensations, and did I not as his maker owe him all the portion of happiness that it was in my power to bestow?" (139). Yet thinking about the monstrous race that might result from their union turns Victor back to hatred and a desire to destroy his creature. Through these fluctuations between hatred and compassion, this breakdown of the distinctions between his love and his hatred for his creature, he has understood the cone of motherhood, its painful and potentially tragic consequences or "afterbirths:" That love and hate may become two sides of the same coin for a mother is an ultimate sort of revelation for Victor, one that perhaps makes him—and the reader—rethink the relationship with his mother, Caroline Beaufort, whom he had idealized for the "tender caresses" that combined with his father's benevolence to make his childhood "but one train of enjoyment" (33). Levine notes that Victor's mother is a forerunner of the Victorian angel in the house (14). Yet if the formerly nurturing Victor has experienced hatred and the desire to destroy the child he had created, may not a reader interpolate through the gaps or absences in the text of the novel that other "angelically" loving mothers have had satanically murderous impulses, even Caroline Beaufort? Perhaps as Kate Ellis argues, Shelley is trying to show "the deficiencies of Victor's family" in order to criticize "the concept of domestic affection" that Percy Shelley claims in his 1818 preface the novel will defend.[26] Surely his mother is in Victor's mind when he "delivers" the monster, as are most women's mothers when they themselves become mothers. In fact, the night the monster is born, Victor dreams of his mother; but she appears in his dream horribly transformed, a corpse in his arms attacked by grave-worms (57). Is his subconscious revealing that he mocks the woman who gave him fife and undermines their son–mother relationship by his unnatural attempts to experience motherhood? Is he expressing Shelley's own fantasy that all newborns are potentially "at once monstrous agents of destruction [of their mothers] and piteous victims of parental abandonment"?[27] These questions of authorial intent are not answerable, but the reader does see, as this dream ominously foreshadows, that Victor must pay a high price in love and blood when he acquires his suprahuman knowledge of motherhood and its potential for tragedy.

Victor's obsession with the mysteries of life is thus transformed into an obsession with destroying the monster. Now beyond all capacity for love of others, the monster having destroyed everyone he ever loved, Victor courts hatred and death (the monster's and his own) by pursuing the monster to the frozen Hell of the Arctic wastes. He dies before the monster, his suicidal double,[28] ascends his own funeral pyre to "exult in the agony of the torturing flames" (211). Such a perverse mother–child relationship is bound to end in this mutual destruction. Yet Victor emerges as a grand tragic hero, for he has had several apocalyptic moments before his death. He has seen beyond himself as a man and as a human being, experiencing an epiphanic, Godlike, womanly insight into motherhood by dissolving the barriers between male and female, love and hate, and life and death. No human being can endure long after such apocalyptic unifying moments—at least in a Romantic context—and death is a fitting tragic end for him. Yet in allowing Victor and male readers to enter female realms, Mary Shelley is creating literary and social consequences that are far-reaching and far from tragic. She, not unlike her husband in "Ode to the West Wind," sounds the clarion calling for a revolutionary understanding between women and men. One hundred and seventy years before the French feminists, Shelley was writing "from the body" and thus creating a "powerful alternative discourse." As some French feminists have claimed, "to write from the body is to recreate the world."[29] In *Frankenstein* Mary Shelley has recreated the world of motherhood in unexpectedly humane and insightful ways.

NOTES

1. Mary Shelley, *Frankenstein, or The Modern Prometheus* (New York: NAL, 1965) 37. All references hereafter are to this edition, cited in the text by page number.

2. Carolyn G. Heilbrun, *Reinventing Womanhood* (New York: Norton, 1979) 151.

3. Ellen Moers, *Literary Women: The Great Writers* (Garden City, N.Y.: Anchor-Doubleday, 1977) 140; Sandra M. Gubar and Susan Gubar, *The Madwoman In the Attic* (New Haven: Yale UP, 1979) 222. See also Moers 145–47.

4. Robert Scholes, *Textual Power* (New Haven: Yale UP, 1985) 4.

5. Toril Moi, *Sexual/Textual Politics: Feminist Literary Theory* (London: Methuen, 1985) 189 (quotes Hélène Cixous, "The Laugh of the Medusa,". tr. Keith Cohen and Paula Cohen, *Signs* 1 [1976]: 875–99. Moi's quotations are from the reprint in Elaine Marks and Isabelle de Courtivron, eds., *New French Feminisms* [Brighton: Harvester, 1980] 254).

6. Moi 9.

7. Moi 92 (quotes de Beauvoir, *The Second Sex*, tr. H.M. Parshley [New York: Bantam, 1970] 249).

8. Ann Rosalind Jones, "Writing the Body: *L'Ecriture Féminine*," in *The New Feminist Criticism: Essays on Women, Literature and Theory*, ed. Elaine Showalter (New York: Pantheon, 1985) 367.

9. Moi 114–15.

10. Moi 166–67.

11. Julia Kristeva, "Women's Time," in *Feminist Theory: A Critique of Ideology*, ed. Nannerl O. Keohane, Michelle Z. Rosaldo, and Barbara C. Gelpi (Chicago: U. of Chicago P, 1982) 49, 51.

12. Moi 110–11.

13. Kristeva 49.

14. Gilbert and Gubar 233.

15. George Levine, "The Ambiguous Heritage of *Frankenstein*," in *The Endurance of Frankenstein: Essays on Mary Shelley's novel*, ed. George Levine and U.C. Knoepflmacher (Berkeley: U of California P, 1979) 9.

16. U.C. Knoepflmacher, "Thoughts on the Aggression of Daughters," in *The Endurance of Frankenstein*, 96.

17. Gilbert and Gubar 233.

18. Jones 362.

19. Gilbert and Gubar 232; see also Moers 147.

20. Knoepflmacher 100.

21. Harold Bloom, Afterword, *Frankenstein*, 217.

22. Moers 142.

23. Levine 16.

24. Quoted by Moers 150.

25. Knoepflmacher 102.

26. Kate Ellis, "Monsters in the Garden: Mary Shelley and the Bourgeois Family," in *The Endurance of Frankenstein* 140.

27. Moers 148.

28. Levine 14–15.

29. Jones 366.

MATTHEW C. BRENNAN

The Landscape of Grief in
Mary Shelley's Frankenstein

"All Romantic horrors," Harold Bloom has said, "are diseases of excessive consciousness" (221). This remark may well explain why interpretations of Gothic novels are almost always psychological, and why in particular Mary Shelley's *Frankenstein* has accommodated such a variety of psychological approaches.[1] In fact, in the introduction she added to the revised 1831 edition, Mary Shelley seems to invite psychological and biographical approaches: "Invention," she writes, "it must be humbly admitted, does not consist in creating out of void, but out of chaos; the materials must, in the first place, be afforded" (8). As she began her novel at age 18, the most prominent materials in Shelley's consciousness (and unconscious) concerned conflicts stemming from the death of her mother, Mary Wollstonecraft, eleven days after giving birth to her second child—Mary. Following the critics who have dealt with this trauma, I intend to emphasize that *Frankenstein* is the result of her unresolved grief for her mother's death, a crisis she vitally needed to work through to forge her own adult identity.[2]

The psychological material most important to my approach here concerns Shelley's attitudes toward daydreams and landscape. What enabled her to endure the chaos of a motherless childhood, she implies in her introduction, was the indulgence in "waking dreams"; "they were," she says,

From *Studies in the Humanities*, vol. 15, no. 1 (June 1988): 33–44. © 1988 by Indiana University of Pennsylvania.

"my refuge." Significantly, though she toured picturesque landscapes—landscapes William Gilpin prized for their external form and firm boundaries—Shelley stresses it was the "blank and dreary" landscapes that "fostered" her youthful flights of imagination. In other words, what produced her escape from an excessive consciousness of her sense of loss were sublime landscapes—landscapes which, in their vast, obscure shapelessness, allow for inner withdrawal from rational consciousness.[3]

Not surprisingly, therefore, as she begins her first novel, she writes of herself through the young adult Victor Frankenstein, who also faces the loss of his mother, Caroline, but never overcomes his grief, which is embodied by the Monster. Through this projection, Mary Shelley releases herself from the censorship the conscious mind places on painful memories and starts to work through her unresolved grief. In the novel these unresolved feelings parallel Victor's desire to resurrect the dead, as well as his longing to escape the Monster—and the grief it symbolizes—through three experiences of Nature: the experience of the natural sublime that induces forgetfulness of sorrow; the experience of the natural sublime that both induces forgetfulness and contributes a comforting maternal power; and the experience of the maternal power of Nature apart from the sublime. Accordingly, after his mother's death, Victor can respond only to sublime and maternal landscapes, experiences of which provide his only escape from grief; in contrast, Henry Clerval, "the image of" his "former self," prefers the picturesque, which amuses the eye but doesn't alter consciousness. To show, then, how Mary Shelley uses landscape to symbolize Victor's regressive and gradually self-destructive response to grief, I want first to explain the preference of Victor's "former self"—his healthy childhood self—for the picturesque; and then to explain his later attraction, after his mother's death, to the sublime—an attraction that Shelley shared but transcended.

I

To enable us to grasp the violence of Victor's grief at his mother's death, Mary Shelley carefully sketches the domestic stability of his childhood. Victor's parents created so favorable an environment for Victor's early psychological development that he tells the Arctic explorer Robert Walton—on whose ship Victor narrates his part of the story—"No human being could have passed a happier childhood than myself" (37). Similarly, Victor remarks on the "exquisite pleasure" he feels "in dwelling on the recollections of childhood" (38). Among his first memories are images of his "mother's tender caresses" (33); and in fact this "mine of love" bestowed upon Victor was so "inexhaustible" that he felt like an "idol" (33): "I was so guided by a silken cord," he imagines, "that all seemed but one train of enjoyment" (34).

"Guided" is an especially apt verb, for his infancy was spent in picturesque rambles through Italy, France, and Germany (33). Because the picturesque typically involves travel with a guide, tutor, artist, or all three, it is an inherently more social mode of landscape appreciation than the sublime, which depends more on solitude. Furthermore, because the aesthetics of the picturesque stress line, form, and other surface qualities, its landscapes do not lead beyond themselves; they encourage attention to reality, not escape from it. So, by associating Victor's childhood with family tours of scenic landscape, Shelley establishes a psychological harmony that parallels the formal harmony of the picturesque. Later in the novel, she returns to this expressiveness of picturesque landscapes to indicate how far Victor has regressed in his grief from his former self, personified by his boyhood friend, Henry Clerval.

As Victor describes the tour he and Henry took through the Rhine valley after the death of his mother and the creation of the Monster, Victor himself remarks on "how great was the contrast between us" (154): for, unlike the solipsistic Victor who prefers the sublime of Switzerland and who abhors society (159), Clerval, being better balanced and more sociable, prefers the more social landscape of the Rhine—a landscape Victor categorizes as picturesque (155). Like William Gilpin in his *Tour of the Wye* (1782), Henry keeps a journal during the trip—a travelogue that records all the picturesque views and qualities in the landscape of the river valley. For instance, like Gilpin in the Wye valley, Henry finds the Rhine valley most picturesque when "the river descends rapidly and winds between hills, not high, but steep, and of beautiful forms" (155).

Furthermore, like Gilpin, Clerval loves "the scenery of external nature" (156) and prizes such qualities in landscape as variety, surprise, and roughness: "the shifting colours of the landscape" (154), "a singularly variegated landscape" (155), "rugged hills, ruined castles," "the sudden turn of a promontory," and "a meandering river" (155)—all these picturesque elements receive mention. Although Mary Shelley does not refer to Gilpin, she certainly knew him, even if only indirectly, for William Godwin's novels include many picturesque descriptions;[4] moreover, to characterize Clerval, she quotes Wordsworth's lines from "Tintern Abbey" that describe the poet's sensibility when he first visited this picturesque ruin, with Gilpin's guide to the Wye in hand. Like Henry, who prefers the surfaces of nature, Wordsworth then found the "colours" and "forms" of nature,

a love,
That had no need of a remoter charm,
By thought supplied, or any interest
Unborrow'd from the eye. (156)

Because Clerval is well-balanced and sane, because he has apparently overcome the loss of his own mother (which the novel merely alludes to), his interest in landscape requires no "remoter charm," just whatever external reality offers: Henry has no need to escape ordinary consciousness.

II

If Clerval is well suited to enjoy the surface charms of the picturesque, Victor, in contrast, is incapable of enjoying the picturesque because he cannot endure external reality. At Oxford, for instance, Victor notes that the colleges are picturesque, but his "enjoyment was embittered" by thoughts of the past (160). Indeed, throughout his picturesque travels in England and the Rhine valley, Victor's consciousness of present reality is tainted, for, as we eventually learn, the Monster has been shadowing him: ever hovering on the threshold of Victor's consciousness, the Monster constantly threatens to obtrude onto the picturesque landscape, thus forcing Victor to face the hideous reality he desires to escape. Clearly, then, the Monster manifests what Victor wants to suppress from consciousness. David Ketterer suggests that the Monster personifies the natural sublime (70), and in fact the Monster appears several times in the savage landscapes of the Alps and the Arctic. But however plausible this view may be, I believe, rather, that the Monster represents what Victor needs to forget—primarily, the fact of his mother's death-and that Victor resorts to the sublime to escape facing the Monster.

So, if the Monster does not personify the sublime, how, then, does Mary Shelley link the Monster with what Victor needs to repress through the sublime? First, not only does she emphasize Victor's idyllic and beneficent childhood, as we've seen; she also reintroduces Victor's childhood alchemical interest in animating the dead almost immediately after Caroline's death— "that most irreparable evil" (43)—and magnifies this interest into an obsession just when the plot's action begins to complicate and to rise. Critically, rather than continue his social development by marrying Elizabeth—the mate provided by his parents—and by creating with her a new generation, Victor instead regresses from the demands of adulthood: his sole motivation becomes the infantile desire to animate the dead.

Mary Shelley herself had fantasies of resurrecting the dead. After her first, nameless infant died, she dreamed of animating it. Significantly, as U. C. Knoepflmacher remarks, not only does Shelley's fantasy parallel Victor's, the fantasy that underlies *Frankenstein*; but "it could hardly have been Mary Shelley's first wishful 'dream' of making the dead come alive" (96)—which suggests she may well have dreamed of resurrecting her mother. In fact, in March 1817 while still at work on the novel, she explains an abrupt end to a letter to Leigh Hunt by stating, "I had a dream tonight of the dead being alive which has affected my spirits" (*Letters* 1:32). In her note to this dream, editor Betty T. Bennett argues that "the dead" could refer to Mary Wollstonecraft (*Letters* 1:33n).

Similarly, though he can never bring himself to say it directly, Victor wants to resurrect his mother, Caroline Frankenstein. In fact, this infantile desire, a projection of Shelley's own unconscious, motivates Victor's scientific progress. After his mother's death has delayed his departure for college, grief-stricken Victor at last leaves, indulging in "the most melancholy reflections" (45). He soon discovers, though, that science can reveal the mysteries of creation, and he becomes not only capable of animating lifeless matter, but also hopeful of renewing "life where death had apparently devoted the body to corruption" (54). This sentiment, however noble-sounding, really amounts to an oblique reference to his infantile desire to resurrect his mother's corpse. Mary Shelley brilliantly makes this clear in the dream Victor has after animating the Monster—a dream that links the dead mother and Monster in an eruption of the uncanny that Victor strives to escape from, through the sublime, during the rest of the novel. In his dream, Victor reports,

> I thought I saw Elizabeth, in the bloom of health, walking in the streets of Ingolstadt. Delighted and surprised, I embraced her, but as I imprinted the first kiss on her lips, they became livid with the hue of death; her features appeared to change, and I thought that I held the corpse of my dead mother in my arms; a shroud enveloped her form, and I saw the grave-worms crawling in the folds of the flannel. I started from my sleep with horror; a cold dew covered my forehead, my teeth chattered, and every limb became convulsed; when, by the dim and yellow light of the moon, as it forced its way through the window shutters, I beheld the wretch—the miserable monster whom I had created. (58)

After the literal animation of the dead, in Victor's unconscious the resurrected, motherless corpse of the Monster becomes the embodiment of his grief; it becomes the uncanny, terrifying reminder that Victor himself is motherless and that his mother is, now and forever, a corpse. As psychoanalyst Marc Rubenstein points out, this dream symbolically presents the return of the hideous, ghastly mother who, opening her arms, welcomes the lost child to her grave. This central conflict—the fulfillment on one level of an old wish (Rubenstein 186)—is underscored when Victor remarks that "a mummy, again endued with animation could not be so hideous as that wretch" (Shelley 58), for as James Twitchell reminds us, mummy is a British homonym also meaning "mother" (177).

To reinforce further that the Monster embodies the grief Victor desperately needs to repress, Mary Shelley elsewhere associates the Monster and Victor's mother. For example, when the Monster encounters little William, his first murder victim, the boy is wearing a locket that contains a portrait of Caroline Frankenstein. At first her image softens the Monster's malignity; then, he becomes enraged again as soon as he remembers that he—like Victor and Mary herself—"was forever deprived of the delights that such beautiful creatures could bestow" (143). A second link between the Monster and Victor's mother comes when, after killing William, the Monster finds Justine asleep in a barn. The Monster seems to intuit that Justine represents Caroline's substitute: not only had Justine successfully modeled her "phraseology and manners" on Victor's mother (65); but she also had "acted toward" William, Caroline's youngest son, "like a most affectionate mother" (85). Consequently, to express his agony of lacking a nurturing mother, the Monster decides to incriminate Justine by placing the locket in her dress; much like an orphaned child who hates his mother for dying, the Monster does this "because," he says, "I am forever robbed of all that she could give me" (144). Therefore, since the Monster embodies knowledge of death (and so of Victor's abandonment by his mother), Victor must repress him. Like Mary Shelley in the bleak Scottish landscape and Wordsworth in the Lake District, Victor achieves this repression through the natural sublime and in regressive solipsism. The sublime escape into maternal Nature, then, becomes Victor's way of playing out the fantasy of returning to the lost mother and of forgetting his grief, "the fiend that lurked in" his "heart" (93).

                                        III

After Justine—the mother substitute—lies, Victor insists that his "abhorrence of this fiend cannot be conceived"; in fact, when he "thought of him [he] gnashed [his] teeth" (92). However, Victor could sometimes handle his overwhelming despair, and so relieve his "intolerable sensations," through three kinds of "change of place" (94). First, the experience of the natural sublime, "the sight of the awful and majestic in nature," he says, had indeed "always the effect of solemnizing my mind and causing me to forget the passing cares of life" (97). Consequently, Victor tours the magnificent, eternal scenes of the Arve, Mont Blanc, and Montanvert—and seeks in these "savage and enduring scenes" "to forget," as he puts it, "myself and my ephemeral, because human, sorrows" (94)—sorrows which include his grief for the lost mother, the lost substitute mother, and the lost child.

In contrast to Byron's Childe Harold who fails to forget his sorrows in the Alpine landscape, Victor receives "the greatest consolation" from the "sublime and magnificent scenes" of the Alps (96): "They elevated me from all littleness of feeling, and although they did not remove my grief, they subdued and tranquilized it. In some degree, also, they diverted my mind from the thoughts over which it had brooded for the last month" (96). In particular, while gazing on the "awful majesty" of Mont Blanc, Victor's "heart, which was before sorrowful, now swelled with something like joy" (98). Similarly, in noting Victor's "constant and deep grief" (27), Walton says, "no one can feel more deeply than [Victor] does the beauties of nature"; he suffers "misery," Walton adds, "yet when he has retired into himself," it is as if he is encircled by a halo that no grief can penetrate (29).

But Victor's sublime withdrawal from external reality not only blots out thoughts of his mother's death; sometimes, this sublime consolation of forgetfulness also provides, through the maternal power of Nature, a second experience—a symbolic reunion with the lost mother. For example, while still in the Alps, Victor explains, "a tingling long-lost sense of pleasure often came across me during this journey" and "reminded me of days gone by, and were associated with the light-hearted gaiety of boyhood" (95), a time when his mother still lived. What produces these feelings of childhood are the maternal qualities of Nature: Nature is "kindly," the winds are "soothing," and the Arve makes "lulling sounds" that act "as a lullaby" bringing Victor the forgetfulness of sleep (95). As in Wordsworth's poetry, here the sublime provides both an escape from consciousness of the monstrous death of the mother and a return to her nurture through maternal Nature.

In yet a third group of passages linking Victor's anguish to his experience of Nature, Mary Shelley downplays the mode of sublimity that diminishes the cares of human beings, and instead privileges just Nature's maternal power to nurture—a power like the sublime that is regressive. For example, after animating the Monster, Victor convalesces from the resulting nervous fever through the help of Nature, specifically, the return of spring (62). Later, Victor's "health and spirits" gain further strength from a tour of the Ingolstadt area. During this trip Nature—"serene sky and verdant fields"—nurses in Victor "feelings of unbridled joy" and "ecstasy," so that he learns "to love the aspect of nature" (70–71). As in childhood, he is "undisturbed by thoughts" (70). Nature likewise nurses Victor when, returning home for his brother William's funeral, he stays for two days at Lausanne. He arrives here in a "painful state of mind"; however, "by degrees the calm and heavenly scene"—the placid lake and snowy mountains— "restored" him (74). Clearly, when Victor is "restored," he is restored to "the light-hearted gaiety of boyhood," that sense of well-being safeguarded by his mother's care. Nature—when sublime, maternal, or both—opposes consciousness of death, as it does not when merely picturesque.

If in his experience of landscape Victor finds both escape from dark thoughts and return to maternal nurture, he nevertheless also makes two sobering discoveries: first, that sublime moments always end; and second, that ultimately only death ensures forgetting, a state he achieves not in the valleys of the Alps, but rather in the icescapes of the Arctic. Significantly, it is when a sublime moment ends, with the mind returning to the "dark melancholy that clouded every thought" (96), that Victor actually faces the Monster for the first time since the night of his dream. Earlier, after the creation, Victor was so "unable to endure" the Monster's "aspect" that seeing it plunged him into a nervous fever. Similarly, when the sublime ecstasy here at Mont Blanc subsides and Victor sees the Monster again, he almost faints. He can bear to hear the Monster's story of agonized motherlessness only because the Monster relieves him "from the sight of [his] detested form" by covering Victor's eyes with his hands (101). As Irving Massey puts it, the Monster's "ugliness seems ... to act as an invisible shutter for the mind" and represents "a truth" that cannot be faced; this ugliness incarnates "an aspect" of Frankenstein's inner self "with which he either cannot or will not come to terms" (128–29).

In other words, what Frankenstein's creature represents is the shock of returning from sublime forgetfulness to the monstrous consciousness of grief. For example, when in the lightning-lit darkness Victor sees the Monster in the distance at Mont Salève, this illumination causes Victor to revolve in his mind "the events which until now [he] had sought to forget" (76–77). And eventually, like the Monster who fails to be engaged by the sublime "prospect of sun setting behind the stupendous mountains of Jura" (142); Victor becomes so haunted that his only escape is death—"the one means," the Monster says, "to overcome the sensation of pain" (120). Like his double, Victor realizes—after Clerval dies and Victor has completely lost touch with his "better self"—that he "had better seek death" (179).

Appropriately, then, Victor's longing for death guides him to the Arctic waste land, where, after collecting his mother's jewels (201), he has stalked in prey of the "fiend." He finds his death here in the land of ice, which symbolizes repression and death, for its numbness brings relief from all feeling. In one sense, then, by leading Victor to death in the Arctic landscape, the Monster ironically fulfills his symbolic function of reuniting Victor with his mother: if Victor failed in restoring her from the grave, he nevertheless now can join her there. As Knoepflmacher says, Victor's longing for death amounts symbolically to longing to return with the lost mother (110). Unlike his sublime moments of infantile regression, which were always temporary, Victor's moment of death is "the only happy one" he had "enjoyed for several years": now, finally, as "the forms of the beloved dead"—which must include his mother—"flit before" him, Victor hastens, he says, to "their arms" (206). Consequently, his death becomes the wish fulfillment of his dream in chapter 5. And as the novel apocalyptically concludes, like his creator, whose agonized grief he manifests, the Monster similarly finds rest in death. In this landscape of death—the ultimate regression—the Monster at last escapes consciousness; for, in death, if his spirit "thinks, it will not surely think thus" (223).

IV

Like Victor Frankenstein and his Monster, Mary Shelley felt the agony and grief of lacking a nurturing mother. Clearly, Mary Shelley has projected into her characterization of Frankenstein her own adolescent attraction to the sublime as a vehicle to escape consciousness of this grief; but, significantly, she also distances herself from Frankenstein through her narrative structure and in so doing mitigates her need to regress. Here, with Walton writing letters about Frankenstein, the narrative frame forms a boundary between, on one hand, the destructive regression of the self at the center of the story and, on the other hand, the more rational, socially adjusted self of the frame—the self represented by Mrs. Saville ("civil") reading Walton's story in her London living room and also, by extension, the self of the novelist herself.[5]

Ultimately, then, Shelley identifies not with Victor Frankenstein, whose sense of self completely collapses at the novel's end, but with Walton, the Arctic explorer: like Victor and Shelley, Walton not only grew up an orphan but also indulges in "day dreams" and suffers depression (15–19). However, Unlike Victor, whose "miseries" Walton learns from (210), he gives up his Arctic daydream, and returns to London. In other words, he stops searching for a sublime "country of eternal light" (16) and accepts a city of limits and adult responsibilities, such as Margaret's to her "husband and lovely children" (213). Like Walton who learns from Victor's destructive regression to abandon his Arctic fantasy, Mary Shelley similarly matures psychologically, and indeed seems to heal herself, by writing this fantastic novel, the offspring of days when death and grief no longer echoed in her heart. Shelley finally reunites with the mother not through regression but rather through creation of a shared identity—that is, a writer. Moreover, as Patrick Brantlinger says, romantic novels may actually capture psychological truth more accurately than realistic novels, since romances resemble dreams and willingly express wish fulfillments (21). Revealingly, when Mary Shelley next writes a work dominated by landscape, she represses Victor's rapture for the sublime. And instead, she privileges Clerval's attraction to the picturesque, the landscape of firm boundaries, and writes a travelogue reminiscent of Victor's sanest and happiest days—*Rambles in Germany and Italy* (1844).

NOTES

1. Several psychoanalytic studies have focused on Victor's character. For example, see Morton Kaplan and Gordon D. Hirsch. More helpful to my approach are studies that include biographical material. Ellen Moers discusses Mary's dark thoughts about teenage pregnancy, and Marc A. Rubenstein explores the effects on Mary of her mother's and her first daughter's deaths. U. C. Knoepflmacher similarly considers Mary's relation to her mother, but in contrast to my argument stresses the lack of nurture she received from her stepmother as well as her ambivalence toward William Godwin, her father.

2. Clearly, Mary had a melancholy nature, which often focused on her mother: we know that before eloping with Percy Shelley she often spent afternoons at her mother's grave and suffered from an especially acute depression at age 15; and after eloping, in the relatively calm spring of 1816—just before the summer spent with Percy and Byron in Switzerland where she began her novel—she again suffered from depression. Moreover, in December 1816, when she finished "the 4 chap of Frankenstein," we know that her mother was on her mind, for she was reading her mother's book *A Vindication of the Rights of Woman*. See Scott. But as she began to write *Frankenstein*, Rubenstein says, "She was in a position of sufficient strength and tranquility to complete ... some of the postponed psychic work of adolescent development. In particular, she was coming to terms with her conflicted identification with the fantasy of her dead mother" (187). In fact, Shelley's "Author's Introduction" of 1831 connects her writing of the novel with the diminishment of grief: the novel, she writes, "was the offspring of happy days, when death and grief were but words which found no true echo in my heart" (10).

3. Though no critics have considered in depth the psychological implications of both the picturesque and the sublime in *Frankenstein*, David Ketterer discusses the presence in the novel of these 18th-century modes of landscape. Using a feminist approach, Fred V. Randel argues that the novel "exuberantly" criticizes "the infantilism latent in supernaturalism or sublime awe and passivity."

4. For brief discussions of Gilpin and his influence, see Christopher Hussey, Elizabeth Manwaring, Samuel Holt Monk, and Carl Paul Barbier. Manwaring comments on Godwin's use of the picturesque.

5. See Patrick Brantlinger. Though his insightful essay does not discuss *Frankenstein*, many of its ideas apply to the novel.

WORKS CITED

Barbier, Carl Paul. *William Gilpin*. Oxford: Oxford University Press, 1963.

Bloom, Harold. Afterword. *Frankenstein*, by Mary Shelley. New York: Signet, 1965. 212–23.

Brantlinger, Patrick. "Romances, Novels, and Psychoanalysis." *The Practice of Psychoanalytic Criticism*. Ed. Leonard Tennenhouse. Detroit: Wayne State University Press, 1976. 18–45.

Hirsch, Gordon D. "The Monster Was a Lady: On the Psychology of Mary Shelley's *Frankenstein*." *Hartford Studies in Literature* 7 (1975): 116–53.

Hussey, Christopher. *The Picturesque*. 1927. London: Frank Cass, 1967.

Kaplan, Morton. "Fantasy of Paternity and the-Doppelgänger: Mary Shelley's *Frankenstein*." *The Unspoken Motive*. Ed. Morton Kaplan and Robert Kloss. New York: Free Press, 1973. 119–45.

Ketterer, David. *Frankenstein's Creation: The Book, the Monster, and Human Reality*. Victoria: University of Victoria Press, 1979.

Knoepflmacher, U. C. "Thoughts on the Aggression of Daughters." *The Endurance of Frankenstein*. Ed. George Levine and U. C. Knoepflmacher. Berkeley: University of California Press, 1979. 88–119.

Manwaring, Elizabeth. *Italian Landscape in 18th Century England*. 1925. New York: Russell and Russell, 1965.

Massey, Irving. *The Gaping Pig: Literature and Metamorphosis*. Berkeley: University of California Press, 1976.

Moers, Ellen. "Female Gothic." *The Endurance of Frankenstein*. Ed. George Levine and U. C. Knoepflmacher. Berkeley: University of California Press, 1979. 77–87.

Monk, Samuel Holt. *The Sublime*. 1935. Ann Arbor: University of Michigan Press, 1960.

Randel, Fred V. "*Frankenstein*, Feminism, and the Intertextuality of Mountains." *Studies in Romanticism* 24 (1985): 515–32.

Rubenstein, Marc A. "'My Accursed Origin': The Search for the Mother in *Frankenstein*." *Studies in Romanticism* 15 (1976): 165–94.

Scott, Peter Dale. "Mary Wollstonecraft Godwin Shelley and *Frankenstein*: A Chronology." *The Endurance of Frankenstein*. Ed. George Levine and U. C. Knoepflmacher. Berkeley: University of California Press, 1979. xvii–xx.

Shelley, Mary. *Frankenstein, or the Modern Prometheus* (1831). Ed. M. K. Joseph. London: Oxford University Press, 1969.

———. *The Letters of Mary Wollstonecraft Shelley*. Ed. Betty T. Bennett. 2 vols. Baltimore: Johns Hopkins University Press, 1983.

Twitchell, James. *Dreadful Pleasures: An Anatomy of Modern Horror*. New York: Oxford University Press, 1985.

IAIN CRAWFORD

Wading Through Slaughter: John Hampden, Thomas Gray, and Mary Shelley's Frankenstein

The recent and extraordinary burgeoning of scholarly interest in Mary Shelley's *Frankenstein* has combined an increasing appreciation of the novel's psychological, mythic, and literary subtexts with a growing respect for the intellectual force and resilience of its youthful author.[1] While following this general trend, my specific concern here is three-fold and touches upon several underlying areas of the text, examining aspects of its intertextuality which have not previously come to critical attention and relating these both to the narratorial postures of the principal male protagonist and to Mary Shelley herself in her relations with her father and her husband. Thus I hope, first, to explore a passing, yet revealing allusion the novel makes to John Hampden, a leader of the Parliamentary cause before and during the English Civil War. Secondly, I shall suggest that, through Hampden, *Frankenstein* is also indebted to Gray's *Elegy Written in a Country Churchyard*. Although this latter debt is one which has passed unnoticed in the attention given to more readily visible intertexts such as *Paradise Lost*, *The Sorrows of Young Werther*, and *The Rime of the Ancient Mariner*, I hope to show that *Frankenstein* does indeed allude to Gray's poem and to argue that, as well as further enriching a novel already permeated with the texture of English literary discourse, these allusions help to develop the presentation of Victor's inner life and to place it in the larger mythic context of rebellion against divine authority.

From *Studies in the Novel*, vol. XX, no. 3 (Fall 1988): 249–61. © 1988 by the University of North Texas.

Finally, and as a matter of some interest in the case of a novel whose very genesis has always been problematic, I shall consider how the allusions to Hampden and Gray not only form an ironic commentary upon Victor's anti-patriarchal revolt but also intimate a covert response by Mary to an enthusiastic idealism in Percy and Godwin that she appears to have found at least partially suspect.

John Hampden, who lived from 1594 to 1643, was "the richest commoner in England"[2] and a figure of considerable importance both during the period leading up to the Civil War and, until his death, in the actual conflict itself. As the principal opponent of the royalist tax known as Ship-Money and as orchestrator of the Grand Remonstrance, a populist petition against the monarch, he was instrumental in focusing discontent with Charles I and thus in preparing the ground for the outbreak of the Civil War. Once the war began, he turned his abilities to military leadership, acting as one of Cromwell's principal generals until being mortally wounded in a minor skirmish near Chillingworth in 1643. Posthumously, Hampden gained the reputation of having been a martyr to the cause of national liberty and, in the words of his most recent biographer, his name thus "entered the language as a symbol for patriotism."[3]

Not perhaps surprisingly, it was in this light that he was viewed by the more liberal writers of the early nineteenth century. Percy Shelley makes numerous enthusiastic allusions to Hampden, commenting, for example, on the less than entirely Glorious Revolution, "my blood boils to think that Sidney's and Hampden's blood was wasted thus." A response containing similar approbation if slightly less hyperbolic language is also to be found in Godwin's 1824 volume, *History of the Commonwealth of England*, where Hampden is described as "one of the most extraordinary men in the records of mankind." Less extravagantly and in a manner characteristic of his influence upon early Victorian thought, Carlyle set the tone for a revival of interest in Hampden with an 1822 notebook entry:

> Hampden and Washington are the two people best *loved* of any in history. Yet they had few illustrious qualities about them; only a high degree of shrewd business-like activity, and above all that honest-hearted unaffected probity, which we patriotically name *English*, in a higher degree than almost any public men commemorated in history.

The Whig historian, Lord Nugent, followed in much the same vein with his 1831 biography of Hampden, a book that occasioned a lively debate over Hampden's historical status and which in particular prompted a celebrated response from Macaulay. Further evidence of a continuing interest in Hampden is offered by the attention John Forster gives him in an 1837 volume in the *Cabinet Cyclopedia* series, and it was only when Carlyle redefined discussion of the Civil War with his 1845 edition of *Cromwell's Letters and Speeches* that Hampden was superseded in early Victorian thought by his more celebrated cousin.[4]

In *Frankenstein*, Hampden makes what at first seems a somewhat gratuitous appearance during chapter 19 when Victor and Henry Clerval prolong their journey towards Scotland by remaining some time in Oxford and indulging themselves with frequent excursions into the surrounding area:

> We visited the tomb of the illustrious Hampden, and the field on which that patriot fell. For a moment my soul was elevated from its debasing and miserable fears, to contemplate the divine ideas of liberty and self-sacrifice, of which these sights were the monuments and the remembrancers. For an instant I dared to shake off my chains, and look around me with a free and lofty spirit; but the iron had eaten into my flesh, and I sank again, trembling and hopeless, into my miserable self.[5]

Hampden's presence at this point in the novel may be owing to any or all of three possible factors: the enthusiasm for him which Percy and Godwin frequently expressed; a perhaps not entirely unrelated visit to his monument which Godwin and his daughter made in October 1817, during the period of preparing *Frankenstein* for the press, and which Mary records in her *Journal*;[6] and, finally, his wider reputation in English writing—in particular, a reference to him in Gray's *Elegy Written in a Country Churchyard*. While the exact reasons for his entering Shelley's novel remain elusive, his significance in the text is, if by no means simple, then perhaps more readily decipherable.

Though Hampden was seen by progressive writers as an opponent of political repression and a martyr who died in the cause of liberty, his life and career were also open to interpretation as an exemplar of the ambivalencies of revolutionary action. In particular, as a leader of the Parliamentary cause and thus an opponent of Charles I, God's representative upon British soil, he could easily be regarded as a precursor of that tendency to resist patriarchal authority which had, since 1789, become such a fundamental and unsettling motif of European culture. The ambivalence of such revolts is, of course, central to *Frankenstein* and, indeed, immediately before he recounts the visit to Hampden's tomb, Victor himself describes Oxford and nostalgically remembers how "the memory of that unfortunate king ... gave a peculiar interest to every part of the city" (p. 159). As is so characteristic of his narrative, he thus incorporates into the text implications of which he is unaware and which, in fact, ironically undermine his own positions. For, while associating himself with Hampden and his usurpation of the monarch's divinely-bestowed power, Victor also appears to be sentimentally bonded to remembrances of the unfortunate king; he thereby articulates an uncertainty that both lies at the very heart of his anti-patriarchal revolt and which also constantly threatens to undermine the stability of his narrative as a whole.

As has been widely noted, Victor's entire project is fundamentally motivated by the terms of his relationship with his own father, since it is in essence his response to that expulsion from domestic bliss into the larger world which initiates the novel's main action. Even here, however, his motivations are characteristically ambivalent and go beyond any simple attempt to revenge himself upon the ostensibly tyrannical parent who orders his initial separation from the secure world of childhood. For he is not unaware that, in being forced out of the nest, he is also embarking upon a voyage of discovery; as M. Krempe reminds him soon after his arrival in Ingolstadt, he has been living in a "desert land" (p. 46) and will only fulfil his potential by embracing the opportunities available in the larger world. Nevertheless, the purity of Victor's scientific pursuits is clearly qualified by a complex of motivations that involves his feelings towards his father, dead mother, and Elizabeth, and, while the exact balance of his inner life may remain open to debate, there can be no doubting the part in it of an intensely rebellious anti-patriarchal impulse. Paradoxically, however, his revolt includes the desire to attain the very degree of control against which he himself rebels:

> Life and death appeared to me ideal bounds, which I should first break through, and pour a torrent of light into our dark world. A new species would bless me as its creator and source; many happy and excellent natures would owe their being to me. No father could claim the gratitude of his child so completely as I should deserve theirs. (p. 54)

In actuality, of course, Victor is to prove a less than happy originator of the species and will be incessantly wracked by the oscillations in his feelings towards the creature he has made.

As his narrative develops, moreover, such confusions in his roles as both son and parent become ever more manifest. On the one hand, he will align himself with the Monster by revealing a submerged self-perception in the terms of Satan's rebellion against his tyrannical father (p. 182). On the other, he greets M. Frankenstein's arrival at the Irish jail rapturously: "the appearance of my father was to me like that of my good angel, and I gradually recovered my health" (p. 181). In an apparent endeavor to resolve this contradiction, he resorts to the stratagem of finding justification for his revenge by presenting it as a mission of justice "enjoined by heaven" (p. 204), which, he feels, guides him across the wastes of Europe in search of his enemy. Notwithstanding this evidently specious device, he and his creation, in fact, move towards and then past one another until, by the final phase of the novel and during the pursuit across the Arctic, hunter and hunted seem almost indistinguishable: for Victor sinks into the obsessive, hateful spirit of revenge that had earlier motivated the Monster, while his quarry takes on that mantle of eloquent sensitivity which had first attracted Walton to the dying scientist. Ultimately, however, each recognizes the sterility of his life and, though Victor never does quite renounce his rebellious ambitions completely, both he and the Monster end the novel in the utter defeat of having destroyed all those to whom they have ties and, in particular, the patriarchs from whom they derive their existences and much of their signification.

While it would certainly be extravagant to suggest that Shelley reinterprets John Hampden as radically as she and other Romantic writers metamorphosed the Satan of *Paradise Lost*, her allusion may nevertheless be seen as offering a somewhat less straightforward interpretation than that widely current in the early nineteenth century. Indeed, such ambivalence is entirely characteristic of a novel whose principal quality is its sense of the final undecidability of human motivation and behavior, a sense evident in the presentations of both Hampden and Victor Frankenstein. If in Victor's eyes Hampden is a glorious rebel and martyr, a prototype of his own struggle against patriarchal authority, both historical precedent and the text itself remind us of the penalty often exacted for such rebellions. For Hampden, the price to be paid was death in an obscure skirmish and the loss of opportunity to see the outcome of his efforts for the revolution; Victor, too, dies, but with a more confirmed sense of failure and defeat. And yet, just as Victor refuses entirely to abandon his dreams at the last, so too Hampden's cause would triumph, even though it may be wondered how he would have reacted to the eventual course Cromwell's revolutionary rule took. Both history and the literary text thus seem to pass mixed verdicts upon their subjects, then: while they condemn Hampden and Victor to their respective defeats, they also still manage to suggest simultaneously both the magnitude of individual aspiration and achievement and yet also a tantalizing sense of the constraints which mortality places upon human ambition, knowledge, and endeavor.

With Victor himself, it is precisely the habit of mind which conditions his comments upon Hampden that leads to failure. For his attitude to the Parliamentary leader suggests an inability to escape from paradigmatic perceptions in his viewing of the world around him. Like the Monster, Victor is incapable of seeing life other than through inherited patterns of literary discourse, and, while the Monster has good reason for basing his perceptions upon the texts which are almost his only source of knowledge, Victor himself cannot be so readily excused. William Veeder has recently argued that Victor has the mind of a Gothic protagonist and that he sees the entire world in the terms of Gothic fiction.[7] Similarly, I would suggest, he also regards himself as a latter-day Hampden, a Romantic version of the figure Clarendon described as almost the savior of his age: "And I am persuaded his power and interest at that time was greater to do good or hurt than any man's in the kingdom, or than any man in his rank hath had in any time."[8] Victor likewise considers himself to possess the ability to bestow unique blessings upon mankind, a notion which proves extremely corrosive since it enables him to cloak the chaos of his inner life in a veil of benevolence and thus to proceed along his grisly trail unhindered, indeed perversely encouraged, by the proddings of his conscience. And yet, so great is the need to construct layers of protective auto-valorization about himself that even this level of self-defence does not prove sufficient, and he appears ever more concerned to present himself as speaking his own elegy and to justify, if hardly the ways of God to man, then surely his own motivations and actions.

For, if his allusion to Hampden derives in part from a broad cultural interest in the man, it may also simultaneously owe something to a parallel literary source—that of Gray's *Elegy Written in a Country Churchyard*, where reference is made to the fallen martyr:

> Some village-Hampden, that with dauntless breast
> The little Tyrant of his fields withstood;
> Some mute inglorious Milton here may rest,
> Some Cromwell guiltless of his country's blood.[9]

Circumstantially, there are several reasons to assume that the *Elegy* was, indeed, an influence upon *Frankenstein*: the emphasis here is evidently in the mainstream of historical interpretation of Hampden's role; the poem itself was a central intertext in the Romantics' definition of the nature and function of poetry; and its elegiac stance towards a melancholy subject is a posture which offers considerable attractions to Victor's sense of his own narrative.

Gray's poem achieved enormous popularity upon its publication in 1751 and rapidly became a touchstone of the English literary imagination. Johnson's celebrated description of its abounding with "images which find a mirror in every mind, and with sentiments to which every bosom returns an echo," and his judgement that "Had Gray written often thus, it had been vain to blame, and useless to praise him" readily suggest the power the *Elegy* soon came to have. The duality lurking in this latter comment, however, is developed further in Romantic responses both to the poem itself and to its author's wider achievement. Thus while Wordsworth in the Preface to *Lyrical Ballads* was to pillorize Gray as epitomizing the limitations of eighteenth-century poetic style, the *Elegy* itself seems to have remained immune to attack and become a text held in near universal affection and respect. In *Biographia Literaria*, for example, Coleridge, too, is willing to express considerable criticism of Gray's work at large, but steadfastly defends the *Elegy* itself as a poem he cannot read "without delight, and a portion of enthusiasm." In the writings of Shelley's circle, we also find evidence of this divided response: Percy Shelley alludes favorably to there being "a line to be drawn between affectation of unpossessed talents, and the deceit of self distrust by which much power has been lost to the world for 'full many a flower is born to blush unseen, and waste its sweetness on the desert air.'— This line may be called the 'modesty of nature.'" On the other hand, in her unfinished short story, "The Cave of Fancy," Mary Wollstonecraft quotes the same lines, only to then deny that a true poet remains "mute" and "inglorious"; rather, "those only grovel who have not power to fly."[10] While specific evidence of Mary Shelley's acquaintance with the poem does not appear to exist, there seems every reason to believe that such a precociously well-read author as she was in 1816 would have known what was already a standard text. Moreover, in both the direct allusion to Hampden and then in the more general nature of his motivation, Victor Frankenstein suggests that the *Elegy* is indeed of considerable importance to his own narrative. For, to borrow Michael Rifaterre's term, what Victor apparently does is "scramble" his intertext in order to generate a meaning for his own narrative that is both wedded to and yet subtly distinct from its model.[11]

Linking *Frankenstein*'s three narratives is a single underlying conflict that is at the heart of the *Elegy* and which George Levine has seen to be central to nineteenth-century realistic fiction: that between "a simultaneous awe and reverence toward greatness of ambition, and fear and distrust of those who act on it."[12] It is this tension that both drives Victor, Walton, and the Monster in their journeys of discovery and self-discovery, yet which also leaves them naggingly dissatisfied with their lives. While in each case this opposition clearly overlays a more complex psychology, the actual tension between the desire for ambitious exploration of the universe at large and a yearning towards the passive satisfactions of domesticity is evidently central to the text as a whole and forms a vital part in the motivations of each of the three male narrators. It is perhaps Victor who most clearly articulates the dilemma they all feel in the contrast that emerges between two of the intertexts upon which he draws in the framing of his narrative.

For, on the one hand, he is eager to liken his scientific explorations to the voyage of Coleridge's Ancient Mariner; on the other, he structures his text in cautionary terms close to those of Gray's *Elegy*. The debt to Coleridge has been widely noted and, in fact, not only Victor but also Walton, and Mary Shelley herself in the Introduction to the novel's 1831 edition make reference to the *Ancient Mariner* as a means of describing their explorations beyond the pale of normal human endeavor (pp. 9, 21, 151–52). Although the novel thus might at one level partake of the poem's ostensible moral edict to love both creatures great and small, the relationship between the two texts is perhaps more profoundly seen in their common focus upon the forces of creative obsession, the demonic capacities of the human mind, and the destructive energies released when these two clash.

In this context, Victor's submerged allusions to the *Elegy* appear to stand as a corrective admonition intended to deter Walton (and, by implication, the reader) from following in his footsteps: "Learn from me, if not by my precepts, at least by my example, how dangerous is the acquirement of knowledge, and how much happier that man is who believes his native town to be the world, than he who aspires to become greater than his nature will allow" (p. 53). Though this quietist sentiment and the "apt moral" (p. 30) it implies for the text at large are almost a commonplace of eighteenth-century writing, the particular phrasing here is close to that of Gray's narrator in the *Elegy*. For the speaker and protagonist of the poem also repeatedly evokes the stable tranquillity of rural life as an antidote to the dangerous temptations of ambition:

> Let not Ambition mock their useful toil,
> Their homely joys, and destiny obscure;
> Nor Grandeur hear with a disdainful smile,
> The short and simple annals of the poor. (29–32)

Both he and Victor find much to praise in those who resist the pull towards the larger world and who, "Far from the madding crowd's ignoble strife ... Along the cool sequester'd vale of life" (73, 75), retain a more measured view of mortal existence. Victor, indeed, sees humanity's recurring failure to achieve such stability as having immense historical significance: "If no man allowed any pursuit whatsoever to interfere with the tranquillity of his domestic affections, Greece had not been enslaved; Caesar would have spared his country; America would have been discovered more gradually; and the empires of Mexico and Peru had not been destroyed" (p. 56). For Victor himself, however, this ideal proves unattainable and must be transposed into Elizabeth and, to a lesser degree, Henry Clerval, both of whom embody the rewards of a life responsive to the language of Nature and the attainment of tranquillity in rural retirement (pp. 36, 64, 156). For the narrator of the poem, the conditioning factor is an inescapable sense of the ultimate frustrations of mortality:

> The boast of heraldry, the pomp of pow'r,
> And all that beauty, all that wealth e'er gave,
> Awaits alike th' inevitable hour.
> The paths of glory lead but to the grave. (33–36)

Clearly, if had Victor taken his own advice—and that of the *Elegy*—Elizabeth, Henry, and his other victims would have been spared the consequences of both his virtues and, more importantly, his vices, since rural immolation could have saved them just as it spared Gray's humble villagers, as it:

>   nor circumscrib'd alone
> Their growing virtues, but their crimes confin'd;
> Forbade to wade through slaughter to a throne,
> And shut the gates of mercy on mankind. (65–68)

And yet, though Victor is unable to accept the finality of death and while his victims could certainly have benefited from an infusion of the temperance he and the narrator of the *Elegy* urge, both texts ultimately remain ambivalent about the ideal they overtly present and suggest a more complex response than that encoded in the moral of simple retirement.

The opposing forces that lie below the surface of the *Elegy* have recently been considered by Howard Weinbrot in a discussion which may also shed light upon Mary Shelley's novel.[13] Weinbrot suggests that, at the outset of the poem, the narrator finds himself in a state of alienation from nature, the village, and his own obscure lot; as the poem develops, it reveals the "flux and counter-flux of an emotionally charged argument"[14] while the speaker endeavors to come to terms with the life of obscure retirement in which he finds himself; and finally, though he never does become a joyful member of the village community, he at least "learns to resign himself to ordinary human affection; he associates himself with his neighboring, humble people and landscape and, in the process, leaves the definition of his hidden, true character to God."[15]

Victor's approximation to yet distinct difference from such a position is evident. Like the speaker of Gray's poem, he is dissatisfied with the whole notion of living a modestly obscure life, and he thus becomes wretchedly self-exiled from the world in which he finds himself. Rejecting the pastoral retreat to which both his father retires and in which Gray's narrator eventually finds peace, he endeavors to aggrandize to himself the entire universe through his creation of life itself. Even in this, however, he lacks a stabilizing "steady purpose" (p. 16), since he also retains his more socialized values and, being made a coward by his own conscience, proves unable to embrace his ambitions wholeheartedly. For, again like Gray's character, if for very different reasons, he too is incapable of blushing unseen in the desert air and is thus tormented by the combination of restlessness in domestic tranquillity and a mixture of attraction to and repulsion from the project through which he endeavors to achieve greatness. Where Victor most essentially differs from his predecessor is in his inability to perceive or accept an overriding value in patriarchal or divine guidance, since he not only rejects his own father but also, until late in his narrative, shows no interest whatsoever in the codes of religious belief. As a result of this solipsism, he becomes isolated. Failing to overcome his isolation, he slides into an ever more dominant obsession with the Monster, its creation and then its—and thus his own—destruction. Gray's protagonist, by contrast, for all his prevarications, never loses a sense of the virtues of the common people amongst whom he finds himself, and so, even though his death is not unlike Victor's in being caused by an overburden of sorrow, he at least has come to some accommodation with his fate:

> Large was his bounty, and his soul sincere,
>   Heav'n did a recompense as largely send:
> He gave to Mis'ry all he had, a tear,
> He gain'd from Heav'n ('twas all he wish'd) a friend. (121–24)

With this distinction in the relations between the protagonist and the external world the two texts are once again both bonded and yet ultimately separate. For it is clearly a similar yearning for companionship which motivates not only Victor but also Walton and the Monster—a hunger which is doomed to go unassuaged. As Stephen Cox has argued, in the case of the *Elegy* the yearning for social sympathy expresses a need for a sense of the significance of individual life and constitutes an alternative to a religious belief which the narrator finds himself unable to sustain. Cox suggests that the conclusion of the poem shows Gray's narrator as having achieved both the ability to trust to the "pure emotion" of a stable sensibility and the capacity to accept human limitations as "a background against which the self can display its dignity of feeling."[16] The triumph may, indeed, be still greater, since the protagonist has also managed to find that larger "trembling hope" in "The bosom of his Father and his God" (127–28). It is, of course, in precisely these respects that Victor and his counterparts are most deficient: in Shelley's text a term such as "pure emotion" is a dangerous oxymoron and Victor is never able to achieve emotional resolutions to match those of Gray's character. Moreover, his narrative, despite all its insistence upon the inescapability of his destiny (pp. 30, 42, 181), not only ignores God but also persistently refuses to distance itself from the individualistic code of Promethean achievement which it ostensibly condemns. For Victor's last words turn out to be anything but the elegiac renunciation of past errors his earlier admonition to Walton might have led one to expect:

> "Farewell, Walton! Seek happiness in tranquillity, and avoid ambition, even if it be only the apparently innocent one of distinguishing yourself in science and discoveries. Yet why do I say this? I have myself been blasted in these hopes, yet another may succeed." (pp. 217–18)

Though Victor dies, the Monster vanishes, and Walton is forced to return to England, the narrative thus refuses to endorse any simple moral as to the value of ambition and the challenging of established authority and thus calls into question its own status as the cautionary tale it has claimed to be.

Finally, the allusions to Hampden and Gray may also have a degree of significance for Mary Shelley and the men who dominated her own life, since they perhaps discretely suggest Mary's commentary upon the intense idealism which marks both her father's and husband's thought and writings. Professor Veeder's useful suggestion that Mary's "critical examination of all paradigms ... is what drives her and her readers beyond Victor's self-justifying explanations to the darker teleology of him and Percy"[17] is relevant here. There is no doubting that both Godwin and Percy knew Gray's poem and were enthusiastic about Hampden; Percy's idolizing, in particular, is entirely characteristic of both his fundamental political views and his general tendency towards hero-worship. That Mary was not quite so taken with this radical version of the blessed martyr may be suggested by the levity of her tone in a letter to Hunt during the composition of *Frankenstein*. Alluding to Hampden's resistance to the Ship-Money levy, she wrote:

> Shelley & Peacock have started a question which I do not esteem myself wise enough to decide upon—and yet as they seem

determined to act on it I wish them to have the *best advise*. As a
prelude to this you must be reminded that Hamden was of Bucks
and our two worthies want to be his successors for which reason
they intend to refuse to pay the taxes as illegally imposed—What
effect will this have & ought they do it is the question? Pray let
me know your opinion.[18]

Similarly, Victor's language—"For an instant I dared to shake off my chains,
and look around me with a free and lofty spirit; but the iron had eaten into
my flesh, and I sank again, trembling and hopeless, into my miserable self"
(p. 160)—in recounting the visit to Hampden's tomb is markedly, if not
indeed parodically Shelleyan in both its terminology and tone. What the
allusions to Gray and Hampden show in the overall text of *Frankenstein*,
moreover, is that such idealization tends to be simplistic, to overlie and
disguise more complex psychological processes, and, when transformed out
of theory and into concrete effect, to become almost wholly pernicious in its
operations. Thus, the fates of both Hampden and Victor, together with the
wider intertextual questioning of Victor's ambitions which the novel offers,
all suggest not only his failings but also, perhaps, limitations in the ideals and
psychology of Godwin and, especially, Percy himself. Accordingly, they may
well represent another facet of that discrete rebellion against the patriarchal
authority of her father and her husband that a number of critics have
discerned in Mary's writings, and, if such indeed be the case, *Frankenstein* can
in this respect also be seen as a critique of the larger character of Romantic
idealism.[19] That Mary should have voiced her qualifications in this covert
manner need hardly be surprising, since there is little cause to assume that
she articulated them fully even to herself and every reason for understanding
why they should have remained disguised in print.

Victor's narrative, then, through its reference to Hampden and allusion
to Gray articulates an ambivalence at the very heart of his revolt and perhaps
also implies a larger critique of the radical ideology to which Mary herself
was exposed by the circumstances of her life. He and, to a lesser degree,
Walton and the Monster attempt to exert control over others and the world
at large through the power that comes from unrivalled possession of unique
forms of knowledge. In each case, however, the endeavor is shown to mask
an underlying psychic instability which eventually, inevitably leads to failure.
For the purposes of this discussion, I have focused upon the anti-patriarchal
character of the struggle, concentrating largely on Victor; a broader
consideration of the novel might valuably also examine Walton and the
Monster in the same light and relate all three male narrators to the
misogynic elements in the text. Nevertheless, even while some part of my

argument must, in the absence of indisputably specific evidence for Mary's debt to Gray, finally remain speculative, Hampden's place in the text is clear. Though his and the novel's connection with Gray's *Elegy* can be claimed only to the extent that I have attempted here, such a link may well indicate yet one more way in which this endlessly suggestive text weds its own delving into the human psyche with an extraordinary sensitivity to the major intertexts of English literature and, out of this union, produces a novel unmatched in its expression of the final undecidability of human emotions and conduct

NOTES

1. The growth of scholarly interest in *Frankenstein* is best evidenced by the listing contained in Frederick S. Frank's compendious survey, "Mary Shelley's *Frankenstein*: A Register of Research," *Bulletin of Bibliography* 40 (1983): 163–88.

2 . Christopher Hill, *Puritanism and Revolution: Studies in Interpretation of the English Revolution of the 17th Century* (New York: Schocken Books, 1964), p. 11.

3. John Adair, *A Life of John Hampden: The Patriot* (London: Macdonald and Jane's, 1976), p. 249.

4. The references in this paragraph are, in the order they appear, to: *The Letters of Percy Bysshe Shelley*, ed. Frederick L. Jones, 2 vols. (Oxford: Clarendon Press, 1964), 1:264; Godwin, *History of the Commonwealth of England, from its Commencement to the Restoration of Charles the Second*, 4 vols. (London: n.p. 1824–1828), 1:11; Carlyle's notebook is cited in Charles Richard Sanders, *Carlyle's Friendships and Other Studies* (Durham, NC: Duke Univ. Press, 1977), p. 28; Lord Nugent's 1831 biography, *Memorials of John Hampden*, encountered Macaulay's response in the *Edinburgh Review* for December of that year.

5. *Frankenstein or The Modern Prometheus*, ed. M. K. Joseph (Oxford: Oxford Univ. Press, 1969), p. 160. All references are to this edition and will be inserted parenthetically.

6. *Mary Shelley's Journal*, ed. Frederick L. Jones (Norman: Univ. of Oklahoma Press, 1947), October 20, 1817, p. 85. Mary also records here that she was transcribing *Frankenstein* during the previous week.

7. William Veeder, "The Negative Oedipus: Father, *Frankenstein*, and the Shelleys," *Critical Inquiry* 12 (1986): 378.

8. Cited in Adair, *A Life of John Hampden*, p. 2.

9. *The Complete Poems of Thomas Gray*, H. W. Starr and J. R. Hendrickson, eds. (Oxford: The Clarendon Press, 1966), II. 57–60. Further quotations will be taken from this edition and inserted parenthetically.

10. The references in this paragraph are, in the order, they appear, to: "Johnson's *Life of Gray*," in *Samuel Johnson: Selected Writings*, R. T. Davies, ed. (Evanston, IL: Northwestern Univ. Press, 1965), p. 376; Wordsworth, "Preface and Appendix to *Lyrical Ballads*," in *Wordsworth's Literary Criticism*, ed. W. J. B. Owen (London: Routledge and Kegan Paul, 1974), pp. 75–76; Coleridge, *Biographia Literaria*, ed. James Engell and W. Jackson Bate, 2 vols. (Princeton: Princeton Univ. Press, 1983), 1:41; Shelley, *Letters*, 1:231; and Mary Wollstonecraft, cited in Ralph M. Wardle, *Mary Wollstonecraft: A Critical Biography* (Lincoln: Univ. of Nebraska Press, 1951), pp. 81–82.

11. Michael Rifaterre, *Semiotics of Poetry* (Bloomington: Indiana Univ. Press, 1978), pp. 138–50.

12. George Levine, *The Realistic Imagination: English Fiction from Frankenstein to Lady Chatterley* (Chicago: Univ. of Chicago Press, 1981), p. 27.

13. Howard S. Weinbrot, "Gray's *Elegy*: A Poem of Moral Choice and Resolution," *Studies in English Literature: 1500–1900* 18 (1978): 537–51.

14. Weinbrot, p. 538.

15. Weinbrot, p. 551.

16. Stephen Cox, *"The Stranger Within Thee"*: *Concepts of the Self in Late Eighteenth-Century Literature* (Pittsburgh: Univ. of Pittsburgh Press, 1980), pp. 92, 94.

17. Veeder, p. 379.

18. *The Letters of Mary Wollstonecraft Shelley*, ed. Betty T. Bennett, 2 vols. (Baltimore: Johns Hopkins Univ. Press, 1980–83), 1:29.

19. The breadth of Mary's concern with contemporary political issues and her belief in "evolutionary radicalism" rather than violent revolt is apparent from a series of letters recently discovered in Australia which will appear in the forthcoming third volume of Betty T. Bennett's definitive edition of the correspondence. These letters, as described by Herbert Mitgang, "A Hunch on Mary Shelley Pays Off," *The New York Times*, 2 Dec. 1987, national ed., p. 29, suggest that, while deeply committed to libertarian ideals, Mary was more pragmatic than either Godwin or Percy in her sense of how they might be achieved.

PAUL A. CANTOR

Mary Shelley and the Taming of the Byronic Hero: *"Transformation" and* The Deformed Transformed

Having long been viewed as peripheral to the study of Romanticism, *Frankenstein* has been moved to the center. Critics originally tried to assimilate Mary Shelley's novel to patterns already familiar from Romantic poetry. But more recent studies of *Frankenstein* have led critics to rethink Romanticism in light of Mary Shelley's contribution. Gradually emerging from the shadow of her husband, she is increasingly being recognized as a distinct voice within Romanticism, a distinctly feminine voice within what seems to be a male-dominated movement.[1] The trend of recent studies of *Frankenstein* has been to view it as a critique of Romanticism, particularly as developed in Percy Shelley's poetry. Critics have argued that *Frankenstein* is a protest against Romantic titanism, against the masculine aggressiveness that lies concealed beneath the dreams of Romantic idealism. They characterize Victor Frankenstein as a man claiming to be acting for the benefit of humanity but in his egotism only succeeding in destroying himself and all those he loves.[2] As a story focusing on an aggressively male attempt to displace the female from her role as creator and nourisher of human life, *Frankenstein* embodies on several levels Shelley's distinctive concerns as a woman in the early nineteenth century. Above all, the novel can be viewed as a protest in the name of domesticity against the destructive effects of the Romantic heroic ideal.[3]

As Shelley's most powerful work, *Frankenstein* has inevitably played the

From *The Other Mary Shelley: Beyond Frankenstein*, eds. Audrey A. Fisch, Anne K. Mellor and Esther H. Schor. © 1993 by Oxford University Press.

most important role in helping reshape our notions of Romanticism. But *Frankenstein* is not unique among Shelley's works in providing a critique of male Romanticism. In 1822–23, she transcribed Byron's *The Deformed Transformed* at his request with a view to publication.[4] This unfinished poetic drama involves a bizarre twist on the Faust legend, telling the story of a tormented hunchback who invokes the devil's aid to give his spirit a new lodging in a scaled-down version of Achilles' body. In 1830, Shelley published in *The Keepsake* annual a story called "Transformation," which clearly constitutes a rewriting of Byron's work. First published in 1824, *The Deformed Transformed* has never received much attention from critics, partly because as a fragment it is hard to analyze, partly because in conception it is derivative from Goethe's *Faust*, and partly because its poetry is uneven in quality.[5] "Transformation" has lived largely in the shadow of *Frankenstein*, which it resembles in its use of the *Doppelgänger* motif and its treatment of the body as the prison of the soul. Read separately, *The Deformed Transformed* and "Transformation" may seem relatively unimportant to our understanding of Romanticism. But viewing "Transformation" as a feminist revision of *The Deformed Transformed* does allow us to see this confrontation as a significant episode in the history of English Romanticism. I want to use "Transformation" to help reread its precursor text in Byron, and at the same time use *The Deformed Transformed* to help rethink a central pattern in Byron's poetry, the relation of love and aggression. This rereading of Byron should have implications for our understanding of *Frankenstein* as well.

What works like *Frankenstein* and "Transformation" call attention to in Romantic literature in general and in Byron's poetry in particular is the remarkable prevalence of aggression and violence in a movement that claimed to promote peace and love. In many ways Wordsworth shaped the image of Romanticism that traditionally prevailed in the Anglo-American world, with the result that critics tended to picture the Romantic poet typically at peace with nature. This characterization is in fact inadequate to the complexity of Wordsworth's poetry; it cannot account for the massive scenes of warfare throughout Blake; and it certainly gives a false impression of the second generation of the English Romantics. It is indeed hardly surprising to find so much violence in Romantic literature, given the fact that it was a product of a revolutionary age. It would in fact be strange if the violence of the French Revolution and the Napoleonic Wars were not somehow reflected in Romantic literature. Even though the Romantics typically posited nonviolent goals for humanity, like liberty and equality, they did not always advocate nonviolent means to those ends. To the extent that the Romantics supported the cause of political revolution, they often found themselves in the position of portraying and even celebrating political violence.

But Byron goes a step further: he seems fascinated with violence per se, especially with the crime of murder. And Byron does not confine himself to political violence: the murders he portrays often grow out of disputes between men competing for women and thus could be classified as domestic violence. But in fact in Byron, it is not always possible to draw a clear line between domestic and political violence. In a series of works beginning with the Oriental tales, such as *The Giaour* and *The Corsair*, and continuing on through poems such as *Parisina*, Byron seems to dwell obsessively upon a pattern which has many variations but in some ways stands most clearly revealed in *Mazeppa*. A younger man wins the love of a beautiful woman away from an older man; the older man, who is somehow socially and politically superior to the younger, metes out a dreadful punishment to him; out of the depth of his defeat, the younger man somehow reconstitutes his strength and lives to exact a terrible vengeance upon the older man and anyone associated with him. This narrative pattern is of course not unique to Byron: in its outline it provides the staple of romantic plots in all ages. But what is peculiar to Byron is the proportions of his narratives. For a Romantic poet, he seems curiously to downplay the role of romance in his poetry. One might expect the love element in these stories to be primary and the revenge element to be secondary, but exactly the reverse happens. The imaginative core of these poems—the most fully realized moment poetically—is almost always a scene of brutal and devastating violence: an army wiped out, a castle obliterated, an enemy savagely cut down. Whereas Byron presents the love that provokes the violence in shadowy terms, sometimes merely alluding to it elliptically, he dwells in paradoxically loving detail on the violence itself and the hate it expresses. And if one steps back from these poems to survey their pattern, one cannot help being struck by the disproportion of the violence they portray. A comparatively isolated incident of domestic violence triggers an outpouring of community-wide violence that may eventually lay an entire kingdom waste.

It is this pattern in Byron which struck Mary Shelley, this interweaving of love and hate, romance and war, a pattern in which the aggressive elements tend to predominate. As Mazeppa speaks of his beloved, we see how love and hate blend in his mind:

> I loved her then—I love her still;
> And such as I am, love indeed
>   In fierce extremes—in good and ill.
> But still we love even in our rage.
>
> (225–28)[6]

In *The Giaour* the equivalence of what appear to be opposite emotions is suggested by the poetic symmetry of a single line: "The maid I love—the man I hate—" (1018). The first in this series of poems, *The Giaour* is the most explicit in portraying hate as an emotion deeper than love:

> But Love itself could never pant
> For all that Beauty sighs to grant,
> With half the fervour Hate bestows
> Upon the last embrace of foes,
> When grappling in the fight they fold
> Those arms that ne'er shall lose their hold;
> Friends meet to part—Love laughs at faith;—
> True foes, once met, are joined till death!
>
> (647–54)

The relationship of the Giaour and his enemy, Hassan, is in fact presented as a kind of marriage (line 718), while the feminine element in the poem is literally and figuratively occluded and suppressed (in terms of the narrative, the hero's beloved, Leila, is placed in a sack and drowned). *The Giaour* appears to be a romantic poem, in which the love of man and woman ought to be at the center. But in practice Byron pushes the love story to the margins, while he focuses on the hate of man for man, which is paradoxically presented as a kind of love. In general, Byron's poetic tales present a hypermasculine world, in which women function largely as pawns in the power struggles of men.

One can readily see why Shelley might have reacted negatively to the portrayal of women in Byron's Oriental tales, but before discussing her revision of Byron, it is important to analyze this pattern in greater depth. It is only when we read his works in conventionally romantic terms that the violence in them seems disproportionate. Our first impression in the Oriental tales is that romantic love is the cause and violence is the effect, and in that case the effect does seem out of proportion to the cause. At first sight Byron seems to be portraying situations in which men become rivals because they have fallen in love with the same woman. But the poems suddenly appear in a new light if we experiment with reversing our sense that love is the primary phenomenon and aggression the derivative. Suppose for a moment that in Byron's poetry the men fall in love with the same woman because they are rivals. Then the violence would no longer seem as peculiar, for the love conflict would merely be providing the excuse for a more basic hostility that was already latent in the situation.

Readers familiar with the writings of René Girard will recognize that I am applying his theory of mimetic desire and mimetic violence to Byron.[7] Girard's reconception of the nature of desire is best understood in terms of his polemic against Freud and specifically the idea of the Oedipus complex.[8] In Freud's conception of the oedipal triangle, the primary fact is the son's desire for his mother, from which his hostility to his father as his competitor is derived. More generally, for Freud the foundation of all explanation is the fact of human desire, and he views aggression as a derivative phenomenon.[9] Girard, by contrast, treats desire as learned rather than spontaneous. For Girard the primary fact is the son's identification with his father; wanting to be like his father, he comes to desire what his father desires, namely, his mother. Thus Girard views the rivalry between father and son as the cause rather than the effect of the son's desire for his mother. Byron's poetry offers unusually fertile ground for applying Girard's theories. To be sure, at first glance the poetic tales seem to be readily explicable in Freudian terms. The basic situation repeatedly seems oedipal: a younger man in conflict with an older over a woman who is usually midway between them in age and sometimes related to the younger man (in *Parisina*, for example, the younger man is the illegitimate son of the older, and falls in love with the woman who becomes his father's wife). In *The Bride of Abydos* the language becomes pointedly oedipal, as Old Giaffir speaks with contempt for his nephew-son Selim in clearly phallic terms:

> But if thy beard had manlier length,
> And if thy hand had skill and strength,
> I'd joy to see thee break a lance,
> Albeit against my own perchance.
>
> (I.122–25)

But as the inversion of Freud's theory of the Oedipus complex, Girard's theory of mimetic desire can explain these patterns in Byron's poetry equally well. The question becomes, Where does the emphasis fall in Byron's poetic tales: on the sexual aspects or the aggressive behavior?

I would argue that what energizes these poems is Byron's portrayal of masculine rivalry and specifically the way mimetic desire leads to violence. At one point Byron even speaks of "mimic slaughter" (*Abydos*, I.247). He constantly dwells upon how protagonist and antagonist, despite their apparent differences in age, nationality, and faith, are mirror images of each other. Consider the striking moment when the Giaour stands over his defeated foe:

> Fall'n Hassan lies—his unclos'd eye
> Yet lowering on his enemy,

As if the hour that seal'd his fate,
Surviving left his quenchless hate;
And o'er him bends that foe with brow
As dark as his that bled below.—

(669–74)

Thus what seems to draw Byron's characters into conflict is not the accidental conjunction of their desires but some fundamental similarity in their natures that from the beginning sets them on a collision course of imitation.

The advantage of a Girardian rather than a Freudian reading of Byron's poetic tales is that it allows us to see the hidden agenda of the Byronic hero. At first sight the characters in the poetic tales seem to stumble into criminality. Because their desires are for one reason or another illicit, they end up at odds with society. But a Girardian reading suggests that something deep within these characters makes them antisocial to begin with, and the desires that ostensibly ruin their lives paradoxically serve the function of bringing about the break with society they secretly crave. Along with such writers as Kleist and Dostoevsky, Byron must be credited with discovering what might be called the metaphysics of criminality as a theme for literature.[10] Byron's characters are not antisocial because their desires are criminal; they generate criminal desires because they are by nature antisocial. Something in them cannot stand ordinary contentment and a peaceful life within society, and thus they in effect seek out a way of life that will prevent them from becoming trapped in a conventional existence. What seems to be merely the result of fatal accidents in their lives turns out to correspond to their deepest longing.

This approach helps account for the fact that, despite the way the violence is generated domestically in Byron's poetic tales, he supplies a political dimension to the stories. Mazeppa's tale is doubly framed by political events: it is narrated in the context of Peter the Great's victory over Charles XII of Sweden at Pultowa, which is in turn associated with Napoleon's later defeat at Moscow. The Oriental tales all take place against the background of Greek–Turkish conflicts, and specifically the issue of Greek independence. In *The Giaour* Byron harks back to the great battles of Thermopylae and Salamis and hence to the conflicts between the ancient Greeks and Persians. Thus the domestic violence in these poetic tales takes place within a larger political context, which suggests that aggression is a pervasive phenomenon in human life. Once again, what is characteristic of Byron is the way the domestic violence tends to spill over into political. If as I have been arguing Byron's heroes are in effect looking for a fight, then we can understand why what initially seems like a limited occasion for conflict in his poetry swiftly generates uncontrollable violence. Feeling at odds with the fabric of society, his heroes seize upon the first excuse to tear it down. What is most modern in Byron's poetry is his portrayal of violence as a symptom, a symptom of a root dissatisfaction with human existence driving his heroes into an escalating pattern of aggression and destruction that ultimately aims at nothing less than dislodging the frame of the universe.

Though incomplete as a poem, *The Deformed Transformed* provides the fullest realization in Byron of the pattern of mimetic desire and mimetic violence. The hero of the play, Arnold, is a hunchback, who as a result of his ugliness is rejected by everyone, even by his own mother. As a result Arnold becomes a creature of pure negation: he wishes to be anything other than what he is (I.i.347–48). When he reaches the point of attempting suicide, a stranger who we gradually learn is the devil appears to offer Arnold his aid. Conjuring up the shades of some of the greatest heroes of the ancient world, the devil makes Arnold an offer he cannot refuse: he can have the bodily form of anyone he desires. Notice how this differs from the normal scene of satanic temptation. Byron's devil does not corrupt Arnold with promises of worldly goods, with visions of wealth or sexual temptations. He seems to understand that what ultimately motivates human beings is not their appetites but their will to power. If they crave the objects the devil traditionally dangles before their eyes, the reason is that they associate those objects with higher states of being. Byron's devil goes right to the heart of the matter: he knows that what Arnold really wants is to be someone other than himself.

In a curious way Byron has captured in the opening scene the great heritage of Romanticism for modernity, the dream that human beings can be whatever they want to be. The devil gives Arnold a chance to act out the Romantic fantasy of complete autonomy: "You shall have no bond / But your own will" (150–51). At the beginning Arnold's body seems to be his fate, condemning him to a life of tortured isolation, but the devil makes it possible for Arnold's body to become a matter of free choice, as if he could shape his physical being to suit his fancy. This opening scene suggests why Girard's theories are particularly applicable to Byron and Romantic literature. At no point has the ideology of human freedom and equality been stronger than in the Romantic era, and this ideology is the strongest provocation to mimetic desire. Though Girard has increasingly tried to universalize his theories, it is no accident that his studies originally focused on the nineteenth-century novel, which is to say, on the world of postrevolutionary France (Balzac, Stendhal, Flaubert). In an aristocratic and strictly hierarchical society, human beings tend to view their positions in life as natural or divinely ordained, and hence are less prone to dream of rising above their given stations. In a democratic society, by contrast, with the traditional supports of social privilege weakened if not entirely undermined, the barriers to mimetic desire dissolve. In his quixotic wish to become one of the heroes he has read about in books, Arnold is in a sense the perfect embodiment of Romantic-democratic man: the only limits he recognizes are the limits of his aspirations and imagination.

But in a strange twist of plot—one of the most original aspects of the play—Arnold finds he cannot simply leave his old body behind. The devil decides to adopt the body Arnold has abandoned, and thus the transformed hero is shadowed by an image of his former self throughout the play as we have it. Thus the idea of the deformed transformed allows Byron to probe the mysteries of the Romantic self. Is a man's sense of identity bound up with his sense of his body? Is he free to shape a new identity for himself? Or is his destiny linked to the body in which he was created? *Mutatis mutandis*, these are the same questions Shelley explores in *Frankenstein*,[11] which might have borne the subtitle *The Deformed Not Transformed*. The creature Frankenstein creates comes to shadow him in much the same way the devil shadows Arnold. And both works focus on the question of whether human beings can find a way to transcend their physical limitations. Critics are used to speaking of the way Romantic poetry influenced the genesis of *Frankenstein*, but in the case of *The Deformed Transformed* we may be witnessing a flow of influence in the opposite direction. When Byron's devil speaks of those "who make men without women's aid" (I.i.436), he could almost be referring to Frankenstein. Shelley's novel may very well have helped to shape Byron's conception of a creature so deformed that he can find no place in society and above all no one to love him.

Unfortunately the first scene is the high point of *The Deformed Transformed*, and the play thereafter declines in quality.[12] Nevertheless, the way Byron develops the action in *The Deformed Transformed* reveals a great deal about the relation of romance and aggression in his work. Love and war are the explicit themes of the play. When Arnold, like Faust, asks the devil to show him the world, his shadow tells him: "That's to say, where there is War / And Woman in activity" (I.i.495–96). But once again the proportion of the two motifs is unbalanced. This may be only an accidental result of the unfinished character of the work, but in what Byron chose to write of *The Deformed Transformed* war occupies center stage and romance is merely hinted at. What constitutes the heart of the play is the story of Arnold's participation in the siege of Rome in 1527; we see only the bare beginnings of the development of a romance between Arnold and Olimpia.

The fact that Byron places the early sixteenth-century French attempt to conquer Rome at the center of his poem allows him to dwell upon masculine aggressiveness at its most brutal. When Olimpia first appears in the play, she is threatened with rape by a group of pillaging soldiers who clearly are in competition to see who can win her as his prize (II.iii.58–60). Byron heightens the sense of the all-pervasiveness of violence by the historical perspective he creates on the action. He scatters reminders of ancient Rome throughout the play. When the devil takes over Arnold's body, he adopts the name of Caesar. The would-be heroes of the play clearly are acting in imitation of ancient greatness. When Bourbon seems daunted by a vision of the real Julius Caesar, Philibert tells him to copy his model and thus surpass him: "Then conquer / The walls for which he conquered, and be greater!" (I.ii.212–13). Byron repeatedly refers to the legend of the foundation of Rome in an act of mimetic rivalry and violence. The devil reveals:

> I see your Romulus (simple as I am)
> Slay his own twin, quick-born of the same womb,
> Because he leapt a ditch ('twas then no wall,
> Whate'er it now be;) and Rome's earliest cement
> Was brother's blood.
>
> (I.ii.80–84)

As a story of twins—mirror images—engaged in fratricidal strife, the Romulus and Remus myth is one of Girard's examples of how mimetic violence stands at the basis of social organization.[13]

By means of his range of historical reference, Byron develops a strong sense of how mimetic violence breaks down hierarchy and social categories. The conquered are always threatening to turn the tables on their masters and become the conquerers: "'Twas *their* turn—now 'tis ours" (I.ii.283).[14] In particular, family relationships are constantly being subverted by the power of ambition and aggression:

> Rome's sire forgot his mother,
> When he slew his gallant twin.
>
> (II.i.74–75)

> Yield not to these stranger Neros!
> Though the Son who slew his mother,
> Shed Rome's blood, he was your brother:
> 'Twas the Roman curbed the Roman.
>
> (II.i.106–9)

In the chaos of mimetic violence, even sexual differentiation begins to break down. In a remarkable passage, Rome itself switches gender:

> now to be
> Lord of the city which hath been Earth's lord
> Under its Emperors, and-changing sex,
> Not sceptre, an hermaphrodite of empire—
> *Lady* of the Old World.
>
> (I.ii.6–10)

The fact that when Rome becomes the object of rival heroes, the city becomes figured as symbolically female is one of the most telling moments in the play, another sign of how the feminine tends to be equated with the oppressed in Byron and of how romance tends to be subordinated to aggression.

The fragmentary part III of the play opens with the promise of a reversal of this pattern:

> The wars are over,
>   The spring is come;
> The bride and her lover
>   Have sought their home.
>
> (III.i.1–4)

But like much else in this play, the promised triumph of domesticity over warfare was likely to prove abortive. Though part III was going to be devoted to the love of Arnold and Olimpia, that story was almost certainly going to end in violence, probably at least one act of murder. It is of course impossible to come to any firm conclusions about the unwritten ending of the work. Mary Shelley reports that Byron knew how he was going to end the play,[15] but he left no more than hints of what he had in mind. Various attempts have been made to figure out how *The Deformed Transformed* would have ended, based largely on the study of proven and hypothetical sources of the play.[16] Whatever the exact shape of the ending, one thing seems clear: part III was to tell a story of mimetic desire. Arnold, Olimpia, and Caesar were to become involved in a Girardian love triangle, reflecting the underlying tension between the two males. Byron was preparing for this outcome, as Caesar learns to imitate Arnold in his love for Olimpia in part II:

> *Caes.*   I am almost enamoured of her, as
>   Of old the Angels of her earliest sex.

Arn.   Thou!
Caes.   I. But fear not. I'll not be your rival!
Arn.   Rival!
Caes.   I could be one right formidable.

(II.iii.177–80)

In fact, as early as the beginning of the second scene of the play, Arnold has begun to sense that the devil is chafing under his position of servitude and hoping to reverse their positions:

Caes.   Your obedient humble servant.
Arn.   Say *Master* rather.

(I.iii.18–19)

Too proud to accept a position of inferiority vis-à-vis a mortal, the devil was evidently going to reassert his superiority by accepting a remarkable challenge, to win Olimpia by getting her to fall in love with him in Arnold's old body.

This is the brilliant direction in which Byron hoped to develop *The Deformed Transformed* according to a note he left:

Mem. Jealous—Arnold of Caesar. Olympia [*sic*] at first not liking Caesar—then?—Arnold jealous of himself under his former figure, owing to the power of intellect, etc., etc., etc.[17]

The one substantial fragment we have of the dialogue between Arnold and Caesar in part III confirms that jealousy was going to be the focus of the last section. Arnold has become disillusioned with the deal he made with the devil. Originally his desires were purely other-directed: he wanted the beautiful appearance of somebody else so that he could be the envy of all eyes and above all be attractive to women. But now he has come to sense the absence of integrity in his situation and feels dissatisfied with being loved on the basis of externals, loved for anything other than his innermost self. As the devil explains to him:

> you would be *loved*—what you call loved—
> *Self-loved*—loved for yourself—for neither health
> Nor wealth—nor youth—nor power—nor rank nor beauty—
> For these you may be stript of—but *beloved*
> As an Abstraction—for—you know not what—

(III.61–65)

Arnold is on the verge of realizing the irony of the situation he has brought upon himself. His original wish was based on the premise that the self is wholly separable from the body, that he could maintain his identity in somebody else's form. But if that is so, when Olimpia falls in love with him in Achilles' form, then she is not falling in love with *him*, but in effect with someone else. In articulating a truly Romantic sense of self-that the human spirit transcends any concrete embodiment of it—the devil condemns Arnold to a perpetual sense of self-alienation in his newfound body and hence to a life of frustration in love.

This frustration was evidently to be compounded by the spectacle of the devil proving that Olimpia could have learned to love Arnold in his original deformed appearance. From Byron's comment "owing to the power of intellect," we may surmise that Caesar was to play a kind of Richard III to Olimpia's Anne, and win her despite his ugliness by the strength and daring of his spirit.[18] Arnold himself had earlier claimed that virtue is independent of physical appearance. When the devil offered to go beyond giving him a new body and include some new virtues in the bargain, Arnold refused, saying: "I ask not / For Valour, since Deformity is daring" (I.i.312–13). Citing the case of Timor the lame Tartar, Arnold claims that he already has the valor of Achilles, though not the beauty; indeed he argues that his ugliness acts as a spur to his virtue. In trying to distinguish the quality of his soul from his outward appearance, Arnold echoes Frankenstein's monster.[19] But if his assertions are correct, then there is no reason why Caesar in Arnold's old form should not be able to woo Olimpia with a demonstration of the superior quality of his intellect, thus leaving Arnold to curse his fate in bargaining away his chances for true love. How exactly the story was to end we cannot be sure—if tragically, either Arnold or Caesar might have accidentally or deliberately killed Olimpia. The most probable scenario for the denouement was for Arnold to attempt to kill Caesar, only to discover that in slaying his double he had slain himself. This ending would have provided a powerful image of the self-destructive character of mimetic desire.

Even though a fragment, *The Deformed Transformed* provides a relentless working out of the self-defeating logic of mimetic desire. In a variant of the proverb "the grass is always greener in someone else's yard," in the world of mimetic desire the pole of satisfaction always remains elusively in the Other. If one somehow gets one's wish and becomes the desired Other, the positions of superiority and inferiority are reversed and one finds oneself jealous of one's original self. Arnold is drawn into an increasingly destructive—and ultimately self-destructive—world of violence because of his nagging sense that his life is governed by a defective providence, that he was not made to be happy (see especially I.i.35–37). Out of this frustration, which is only increased by attempts to overcome it, Arnold is driven to strike out in hopes of bringing the world around him down in ruins.

Having transcribed *The Deformed Transformed* for Byron, and perhaps in the process even influenced in minor details the way the work appeared in print,[20] Shelley had a special interest in the work, which culminated in her attempt to rewrite it in "Transformation." And the phenomenon she chose to focus on is the triangulation of desire. This should not be surprising, since she shows interest in the subject as early as *Frankenstein*.[21] The monster is in fact a veritable case study in mimetic desire. As the book makes clear, his spontaneous desires are few and simple, based in his physical needs and thus involving food and shelter. The monster's desires begin to get complicated only when he starts observing and imitating human beings. It is from watching the De Lacey family that he learns to desire human companionship and love. In his variant of the Quixote syndrome, the monster gets his idea of what he wants to be from reading books, in his case not *Amadis of Gaul* but *Plutarch's Lives*, *Paradise Lost*, and *The Sorrows of Young Werther* (all three of which, incidentally, deal with the issue of heroism and mimetic desire in one form or another).

The logic of mimetic desire explains why the monster gets locked into a life-and-death struggle with his creator. In some sense the monster's desire for a mate reflects his rivalry with Frankenstein: if his creator is going to have a bride, then the monster should have one, too. His fundamental desire is not for any particular object but for a certain state of being. What he wants above all is to be human, or at least as human as possible, and as he learns from observing the De Laceys, for a male that state requires female companionship. As the monster comes to understand, his sense of his own identity ultimately rests on his ability to define himself in relation to another being of his own species. That consideration explains the seemingly curious fact that he does not desire a beautiful mate, but rather one who would be a mirror image of himself: "one as deformed and horrible as myself would not deny herself to me. My companion must be of the same species and have the same defects" (137).[22]

When Victor destroys the bride intended for the monster, he replies with mimetic violence: Frankenstein's bride must be destroyed on their wedding night. As in Byron's poetic tales, the females in *Frankenstein* become pawns in the power struggles of the males. The murder of Elizabeth precipitates a mortal conflict between Frankenstein and the monster, in which they keep exchanging roles; we cannot tell from one moment to the next who is the hunter and who the hunted, who is the master and who the slave. *Frankenstein* is in fact filled with examples of masculine rivalry and aggression. Frankenstein seeks to create life very much out of a spirit of

rivalry with his scientific predecessors and colleagues. Similarly, in the frame
tale, Walton hopes to become preeminent among polar explorers. Wherever
one turns in the book one finds masculine pairs, men who are in some way
bonded together but in some way torn apart by a spirit of competition
(Frankenstein and Walton, Frankenstein and his father, Frankenstein and
Clerval, Frankenstein and the monster, and so on). Well before she read *The
Deformed Transformed*, Shelley shows her awareness of the potentially
destructive effects of a masculine ethos so strong that it tries to displace
women even from their role in the creation of life.[23]

What is distinctive about Shelley's rewriting of *The Deformed
Transformed* in "Transformation" is her attempt to shape a happy ending to
the tale, to find a way out of the vicious circle of mimetic desire. Like
Frankenstein, "Transformation" is a retrospective narrative, but unlike the
novel, the story is told solely by its hero, who in this case has survived and
learned to reform his character. Again as in *Frankenstein*, to understand her
principal character Shelley goes back to his childhood. Like Victor
Frankenstein, Guido is an only child, and even more explicitly than his
counterpart, he is corrupted by overindulgence: "I became a spoiled child"
(123/887).[24] Guido grows up in an even more exclusively masculine world
than Frankenstein does. Both his father and his father's one friend, the
Marchese Torella, are widowers. It is no accident, then, that masculine
aggressiveness becomes the hallmark of Guido's character:

> I was born with the most imperious, haughty, tameless spirit, with
> which ever mortal was gifted. I quailed before my father only; and
> he, generous and noble, but capricious and tyrannical, at once
> fostered and checked the wild impetuosity of my character,
> making obedience necessary, but inspiring no respect for the
> motives which guided his commands. To be a man, free,
> independent; or, in better words, insolent and domineering, was
> the hope and prayer of my rebel heart. (121–22/886)

We can observe here the fruits of Shelley's reading of Byron: "generous and
noble, but capricious and tyrannical" is an apt characterization of the typical
Byronic hero. In the words "fostered and checked" Shelley captures the
double bind mimetic rivalry inevitably produces. Guido's father both wants
his son to resemble him and does not want him to. The rivalry between
father and son leads to the development of an extreme masculinity which
Shelley calls into question (notice her equation of "to be a man" with to be
"insolent and domineering").

Into this hypermasculine world, Shelley introduces a single female,

Juliet, the daughter of Torella, who is left in the care of Guido's father when her own father is banished from Genoa. Guido becomes her protector, but he does not begin to love her until a rival for her affections intervenes:

> When I was eleven and Juliet eight years of age, a cousin of mine, much older than either—he seemed to us a man—took great notice of my playmate; he called her his bride, and asked her to marry him. She refused, and he insisted, drawing her unwillingly towards him. With the countenance and emotions of a maniac I threw myself on him—I strove to draw his sword—I clung to his neck with the ferocious resolve to strangle him: he was obliged to call for assistance to disengage himself from me. On that night I led Juliet to the chapel of our house: I made her touch the sacred relics—I harrowed her child's heart, and profaned her child's lips with an oath, that she would be mine, and mine only. (122/886)

This passage betrays all the familiar signs of mimetic desire. Guido is prompted into falling in love with Juliet by observing the attentions of an older male and indeed we get the impression that Guido feels that in order to prove himself a man, he has to win a woman for himself, preferably one already shown to be desirable in the eyes of another male.[25] The outbreak of mimetic violence is sudden and powerful, thus presaging the destructive behavior Guido exhibits later in life. From the very beginning his love for Juliet is bound up with his will to power; he regards her as a possession: "she would me mine, and mine only." Here Shelley gives Guido exactly the same words she gave Frankenstein in his account of his childhood bond with Elizabeth (who like Juliet also grows up in the same household as her lover): "since till death she was to be mine only" (35).

As he matures, Guido's possessiveness continues to dominate his love for Juliet. When he finally decides to ask for her hand in marriage, his sense of masculine triumph overwhelms his initial appreciation of her beauty: "Admiration first possessed me; she is mine! was the second proud emotion, and my lips curled with haughty triumph" (124/888). (The curled lip is of course another trademark of the Byronic hero.) Threatened with losing Juliet, Guido is less troubled by the thought of being deprived of her beauty than by the prospect of another man enjoying it:

> And Juliet!—her angel-face and sylph-like form gleamed among the clouds of my despair with vain beauty; for I had lost her—the glory and flower of the world! Another will call her his!—that smile of paradise will bless another! (126/890)

More concretely, Guido's love for Juliet becomes bound up with his rivalry with her father Torella. After Guido's father dies, Torella becomes his guardian and hence his symbolic father ("Torella was to be a second parent to me", 122/887). Guido's sense of competition with his own father thus gets transferred to Torella, and winning the daughter away from him becomes Guido's way of triumphing. In an odd twist of plot, at one point he kidnaps both Torella and Juliet, as if conquering the father were as significant to him as conquering the daughter. At the culminating moment of Guido's mad aggressiveness, his real motive in possessing Juliet comes to the surface: "To bring Torella to my feet—to possess my Juliet in spite of him" (130/894). In effect Juliet has no intrinsic value for Guido; what matters to him is that she is a prize to be won away from a masculine rival.

Thus in "Transformation" Shelley recreates the typical configuration in Byron's poetic tales: a younger man in competition with an older man for a woman's affections, with the characters tangled in a web of real and symbolic ties that gives a vaguely incestuous aura to the situation. Like Byron, Shelley even gives a political dimension to the story by sending Guido to Paris at one point and associating him with dynastic intrigue in France, a struggle within the royal family, who are "alternating friends and foes—now meeting in prodigal feasts, now shedding blood in rivalry" (122–23/887). This "savage strife" culminates in a moment of mimetic violence: "The Duke of Orleans was waylaid and murdered by the Duke of Burgundy" (123/887). Up to this point, Shelley could be imitating many of Byron's works, but in the crucial plot development of "Transformation," she focuses on *The Deformed Transformed*. In the depths of his despair over losing Juliet, Guido observes a storm and a shipwreck. Only one person survives the shipwreck: Shelley's equivalent of Byron's Arnold: "a misshapen dwarf, with squinting eyes, distorted features, and body deformed" (127/891).[26] The dwarf offers to exchange bodies with Guido for a period of three days; in return he will give Guido a chest filled with treasure which will allow him to buy his revenge against Torella. Thus. Shelley refashions the central motif of the exchange of bodies in *The Deformed Transformed*.

Shelley develops a number of interesting variations on her central Byronic theme. She hints at the undercurrent of homosexuality that always seems to lie just beneath the surface in these intense male relationships.[27] The dwarf tells Guido: "something does please me in your well-proportioned body and handsome face" (128/892). And in one of the most emotionally charged moments in the story—Guido shivers—the dwarf replies to the question, What can he possibly desire of a man who has lost all his possessions?: "Your comely face and well-made limbs" (129/893). In view of the fact that the dwarf is clearly Guido's *Doppelgänger*, or shadow, and hence a reflection of part of his self, one could also read these passages as an expression of the hero's narcissism. The dwarf gives voice to Guido's love of his own "comely face and well-made limbs," which is at the root of all his problems. His pride, vanity, and self-centeredness make it impossible for him to love another human being as anything other than an extension of his self, which explains why he treats Juliet as a possession. Guido's narcissism is in many respects the keynote of his character. Even after his destructive encounter with the dwarf, he does not fully renounce his narcissistic tendencies: "my first broken request was for a mirror" (134/897). Shelley seems to dwell upon this aspect of his character, even at the end of the story:

> I thought myself a right proper youth when I saw the dear reflection of my own well-known features. I confess it is a weakness, but I avow it, I do entertain a considerable affection for the countenance and limbs I behold, whenever I look at a glass; and have more mirrors in my house, and consult them oftener than any beauty in Venice. Before you too much condemn me, permit me to say that no one better knows than I the value of his own body; no one, probably, except myself, ever having had it stolen from him. (134–35/897)

If "Transformation" is a commentary on Byron, then this is a telling passage, revealing the narcissistic tendencies that shadow the Romantic self, even— and perhaps especially—in its moments of greatest self-consciousness (a theme Shelley had already explored in *Frankenstein*).[28] And the importance of mirrors and reflections in "Transformation" is another sign of the centrality of mimetic desire in the story.

Shelley's rewriting of Byron is most evident in the way she inverts the pattern of *The Deformed Transformed*. In Byron's play, the hero begins as ugly, and becomes handsome as a result of his meeting with a demonic figure. In "Transformation" just the opposite happens: the hero begins as handsome, and becomes ugly as a result of the bargain he makes. Indeed, Shelley might have entitled her story "The Transformed Deformed." The psychological implications of these contrasting patterns are interesting. Byron's story seems to reflect a typical masculine fantasy: "Despite appearances, I am not ugly: inside me is a handsome man just waiting to get out." Shelley's story seems to reflect the corresponding feminine fear: "The handsome appearance of this man conceals an inner ugliness: inside is a hideous demon just waiting to get out." "Transformation" repeatedly suggests that the hidden ugliness of the male is his aggressiveness and will to power. In that sense, Guido's transformation is in fact a revelation of his inner character. As in *Frankenstein*,

Shelley imaginatively depicts the release of a man's dark, violent urges in the form of a shadowy companion. Guido even thinks of himself in terms reminiscent of Frankenstein's creature: "I was not quite sure that, if seen, the mere boys would not stone me to death as I passed, for a monster" (131/895).

Thus "Transformation" appears to be headed for the kind of tragic conclusion we have seen in all the other tales of mimetic desire we have examined. The dwarf violates his bargain with Guido and uses his newly acquired body to win Juliet for himself. Guido thus experiences the horrible emotion Arnold has to live with: in the purest distillation of mimetic desire, he becomes jealous of himself: "But it was not I—it was he, the fiend, arrayed in my limbs, speaking with my voice, winning her with my looks of love" (130/894). One might expect Guido's sense of rivalry with himself to result in the kind of self-destruction that Byron was evidently going to portray in *The Deformed Transformed*. But Shelley was out to revise the Byronic myth, not repeat it. In her variation, the release of Guido's aggressive impulses in the hideous form of the dwarf turns out to be purgative, a way for Guido to get them out of his system. In fact, the dwarf points the way to Guido's salvation: he wins Juliet precisely by swallowing his pride and humbly begging Torella for forgiveness. Guido's realization—"O! had an angel from Paradise whispered to me to act thus!" (132/896)—suggests how to interpret the climax of "Transformation." When Guido murders the dwarf he is in effect killing the "demoniac violence and wicked self idolatry" (131/895) within himself, which have come to be crystallized and externalized in this hideous form. Only by destroying part of himself—his masculine pride—can Guido be freed to experience true love with Juliet.

Shelley thus tells the story of the taming and domestication of the Byronic hero (in some ways resembling what Charlotte Brontë does in *Jane Eyre*). Leaving behind the hypermasculine world to which he was attracted, Guido becomes *il Cortese*, the "courteous one," now fit for the society of women. Shelley is aware of the price Guido must pay for his transformation but suggests that the result makes the bargain worthwhile:

> I have never, indeed, wholly recovered my strength—my cheek is paler since—my person a little bent. Juliet sometimes ventures to allude bitterly to the malice that caused this change, but I kiss her on the moment, and tell her all is for the best. I am a fonder and more faithful husband—and true is this—but for that wound, never had I called her mine. (135/898)

Here the domestic world finally triumphs over the heroic, as Guido loses his aggressiveness and settles down to a peaceful life within society, for the first time speaking of his "fellow-citizens" (135/898). To be sure, Juliet must settle for something less of a man: Guido no longer has the same strength. But in return for accepting a diminished version of her lover, she wins his undying loyalty. With characteristic sobriety and restraint, Shelley carries out her struggle with Byron and reshapes one of the central myths of his poetry. As in *Frankenstein*, she exposes the dark side of Romanticism, the destructive potential of the egotism and narcissism that lies barely concealed beneath the new Romantic premium on the self. However one may side in the quarrel between Shelley and Byron, one must acknowledge that "Transformation" displays remarkable insight into the pattern embodied in its precursor text. And in helping to uncover the centrality of triangulated desire and mimetic rivalry in Byron, Shelley once again, as in *Frankenstein*, provides a profound clue as to the character of Romanticism in general.

NOTES

1. To survey developments in the contemporary criticism of *Frankenstein*, see the excellent collection of essays, edited by George Levine and U. C. Knoepflmacher, *The Endurance of Frankenstein* (Berkeley: University of California Press, 1979), which contains several feminist essays on the novel. For further feminist approaches, see, among others, Sandra M. Gilbert and Susan Gubar, *The Madwoman in the Attic: The Woman Writer and the Nineteenth-Century Literary Imagination* (New Haven: Yale University Press, 1979), 213–47; Mary Poovey, "My Hideous Progeny: Mary Shelley and the Feminization of Romanticism," *PMLA* 95 (1980): 332–47; and Gayatri Chakravorty Spivak, "Three Women's Texts and a Critique of Imperialism," *"Race," Writing, and Difference*, ed. Henry Louis Gates, Jr. (Chicago: University of Chicago Press, 1986), 262–80.

2. For an example of this approach, see my book, *Creature and Creator: Myth-making and English Romanticism* (Cambridge: Cambridge University Press, 1984), 103–32.

3. For an approach to Shelley which focuses on her concern for the integrity of the family, see Anne K. Mellor, *Mary Shelley: Her Life, Her Fiction, Her Monsters* (London: Methuen, 1988). For a contrary view—that *Frankenstein* constitutes a critique of the bourgeois family—see the essay by Kate Ellis, "Monsters in the Garden: Mary Shelley and the Bourgeois Family," in Levine and Knoepflmacher, *Endurance*, 123–42.

4. Shelley's letters indicate that she had an unusually high opinion of the drama. See, for example, her letter to Byron of February 2, 1823: "The more I read this Poem that I send, the more I admire it. I pray that Your Lordship will finish it.... You never wrote any thing more beautiful than one lyric in it—& the whole, I am tempted to say, surpasses 'Your former glorious style'—at least it fully equals the very best parts of your best productions." See *The Letters of Mary Wollstonecraft Shelley*, 3 vols., ed. Betty T. Bennett (Baltimore: Johns Hopkins University Press, 1980–88), 1:311.

5. For such judgments, see George Steiner, *The Death of Tragedy* (New York: Hill and Wang, 1963), 211; and Leslie A. Marchand, *Byron's Poetry: A Critical Introduction* (Cambridge, Mass.: Harvard University Press, 1968), 94.

6. All quotations from Byron are taken from Jerome J. McGann, ed., *Lord Byron: The Complete Poetical Works* (Oxford: Clarendon Press). All poems cited appear in volume 3 (1981), except *Mazeppa* (volume 4, 1986) and *The Deformed Transformed*, ed. Barry Weller (volume 6, 1991).

7. See, for example, René Girard, *Deceit, Desire, and the Novel*, trans. Yvonne Freccero (Baltimore: Johns Hopkins University Press, 1966), esp. chapter 1, "'Triangular' Desire," 1–52; *Violence and the Sacred*, trans. Patrick Gregory (Baltimore: Johns Hopkins University Press, 1977); and *Things Hidden Since the Foundation of the World*, trans. Stephen Bann and Michael Metteer (Stanford: Stanford University Press, 1987).

8. See especially *Violence*, 169–92.

9. In his later writings, in particular, *Beyond the Pleasure Principle*, Freud did come to recognize two basic drives, but it is significant that even here he chose not to call the second drive *aggression* but to reinterpret it in negative terms as the *death instinct*.

10. For a more general discussion of this point in Byron, with particular regard to *Cain*, see the chapter "The Metaphysical Rebel" in my *Creature and Creator*, esp. 144–45.

11. For a brief comparison of *Frankenstein* and *The Deformed Transformed*, see Daniel P. Watkins, "The Ideological Dimensions of Byron's *The Deformed Transformed*," *Criticism* 25 (1983): 31.

12. See Charles E. Robinson, "The Devil as Doppelgänger in *The Deformed Transformed*: The Sources and Meanings of Byron's Unfinished Drama," *Bulletin of the New York Public Library* 74 (1970): 177.

13. On the importance of Romulus and Remus in *The Deformed Transformed*, see Robinson, 195–96. For Romulus and Remus in Girard, see *Violence*, 61–65, and *The Scapegoat*, trans. Yvonne Freccero (Baltimore: Johns Hopkins University Press, 1986), 91–94.

14. See also Caesar's comment: "Aye, slave or master, 'tis all one" (II.iii.137).

15. In the flyleaf of her copy of *The Deformed Transformed*, Shelley wrote: "I do not know how he meant to finish it; but he said himself that the whole conduct of the story was already conceived." See Ernest Hartley Coleridge, ed., *The Works of Lord Byron* 7 vols. (London: John Murray, 1898–1904), 5:474.

16. For the most plausible account, see Robinson, 194–96.

17. Coleridge, 5:531.

18. For an extended comparison of *The Deformed Transformed* and *Richard III*, see G. Wilson Knight, *Byron and Shakespeare* (New York: Barnes & Noble, 1966), 155–59.

19. See *Creature and Creator*, 127–28.

20. See Emily W. Sunstein, *Mary Shelley: Romance and Reality* (Boston: Little, Brown, 1989), 229. In their comparison of Byron's autograph manuscript with the first printed text of *The Deformed Transformed*, Weller and McGann speak of Byron's "tacit sanction of changes, which Mary Shelley may have introduced in the process of transcription" (McGann, 6:727).

21. For a Girardian reading of *Frankenstein* from a feminist perspective, see Mary Jacobus, "Is There a Woman in This Text?" *New Literary History* 14 (1982): esp. 127–37.

22. All quotations from *Frankenstein* are taken from Harold Bloom's edition (New York: New American Library, 1965).

23. We can only speculate as to the extent to which Shelley's awareness of the phenomenon of masculine rivalry was based on her experience of the relationship of her husband and Byron. Certainly there is much evidence of triangular desire in the Shelley–Byron circle.

24. I quote "Transformation" from *Mary Shelley: Collected Tales and Stories*, ed. Charles E. Robinson (Baltimore: Johns Hopkins University Press, 1976). But since the story is at the moment most readily available in M. H. Abrams, ed., *The Norton Anthology of English Literature*, 5th ed., vol. 2, (New York: Norton, 1986), I give two page references, the first to Robinson's edition, the second to the Norton.

25. The phallic dimension of this incident is hinted at in Guido's reaching for his rival's sword, and perhaps even in his forcing Juliet to touch the "sacred relics." Later in

the story, Guido's phallic anxiety becomes evident when he worries about the length of his weapon: "I had no sword—if indeed my distorted arms could wield a soldier's weapon—but I had a dagger, and in that lay my every hope" (132/896).

26. This shipwreck scene recreates a passage from Calderón's *El mágico prodigioso*, which Percy Shelley had translated into English (ii.23–61). The way the dwarf appears before Guido parallels the way Calderón's Daemon appears before his hero, Cyprian. Shelley's reference to a "wizard's wand" (126/890) in her tale reinforces the parallel. The Calderón play is another story of mimetic desire. Two men, named Floro and Lelio, are in love with the same woman (Justina); when Cyprian tries to mediate the dispute, he ends up falling in love with Justina himself. Robinson proposes *El mágico prodigioso* as a source for *The Deformed Transformed* as well (187–89).

27. Here I touch on the work of Eve Kosofsky Sedgwick, who in her book *Between Men* (New York: Columbia University Press, 1985) reinterprets what Girard calls mimetic desire as what Sedgwick calls homosocial bonding (see esp. 16–17, 21–24). Despite the fact that Sedgwick appears to be presenting a revisionary account of Girard, in many respects her theory is less radical than his. Instead of presenting aggression as a genuinely independent drive, she maintains the monolithically erotic bias of Freudian thought. She may be looking at a different kind of eros than Freud did, but her analysis still privileges eros over all other drives. For that reason, whatever the general cogency of her theory may be, I find Girard more relevant to the analysis of Romantic literature, and especially to the relation of Byron and Shelley.

28. See *Creature and Creator*, 124.

MARY LOWE-EVANS

The Groomsmen

He is dead who called me into being; and when I shall be no more, the
very remembrance of us both will speedily vanish.
                              —The Creature to Robert Walton (260)

Throughout this reading of *Frankenstein* I have focused on the question of
marriage, arguing that it is an important subject of the novel. Until recently,
this emphasis would have seemed eccentric, and in fact it deviates from the
norm of *Frankenstein* criticism. That norm, though somewhat amorphous, has
traditionally centered on the relationship between Victor Frankenstein and
his Creature. Even a modern critic can refer to the novel as "the story of
Frankenstein and his monster" without expecting to be contradicted (Baldick,
1), for the urge to concentrate one's attention on the two obviously *main*
characters is almost irresistible.

While this reading has not ignored Victor and his Creature or caused
their "very remembrance [to] speedily vanish," as the chapter epigraph
predicts, it has given prominence instead to minor characters, especially the
women. But to leave the impression that favoring a feminine perspective is the
only correct way of reading *Frankenstein* would be false. "Correct" approaches
to *Frankenstein* are as numerous as the critical schools—psychological,
historicist, mythological, and so on—that treat it, and as varied as the

From *Frankenstein: Mary Shelley's Wedding Guest.* © 1993 by Twayne Publishers.

philosophical issues raised in the novel itself. A truly well informed reading of any complex work like *Frankenstein* would consider all approaches.

Although it is impossible to balance this particular study so that it equally provides, say, a romantic or a science fiction interpretation along with the biographical-historicist one I have attempted, it is possible to recount some of the recurring tenets in these two dominant critical assessments of Victor and his monster. Given two traditional views of the novel along with my modern one, the reader may then discover how interpretations deviate, converge, and become transformed by currents of thought in the text itself, the culture, and the reader's own increasingly sophisticated mind.

The earliest and most persistent treatment of the two antiheroes of *Frankenstein* involves a conflation of their characters, an intentional confusion of master and creature within the framework of the Prometheus myth. In Greek mythology Prometheus is a Titan who, in one version of the myth, creates the first men from potter's clay. In other versions, he steals fire from the gods to benefit humankind. In all versions, the gods punish him for his presumption by restraining him in chains. The full title of Mary Shelley's novel, *Frankenstein; or, The Modern Prometheus*, immediately predisposes the reader to interpret the work in the context of current Prometheus myth variants, like that of Goethe who—to oversimplify—saw the Titan as a rebel against the restrictions of society. The quotation from Milton's Adam in *Paradise Lost* just below the subtitle of *Frankenstein* complicates while reinforcing the novel's Promethean correspondence:

> Did I request thee, Maker, from my clay
> To mould me man?
> Did I solicit thee
> From darkness to promote me?—

This epigraph implies that the story is about a hapless creature as much as it is about an overreaching hero. Taken together, the two allusions imply a conflation of Greek and Judeo-Christian mythologies. References within the text itself also justify reading the novel as a modification of the Prometheus myth as well as an exploration of the creator–creature relationship. For example, when Victor refers to the Creature as "the living monument of presumption" (203), his early nineteenth-century audience, primed by numerous other treatments of the Titanic rebel, would have read "presumption" as an epithet for Prometheus. The Creature then becomes either the legacy of Prometheus (Victor) or Prometheus himself, and Victor stands for either Prometheus or one of the gods who restrained him in chains. The Creature's gift of firewood to his human family, the De Laceys, compares with Prometheus's gift of fire to humankind, but Victor's presumption in creating a new species of being establishes him even more firmly than the Creature in the Promethean camp.

A passage late in the novel makes the interchangeable natures of Victor and the Creature and the confusion of their Promethean roles more obvious. Just after Victor destroys the female Creature, the Creature warns, "I can make you so wretched that the light of day will be hateful to you. You are my creator, but I am your master; obey!" (208). Even the Creature's lament at the opening of this chapter implies an overlapping of his own identity with his maker's. Obvious clues like these have led critics to conclude that *Frankenstein* is one among many romantic reconstructions of Western mythology, one that plays off the Greek and Judeo-Christian world views (Prometheus and Adam being conflated) and incorporates a modern concern about the ways in which civilization is advancing.

This latter-day blend of the two most influential Western philosophies assesses what we might call the primary human conflict differently than does either its Greek or its Christian component. Rather than viewing the universal conflict as an interminable antagonism between the gods, humans, and their mediators, as the Greeks had done, or between God and Satan over the souls of humankind, as the Judeo-Christians do, the romantics saw the conflict as one between the individual and his or her own consciousness. Idealist philosophies like that of Immanuel Kant had done much to reinforce this concern. It is easy to understand how, given the emphasis on human ideas as the foundation and cause of human behavioral systems, a preoccupation with the "psychic split," which the romantics saw as endemic to human nature, would come about. However, the romantic critique of society did not stop at individual consciousness. Becoming increasingly complex, the romantic worldview often projected the fundamental human conflict as one between the individual consciousness and the social, psychological, and physical structures it had itself helped create and within which it had become trapped. Seen through these lenses (which, incidentally, work quite well even for modern readers), *Frankenstein* is "about" Victor's mishandling of his own suppressed desires or fantasies (imaginary constructs), to which he first gives form (as the Creature) and then later rejects. In this reading, Victor may be interpreted as an individual or as humankind's champion or representative. Perhaps the aspect of this romantic schema that is most difficult to accept is the lack of a facile way of determining the difference between good and evil. Judging by romantic tenets, it is not clear, for example, exactly what Victor's sin is: indulging his fantasy, or rejecting it? To complicate the matter, Victor's incarnated fantasy turns out, for many readers, to be more noble than he.

When critics have evaluated Victor in his own right and not as one half of a double-minded protagonist, he has typically been seen as a well-intentioned, brilliant scientist run amok. He may be guilty of Promethean ambition, but he is not necessarily evil. His great mistake is to isolate himself from humankind while purportedly creating a boon for that same humankind. In effect, he fails to balance "solitude" with "sympathy." These two words appear again and again in the novel and are meant to impress the reader with the necessity for both and the dangers of participating in an excess of either. Rousseau strongly influenced romantic notions about the need for solitude and self-reflection balanced with sympathy between individuals and between humankind and nature. Equally influential was Adam Smith's *The Theory of Moral Sentiments*. Published in 1759, the treatise argues that moral behavior is motivated by sympathy for others. According to Smith, acting on our sympathetic feelings not only gives pleasure but moderates our natural egocentricity. Victor Frankenstein clearly exceeds the limits of healthy solitude and, in spite of frequent professions to the contrary, has no *active* sympathy for anyone but himself. He talks about his strong feelings for others but seldom takes action on their behalf.

Mary Shelley's depiction of Victor as a scientist obsessed with his research grew out of real concern about eighteenth- and early nineteenth-century advancements in chemistry, biology, and electrical engineering. For example, some critics believe that Victor Frankenstein's character may have been partly inspired by Mary Shelley's interest in the life of Sir Humphrey Davy, a professor of chemistry at the Royal Institution in London who enthusiastically anticipated a brave new world of perfect people realized through advances in chemistry. In any case, Victor's character fits the profile of the brilliant but eccentric, preoccupied scientist and has done more to ensure the permanence of that model in our cultural consciousness than any other fictional character.

The model Victor typifies features a scientist who begins with noble, humanitarian ideals but becomes so obsessed with his project that he loses sight of its possible negative consequences. A descendant of Victor Frankenstein who incorporates both the idea of the psychic split and the benevolent-scientist-turned-fanatic is Dr. Henry Jekyll, the altruistic side of the abhorrent Mr. Hyde. This scientist-demon model was a natural for the romantic imagination since it could readily be accommodated to the Promethean myth. Having stolen fire or light from the gods to give to man, Prometheus is the prototypical scientist as well as the champion of the imagination. Both "light" and "fire" may be interpreted symbolically *and* realistically to mean either inspiration or physical energy. Either way, Prometheus's gift, with its potential for destroying or enhancing existence, can be viewed as a curse as well as a blessing. Victor's right to the title of "the Modern Prometheus" is firmly established by his assertion that

> life and death appeared to me ideal bounds, which I should first break through, and pour a torrent of light into our dark world. A new species would bless me as its creator and source; many happy and excellent natures would owe their being to me. No father could claim the gratitude of his child so completely as I should deserve theirs. Pursuing these reflections, I thought that if I could bestow animation upon lifeless matter, I might in process of time ... renew life where death had apparently devoted the body to corruption. (98)

The Promethean and even Satanic lust for power that pervades this passage, in spite of its overt statement of concern about "our dark world" and bodily "corruption," locates Victor securely in the ranks of the criminally obsessed scientist. Assuming this reading of Victor's character, the Creature must be viewed as the product of Victor's scientific labor and judged an incarnation of energy indiscriminately released into an unsuspecting and unprepared world. The Creature thus becomes a threat to the very community whose lives he was meant to enhance. Like chemical waste or nuclear power that is not carefully channeled toward life-supporting ends, he haunts the community and his creator, demanding attention and threatening revenge.

Recently the scientific community in the United States has registered concern about the image of the irresponsible, obsessed scientist who is insensitive to human concerns and devoted either to abstract science for science's sake or to the advancement of industry and commerce. *Frankenstein* and its variants have actually been cited as being partially responsible for promulgating that image.[1] This response from the scientific community attests to the tenacious hold *Frankenstein* has on our collective imagination and justifies the novel's position as the archetypal work of science fiction.

No discussion of *Frankenstein*'s men would be complete without fully acknowledging the role Percy Shelley played in their formulation. Although some recent critics feel that his direct responsibility for the novel has been greatly exaggerated, there seems little doubt that he inspired certain aspects of Victor, Felix, Henry Clerval, and even the Creature. A consideration of Percy Shelley's influence will naturally take us back into the realm of biographical-historicist criticism where this study began. It should be clear by now, however, that the romantic and science fiction readings of *Frankenstein* briefly summarized above rely on a knowledge of the cultural context Mary Shelley inhabited almost as much as a biographical-historicist interpretation does.

We know by way of a 21 August 1816 entry in her journal that Mary Shelley talked about her "story" with Percy Shelley. We also know that he encouraged her to expand the story into a novel, that he helped correct the manuscript, and that he wrote a preface for it. Her permission, given in a letter written when he was away taking care of publishing problems, allowing him "carte blanche to make what alterations" he pleased has led some critics to view him as a co-author (or "ghostwriter," as I have suggested earlier). However, careful comparison of the text to both Mary's and Percy's writing styles, and extensive examination of notes, letters, and journals, has convinced recent scholars that Mary Shelley was indeed the real author of *Frankenstein* and that Percy Shelley was nothing more than her well-informed, responsible, and sympathetic editor (Sunstein, 124, 127, 131, 144, 392, 430–31, 433; Mellor, 57–68).

From my point of view, Percy Shelley's most important contribution to *Frankenstein* was the inspiration of his volatile and unusually complex persona. Mary Shelley may even have chosen "Victor" for her protagonist's name because as a young boy Percy had sensed the power that the name implied and assigned it to himself. Victor Frankenstein's interest in science, his tendency to become obsessively enthusiastic about whatever project he had currently under way, his need for periodic isolation, his powers of persuasion, his alternating fits of anguish and joy—all correspond with the facts of Percy Shelley's life. Even Victor's reluctance to marry, his use of laudanum, and the frequent contradictions between what he says and does match Percy Shelley's profile. Like Victor, Percy had been spoiled in early childhood by his mother and sisters, but his later unconventional beliefs and behavior estranged him from them. Percy Shelley was surely more balanced than Victor, however, and some critics see in Henry Clerval a more Shelleyan character.

Most likely, both characters were influenced by aspects of Percy Shelley. Clerval's willingness to take on "feminine" roles reflects Percy Shelley's attitude—and indeed it was a general romantic belief—that men should become more feminized. To emphasize his feminine qualities, Clerval is often characterized in the same terms as Elizabeth. He is, for example, a "kind and attentive nurse" (105). He is also interested in literature rather than science, a characteristic considered by many in Mary Shelley's culture (and in our own) to be typically feminine. He is a humanitarian rather than an abstract philosopher. Percy Shelley, of course, was scientist, philosopher, and poet. Thus it seems likely that the characters of Victor and Clerval represent another sort of psychic split, one inspired by contending attitudes within the culture, attitudes that Percy Shelley himself found compatible with each other. Victor's remark "In Clerval I saw the image of my former self" (199) strengthens the argument for viewing the two as parts of a perfect whole. (I have discussed Percy Shelley's kinship with Felix De Lacey, another Clerval-like character, at some length in chapter 6.)

It is not surprising to find so many parallels between the men in *Frankenstein* and the most important man in Mary Shelley's life during its composition. Percy Shelley was not only her lover and husband but her friend and mentor. What's more, he was physically available for her to observe in all his moods during much of Frankenstein's gestation period. We have seen, too, that William Godwin made a mark on the character of Victor Frankenstein in the judgmental-father model he provided. Safie's father may also owe something to William Godwin's example. The indirect impact of his novels, especially *Caleb Williams*, is apparent, too. Caleb is first pursuer and then quarry of his master, Falkland, and like Victor and the monster, the two eventually become psychologically interchangeable.

Still, Percy Shelley remains the most obvious model for Frankenstein's men. Furthermore, he contributed significantly to the Creature's character. As a schoolboy, Percy Shelley, "meek-looking, delicate, narrow-chested, beardless, small-featured, long-haired, shrill-voiced," had undoubtedly felt out of place in the "all-male world of the English public school." His cousin, Thomas Medwin, is said to have remembered that Percy Shelley had been ridiculed for his "girlishness."[2] Later he was expelled from Oxford for publishing the pamphlet *The Necessity of Atheism* (1811) and was all but disowned by his family. Denounced by conservative politicians for championing the Irish cause and by moralists for his irregular sexual liaisons, he was considered by many among the middle classes to be psychologically if not physically deformed. Clearly, then, he knew rejection and must have occasionally felt, like the Creature, "spurned and deserted ... [so that] a kind of insanity ... burst all bounds of reason and reflection" (179).

Perhaps most notable of the Creature's similarities to Percy Shelley is his desire for an equal mate. By today's standards, Shelley's preferences in relationships between the sexes may seem too artificially chivalric on the one hand and too liberated on the other. But for its day, Shelley's philosophy was enlightened. Based partly on the eighteenth-century doctrine of sympathy, Shelley's philosophy for both sexes combined belief in a single standard of education, sexual freedom, and respect for sentiment and desire.

The Creature's demand for a female with whom he "can live in the interchange of those sympathies necessary" for his being (186), echoes Percy Shelley's philosophy. Even the Creature's preference for a mate as "hideous" as himself in a sense corresponds with Percy Shelley's attitude. For, in

Shelley's estimation, the Creature's cultivation, sympathetic nature, and natural, animal-like agility (he "bounded over the crevices in the ice ... with superhuman speed" [140]) would have rendered him beautiful. Presumably, his mate would have been equally endowed.

I have previously made the case that the Creature may have been inspired by Mary Shelley's own guilt. It may therefore seem far-fetched to argue here that he also reflects certain aspects of Percy Shelley. But perhaps it is precisely because the Creature represents a nearly perfect balance of Mary and Percy Shelley at the most unspoiled and honest level of their beings that he has come to be viewed as the most interesting, believable, and complex character in the novel.

Mary Shelley calls the Creature her "hideous progeny," but in reality he is the product of a marriage of minds and sensibilities, those of Mary and Percy Shelley. Chapter 6 of this study emphasizes his sensitivity, a responsiveness to his own and others' feelings that runs the gamut from his wish for "gentle manners" (152) to his "tumultuous," indefinable desires (172) to "rage and revenge" (177). At times he might be Percy Shelley responding as a woman was expected to respond; at others he could be Mary Shelley reacting with typical "masculine" aggression. Even the Creature's education follows a pat-tern that Percy and Mary (and her parents before them) advocated. He is educated along with a "liberated" female, Safie, an arrangement that would have been unlikely in the real world of England. Furthermore, the very books the Creature and Safie learn from are the ones that Mary and Percy Shelley read together and discussed. Thanks to Felix, Safie's (and the Creature's) reading is eclectic; it includes works that cover all branches of knowledge and most of the known literary genres. The result of the Creature's co-education with a female by a male is a relatively balanced, extraordinarily *human* being. He is, of course, ruined by his enforced solitude and failure to meet arbitrary standards of physical beauty.

Yet he endures. After nearly all the beautiful people—the affected and self-deluded members of the Frankenstein family circle—have been destroyed, the Creature remains. In the end he is still the most honest and unpretentiously articulate character in the novel. Promising that his "spirit will sleep in peace" after his death (261), he is the Albatross rather than the Ancient Mariner speaking to us, the wedding guests. Seen in terms of the marriage conundrum considered throughout this study, you might say the Creature *is* a marriage—but too perfect a union of masculine and feminine qualities to be allowed into the mainstream of a civilization that still required that male and female operate in separate spheres.

NOTES

1. I was given this information by a colleague, Mary Hood, Professor of Biology at the University of West Florida, who heard the comments at an annual professional convention.

2. Nathaniel Brown, *Sexuality and Feminism in Shelley* (Cambridge, Mass.: Harvard University Press, 1979), 166.

LUDMILLA JORDANOVA

Melancholy Reflection: Constructing an Identity for Unveilers of Nature

W hen Frankenstein finally left his secluded home for the University of Ingolstadt following his mother's death, his feelings were ambivalent-loss combined with desire:

> I ... indulged in the most melancholy reflection.... I was now alone. My life had hitherto been remarkably secluded and domestic.... I believed myself totally unfitted for the company of strangers.... as I proceeded, my spirits and hopes rose. I ardently desired the acquisition of knowledge.... my desires were complied with....[1]

Shelley's choice of the term 'melancholy' was apt, since it encapsulated ambivalence. Although it suggested sad, gloomy and mournful feelings, it also evoked a sense of pleasure, of the delicious self-indulgence of such feelings. Melancholia was a disease, a neurosis, in the terminology of William Cullen, 'characterised by erroneous judgement'. One image of melancholy, a looser term, which in the early nineteenth century carried both medical and general emotional connotations, associated it with refined, learned and civilized men. While melancholy could be pathological, it also expressed the superior sensibilities of an intellectual elite.[2] Frankenstein's inability to keep

From *Frankenstein, Creation and Monstrosity*, ed. Stephen Bann. © 1994 by Reaktion Books, Ltd.

his intimate, domestic self in a healthy balance with his thirst for knowledge, both of which had a melancholic aspect, constitutes the central monstrosity that the novel explores.

Far from being a simple moralistic tale of masculinist, scientific overreaching, drawing on simple definitions of 'science', 'medicine' or 'surgery', *Frankenstein* is a remarkably precise exploration of the internal conflicts felt by practitioners in a variety of fields, which we can conveniently yoke together as 'natural knowledge', and which are examined by Shelley with acuity. These conflicts are also historically specific, since they surfaced at a time when the expectations and claims of men of science and of medicine were disproportionate to their actual status and power. This mismatch was all the more frustrating because the idiom of scientific heroism, which became increasingly widely available in the first three decades of the nineteenth century, was enticing and seductive, yet insufficiently backed up by state support and cultural rewards.[3] Instability, uncertainty, ambiguity—these are key themes of Shelley's text, and they are explored with particular power through the account of his life that Frankenstein gives to Walton. Walton's character, like Frankenstein's, is portrayed as an uneasy mix. On the one hand he is a daring explorer, a student of nature, possessed of an 'ardent curiosity' and of a desire to triumph over the elements, while on the other he is an isolated, lonely daydreamer, who is ultimately a failure. Walton and Frankenstein recognize their kinship, as the latter asks the former: 'Do you share my madness?'[4]

In order to pursue this argument I need to advance on two fronts, first by discussing the key chapters of Shelley's text, and second by analysing some of the issues portrayals of 'scientists' and 'doctors' raised in her time. Here we must note the anachronism if not of 'doctor' then certainly of 'scientist'. Although the term itself was not coined until the 1830s, there was none the less a sense well before then of men grouped together into some kind of collective, with shared concerns and values, and above all with a common epistemology.[5] This feeling of commonality, well before the word 'scientist' was current among those who produced natural knowledge, is a significant phenomenon. We might cite in support of this point the oil painting *Men of Science Now Living* (1807–8), in London's National Portrait Gallery, which was an attempt to represent a collective and national achievement by means of a group portrait assembled from existing images of those selected as worthy of inclusion.[6]

In Mary Shelley's treatment, what is common to the different pursuits Frankenstein is enthused by is their capacity to open up nature's secrets, or at least they are designed to do so. They reveal or unveil something, personified as female, and presented as mysterious, enticing and potent. I wish to concentrate on the first four chapters, in which Frankenstein narrates his life until the time he is on the brink of completing his creation. From these chapters six themes, all of overriding importance for my argument, emerge. First, seclusion and reclusiveness; these characterize his early family life long before he undertakes his solitary work on making the 'monster'. Second, passion. Even as a child he is described as having a temper, being passionate, and throughout the account of his life his strong desires are foregrounded, above all his desire to learn the secrets of heaven and earth, to possess a kind of knowledge that is full of grandeur. These aspects of his personality were presented by Mary Shelley as overwhelming him, as forces he could not resist or control. Third, there was an absence of satisfaction. Frankenstein was often left unsatisfied by the activities he undertook, by the knowledge available to him, and accordingly he is set apart from others, suffering an inner emptiness. Fourth, he was drawn to particular kinds of natural knowledge. It is striking that he felt attracted to domains that were marginal, contentious or on the boundaries of what could be controlled, such as alchemy and electricity, and that he changed his mind so often about what interested him. This intellectual fickleness led him to discard areas in emotive terms: 'I at once gave up my former occupations, set down natural history and all its progeny as a deformed and abortive creation'.[7] Here fields of knowledge are treated in the way his monster was to be. Fifth, Frankenstein had powerful responses—both positive and negative—to those in positions of intellectual authority over him: his father, his father's friend who explained electricity to him, and his two, very different, teachers at Ingolstadt: Krempe, who repels him, and Waldman, to whom he feels drawn. It is important to note that in the last case this included a strong *physical* reaction to their persons and demeanour. Shelley's account gives credence to the idea that the character of men of science was to be 'read' in their appearance. It was also to be 'read' in their signatures, which were often reproduced beneath their printed portraits.[8]

Finally, the history of natural knowledge is given prominence. The contentious nature of some of the areas to which Frankenstein is attracted derives from the fact that they are archaic: they belong to a past, not a present. Specific mention is made of Cornelius Agrippa, Paracelsus and Albertus Magnus. Humphry Davy's *Elements of Chemical Philosophy*, which Mary Shelley read in 1816, opened with a 'Historical View of the Progress of Chemistry'. His purpose there was to place earlier chemical traditions, including alchemy, in a broad framework, which defined how proper chemical knowledge was to be acquired, specified its usefulness to humankind, and asserted its status as part of an 'intelligent design of the system of the earth'. For Davy, history helps to reveal the stable aspect of experiment, which 'is as it were the chain that binds down the Proteus of nature, and obliges it to confess its real form and divine origin'.[9] For Frankenstein, history and experiment had released an aberrant form of nature, whose origins are profane. Furthermore, Frankenstein revealed his scepticism about the 'modern professors of natural science'.[10] It is true that this refers to his early years, but Frankenstein's evocation of a sense of there being a *history* to natural knowledge is nonetheless significant: 'I had retrod the steps of knowledge along the paths of time ...'.[11] His sense of history was reinforced by Waldman, who 'began his lecture by a recapitulation of the history of chemistry', as did many lecturers in the eighteenth century. And what really inspired Frankenstein was Waldman's way of presenting 'the ancient teachers of science' as mere speculators, and 'the modern masters' as the real miracle-workers.[12] The appeal of performing miracles and probing secrets is still there, but now, thanks to Waldman, it is associated with the moderns. Yet, Waldman's humanity allows the historical figures others dismissed to become those who laid 'the foundations' of modern knowledge. A historical perspective allowed Frankenstein to embrace the present, which he had previously rejected. Here, as elsewhere in the book, Shelley explored different modes of knowledge, not in order to rank and evaluate them, but rather to probe their moral and psychic qualities.

One possible reading of Shelley's depiction of Frankenstein's development and inner life is as an unambiguously critical portrayal of perverted science. And it could be added that it bears no resemblance to the behaviour of medical practitioners and students of nature at the time she was writing. I want to suggest that, on the contrary, she was acutely sensitive to areas of uncertainty and ambiguity felt by those who studied medicine and/or the natural sciences and whose relations with the past of their 'disciplines' were being carefully negotiated at just this time. Many practitioners wrote histories precisely in order to work out the extent of their debt to the ancients and to their other forebears, to give a perspective to 'modern' achievements, to place themselves in a lineage.[13] This was important precisely because they felt deeply implicated by the past, which was not yet separate enough to be put aside safely, but was still sufficiently 'close' to require active management. Those who studied medicine at universities had to read some of the ancients very closely indeed; they would have been well aware of attempts to give a shape to the history of their field, which included compilations and codifications of medical writings.[14] It was because savants felt vulnerable to the suggestion that magic, and an improper concern with death and the supernatural, were still part of the scientific enterprise that they felt the need to repudiate them so firmly. Debates about physiognomy, with its troubling kinship with divination, mesmerism and the violent contests over definitions of 'quackery' can all be characterized in these terms.[15]

In the early decades of the nineteenth century, many, if not most, of those who studied nature in practice worked largely alone, and in a domestic rather than an institutional setting. They more often worked with members of their own families than with their peers. At a time when students of nature were forging their masculine professional identities, they were most likely to be collaborating with female relatives, who were skilled at drawing, and at classifying and preserving specimens.[16] The more formal collective activities, such as those promoted by the British Association for the Advancement of Science, which started in the 1830s, and the specialist, 'disciplinary' scientific societies, which began to be founded in the early nineteenth century, were important because they were new, or relatively so. Indeed it is arguable that provincial medical societies, starting in the 1770s, and medical periodicals, produced by groups of like-minded men from the mid-century on, played a central part in what is conventionally called 'professionalization', and that they were only able to do so because they were strikingly innovative.[17] They worked against the grain of most medical practice, which was solitary, and carried out in domestic settings. The importance of hospitals derives in part from their capacity to bring together medical men, whose other forms of practice were more individual. These features made the personal qualities of practitioners yet more important.

Institutions can be understood as having symbolic functions: they presented the public face of science/medicine as a collective enterprise. It is not contradictory that the late eighteenth and early nineteenth centuries are characterized both by the making of individuals into scientific heroes and by institutionalization; rather, these are complementary faces of the same coin. Heroes on their own could be construed as unstable, their idiosyncracies untethered, while institutions without heroes were impersonal, lacked flair and could be felt to be dull. Even if it was to be decades before stable scientific and medical cultures were firmly established, the tacit goal of early nineteenth-century practitioners was to generate more security—psychic and social—for those who studied nature as a group. The persistence of the amateur is a notable feature of nineteenth-century British science, thus those who insisted that it should be a recognized occupation with collective rights were demanding something for which few indigenous models existed. Medicine, in a limited sense, did provide a model, since its practice could generate a regular source of income. Yet even doctors had little collective power in the early nineteenth century. Despite placing Frankenstein in a European setting, Shelley used themes familiar from the British scene, especially in so far as her hero pursues an individual quest inspired by a thirst for natural knowledge and by a sense of the history of science.

It is true that Mary Shelley makes Frankenstein's reclusiveness and inability to communicate with those close to him into a morbid state, but in doing so she took up a theme that had been common in the medical literature of the eighteenth century. After all, the condition of being a man of thought or reflection was one that, like other social conditions, possessed its own distinctive pathology.[18] To have a well-developed intellect could be seen as a mark of status, a way of differentiating mental refinement from cruder skills based on manual capacities, but it was also a precondition of a particular kind of pathology—introspection, melancholy, obsession. There is also a sexual issue here: masturbation was called the solitary vice and associated with selfish self-absorption; Frankenstein's transgressions rendered him less capable of forming normal adult relationships, especially with the woman destined to be his bride. Perhaps it is also significant that she was chosen for him, above all by his mother, and that she died before their relationship could be consummated. Tissot's famous admonitions concerning male masturbation, first published in the mid-eighteenth century, stressed that its reclusive nature required hunting out and exterminating, and that it disabled the indulger from living a full and productive adult life.[19]

There were many reasons why those who were devotees of science and/or practitioners of medicine wanted to present themselves as men of reason, whose intellectual capabilities combined with deep humanity were their most striking feature, and as the modern equivalents of earlier philosophers, using as vehicles for this presentation styles and idioms that had authoritative connotations. This entailed a distancing from trade, from manual labour, from crude manners and from rudimentary educational attainments. At the same time, a thirst for knowledge, which produced an uncommon commitment to unveiling nature, was an important element of scientific/medical heroism. Natural knowledge was best produced by conspicuously disinterested behaviour, by a desire to generate knowledge for its own sake, for the sake of mankind and not for one's own personal advancement, for mere selfish gratification. Philanthropic activities were one vehicle through which these points could be made. The desire for knowledge came to occupy a different category from other kinds of desire, with which it might otherwise be confused. Two pairs of prints from the 1780s are relevant here; they both contrast the Benevolent Physician, who gives to his patients, with the Rapacious Quack, who robs them. The dominant issue was clearly money, but the broader implications of setting benevolence (the desire to do good) against rapaciousness (desire as greed for money, possessions and sexual domination) are unavoidable.[20] Just as there was a potentially pathological aspect to solitary, contemplative work, so there was to the desire to know nature, which could become a consuming passion, and, by that token, something abnormal. In all these cases—history, seclusion, thirst for knowledge—a careful balancing act was required in practice. Mary Shelley picked this up, and showed the absence of balance. She thereby pointed up the importance of balancing acts, not the unproblematically 'bad' qualities of scientists in general or of Frankenstein in particular.[21]

One of the most striking features of Frankenstein's personality is that he feels driven to act on his new enthusiasm for natural knowledge, and that his efforts meet with success. He is portrayed as, in a specific sense, highly interventionist. Although no mention is made of it in the text, one recent edition of the book associates his activities with surgery: 'she was of course writing in the early 1800s when liver transplants and open heart surgery were but considered fantasies in the minds of a few inventive surgeons'.[22] In Mary Shelley's time, surgery consisted largely of bleeding, the removal of limbs, the treatment of wounds, and dealing with ailments such as bladder stone. Other operations were performed, but these mostly consisted of *removing* growths and related procedures. Thus surgery was active and manual, but not until the second half of the nineteenth century did it entail much entry into body cavities. Surgery was clearly not what Mary Shelley had in mind. Her emphasis was on anatomy and physiology, on understanding life through the processes of death. Opening organic beings for inspection, and then using them, or parts of them, again, was Frankenstein's concern.

The fluid boundary between death and life—a dominant theme in the bio-medical sciences of this time—was of such importance that Frankenstein imagined that, in time, he might be able to 'renew life where death had apparently devoted the body to corruption'.[23] The belief that the boundary between life and death was reversible was widely held at the time, indeed for most of the eighteenth century there had been sustained interest in suspended animation, techniques for reviving the drowned and the hanged, premature burial—indeed in any aspect of medicine that held out the hope that death could be delayed, avoided, held at bay.[24] Medical writers imagined doctors in a quasi-divine role, shedding new light on nature's processes. For example, according to David Ramsay, medical practitioner and early historian of the American Revolution, experiments on animals have 'tended to enlighten physicians in the god-like work of alleviating human misery'.[25] Ramsay was eloquent about the medical benefits of treating the drowned: 'How many must have been lost to their friends and the community, before mankind were acquainted with the god-like art of restoring suspended animation?'[26] Ramsay often used metaphors of light, referring, for example, to 'a blaze of medical knowledge'.[27] 'From the midst of this darkness a sudden light broke in upon me—a light so brilliant and wondrous, yet so simple, that ... I became dizzy with the immensity of the prospect which it illustrated'; this is Frankenstein's description of his discovery of 'the cause of generation and life'.[28] Mary Shelley has grasped perfectly the fantasies of (at least some) medical practitioners of the time, which involved imagining transcendent powers that were almost their own.

These fantasies comprised claims both to intellectual penetration and to active skills. They were nurtured by a new breed of metropolitan medical men, who were becoming successful in acquiring institutional power and social prestige and were rather assertive about their achievements as medics. Examples of the phenomenon include John Abernethy, Matthew Baillie, Sir Astley Paston Cooper and Samuel Foart Simmons, all of whom were painted by Sir Thomas Lawrence, who also put the likenesses of other medical and scientific heroes on canvas—Sir Joseph Banks, Sir Humphry Davy, Edward Jenner and Thomas Young.[29] Also members of this new breed were Sir Anthony Carlisle, professor of anatomy at the Royal Academy, and Sir Charles Bell, author of one of the Bridgewater treatises of the 1830s, who shared an interest in the relationships between medicine and the fine arts.[30] Measuring power is impossible, but the power of these men was probably more symbolic than it was real; however, creating a *culture* of medical and scientific power was one way of securing power itself. The portraits of such men are, in a significant sense, romantic; they make their subjects assertive and exciting but are not afraid to suggest the kinship between medicine and death. At first sight, the inclusion of skulls and bones in a number of these images is surprising, since they evoke a topic, death, which practitioners generally found difficult to cope with. After all, doctors were widely seen as the agents of death, and, in their anatomical role, as tormenters of the dead.

The most unpleasant sides of Frankenstein's activities suggest an inappropriate contact with and disturbance of dead bodies. There is no evidence to indicate that the links between medicine and death became any less troublesome in the years leading up to 1831—the year the second edition of *Frankenstein* appeared—and Ruth Richardson's work suggests that, with the Anatomy Act of 1832, they became far more so, especially at a popular level.[31] How, then, are we to account for the fact that such troubling associations surface in portraits of elite medical practitioners?

Three possibilities present themselves, which are by no means mutually exclusive. The first is that these are the men who *legitimately* look death in the face, who know mortality in a way that *they* are claiming to be acceptable. They may be making such claims in the face of opposition, but they are making them none the less from a position where their rights were gradually being acknowledged by members of social groups whom they could accept as their peers, and by those who were still clearly their superiors. Second, being an old emblem, the skull could be used in this context to evoke long traditions of *memento mori* and of the contemplative life. Precisely because these were part of established traditions in high culture, they might be understood as alluding to the medical contact with death and with the human condition in its morbid states, in a manner that was softened, rendered elegant, by centuries of conventionalized use.[32] If skulls and bones had a certain formulaic quality, then the possibility that associations with death suggest a sharp, urgent critique of science and medicine would be lessened or undermined. The third possibility is that the presence of skulls may be understood in terms of a romantic portrayal of science and medicine at this time as domains of daring. There is absolutely no doubt that in building a set of self-images for those who unveiled nature, the vocabulary of romantic heroism and genius had huge importance.[33] Thus the frisson generated by the macabre side of medicine/death, added something to the image and self-image of those who studied such subjects.

The language of genius was also taken up by those in scientific circles more strictly defined, the pre-eminent example being Humphry Davy.[34] Certain biographical traits were commonly picked up in accounts of students of nature. Individual struggle was a frequent prelude to discovery, suggesting a sustained commitment to an overarching ideal. Uncommon talent was made manifest at a young age. Such men showed a predilection for long hours of work, for solitary study, with the implication that they sacrificed their own health in the process. They also possessed the ability to stick with ideas, even in the face of opposition, displaying bravery, tenaciousness, even a zeal, a passionate commitment. These themes were developed in the growing number of published biographical accounts in the early nineteenth century.[35] It was not even necessary for individuals to be at the top of their field or in the eye of a wide public for a romantic idiom to be applicable.[36] The traits I have just noted were present in Frankenstein's life and labours, but developed to such a degree that they became pathological. This was *always* a possibility for scientists and medical practitioners, and the extreme importance attached to reputation at this period suggests how fragile—both in their internal lives and in their material circumstances—their careers were. Perhaps 'careers' is not the best term, because it suggests a far more structured course of life than was usually the case. Although by the 1830s many doctors had institutional affiliations, these rarely offered them any kind of security and most were 'honorary', while those about to be designated 'scientists' had far fewer such niches available to them. Often a scientific and/or medical life was pieced together, like Frankenstein's monster, made up of bits of lecturing, writing and practising medicine, with the possibility of patronage from friends, relations or sympathetic aristocrats.

In these circumstances, it was attractive to create a certain aura around scientific and medical activities that presented them not just as worthwhile in terms of contributing to the progress of knowledge and to human well-being, but as thrilling. A good deal of mythologizing was involved in terms already established as plausible at this particular historical moment. None the less, this image/self-image was fragile, it was delicately poised between social benefits deriving from knowledge well used, and disasters derived from certain kinds of excess. Practitioners had recourse to a range of devices to cultivate the former and keep at bay the latter. Histories of their subjects did just this. These were quite explicitly about fatherhood in both its good and bad forms. Hippocrates was the father—the good progenitor—of medicine, Galen was the self-indulgent obscurantist—the bad father—just as Frankenstein was.[37] Portraits of practitioners, which would embody—literally—desired values, can be viewed in a similar way. Other devices included the elaboration of intra-professional etiquette, cultivation of patronage relations, and assertions of moral and/or religious conformity.[38]

My argument has been that, in the early nineteenth century, the ambivalence surrounding a thirst for natural knowledge could not be laid to rest. Perhaps it never has been—the afterlife of *Frankenstein*, the history of science fiction as a genre, and the interest in films such as *Dead Ringers* suggest as much. The resulting tensions and ambivalences had to be actively negotiated. In the area of gender and sexuality there was a need to create a secure masculine identity for practitioners of science and medicine, which allowed that natural knowledge was exciting and to be sought in the fashion of a quest, but which resisted any suggestion that it was totally seductive. This would have led to a loss of self-control, or generated auto-eroticism. It was important that the power flowing from natural knowledge was purged of its magical and hubristic elements. In other words, the cardinal tenet of the Enlightenment, that rational knowledge was a proper source of secular power, had to be further refined and clarified. The unveiling of nature, that profoundly instable term, was a source of valued insights, but it could also unleash that which was dangerous. This tension is much more apparent in languages like English, where gendered personifications stand out. And, as I have pointed out elsewhere, it is evident in the very idea of a veil, which simultaneously conceals and reveals and is thereby erotically charged.[39]

I am not claiming for *Frankenstein* some kind of 'documentary' status it does not possess. Rather, in its powerful evocation of the internal life of a student of nature, it tapped into a turbulent unconscious life that was experienced in a variety of ways by practitioners of the time. They tended to present this in its most stable form, Shelley in its least stable one. One of the monstrosities of the book is, of course, Frankenstein's psyche. We cannot understand the scientific/medical enterprises of the time without paying due attention to their internal psychic dimensions. Admittedly, such a claim is not unproblematic, since it raises questions about that which constitutes evidence of the psyche and about the manner in which it is to be interpreted. There are sources, however, in which these dimensions are so dramatically expressed that it seems perverse not to respond accordingly. For example, the theme of monstrosity was taken up quite explicitly in one place within medicine—man-midwifery. This is an important area because of the ways in which it has been invoked in writings on *Frankenstein*, as if Mary Shelley were mounting an explicit critique of men as midwives.[40] This was not, I believe, her concern, but the remarkable diatribe *Man-Midwifery Dissected* of 1793 is relevant to my argument because it indicates the depth of feeling aroused by the unstable identities of medical and scientific practitioners.[41]

Man-Midwifery Dissected contains a well-known frontispiece, that of a figure divided down the middle by a straight line; on one side is a male midwife with his drugs and obstetrical instruments, on the other is a female midwife, who requires few aids. Although the image is familiar, it is rarely analysed in any detail. It is all of a piece with the text, by a man, which decries man-midwifery as a French perversion, a threat to the nation's morals. In the caption beneath the image, the man-midwife is referred to as a monster lately discovered but not known in Buffon's time. Buffon's natural history, with which Mary Shelley was familiar, was not only a huge compendium of the natural world written by a prominent and powerful French savant, but a work widely read and appreciated for its literary elegance.[42] The monstrosity alluded to is of many kinds, but it is especially sexual. It rests partly on the idea that to join two utterly unlike things together—a man and a woman—is going against nature, and by that token, against morality. This example indicates the heightened language that already existed in the 1790s around the practice of medicine, and, by extension, science, a point that is reinforced by the equally vitriolic disputes about quackery.[43] Practitioners knew this, feared charges of improper conduct, and hence were already anxious about their identities on these grounds by the end of the eighteenth century, and the more they strove for respectability, the worse the fear, the higher the stakes became.

It is clear from her journals that Mary Shelley both read widely in what I have called natural knowledge, and that she was acquainted with a number of medical practitioners.[44] Percy Shelley was often preoccupied with his own health, and construed the resulting experiences as integral to his imaginative life.[45] In this sense the Shelleys drew on a cultural context in which science and medicine were not set apart, but were openly available to educated persons as intellectual and emotional resources. They were vehicles for general thought. It is mistaken, on a number of grounds, to see *Frankenstein* as a direct critique of science. Rather it is more helpful to interpret it as an exploration of intellectual energy, of practices that manipulated nature, and of the desire for mastery. Put this way it becomes clear that Mary Shelley was probably thinking about a number of different modes of knowledge—literary and philosophical as well as magical, scientific and medical, and possibly also about their diverse manifestations in different geographical and historical locations. Thus science was not unique, but like other activities in some respects, if not in others. Historians of science are likely to be intensely aware of its uniqueness— scholars often carry the baggage of the domain they study—and to wish to trace that uniqueness backwards. This accounts for the widespread tendency to see *Frankenstein* as a prophetic work, and to present twentieth-century science as the direct legacy that confirms its prophetic status.[46]

I have suggested another point of view, one in which Mary Shelley is a cultural commentator on a highly fluid situation, in which medical and scientific practitioners were striving to carve out niches for themselves, often against the grain of their actual situations. They wished for forms of social and cultural stability they could only fantasize about, while Mary Shelley imagined knowledge in its most unstable, transgressive form. This was possible, I have hinted, not so much because of the content of natural knowledge at the time, which is only lightly sketched in by her, as because she sensed something of the psychological complexities of a thirst for grand knowledge. Since the idioms she deployed were of her time, we can appreciate their immediacy in the context of late eighteenth- and early nineteenth-century anxieties about what unveilers of nature were like. Such people were potentially monstrous, in historically specific ways. At the same time, we, like Mary Shelley, also appreciate that the dangers of desiring knowledge are not limited to a particular historical moment, hence fears of monstrous forms of knowing can never be assuaged.

NOTES

This essay was presented, in a slightly different form, to an interdisciplinary seminar at the University of Victoria, BC, in January 1994. I am most grateful to my hosts, Paul Wood and Carol Gibson Wood, and to the participants, for their helpful comments. I owe a particular debt to Gregory Dart, not only for his detailed responses to my draft, but also for his support and encouragement in preparing the finished essay.

1. Mary Shelley, Frankenstein (Harmondsworth, 1985), p. 89. All subsequent references to Shelley's text are from this edition, edited by Maurice Hindle, hereafter cited as *Frankenstein*.
2. Robert Morris, James Kendrick and others, *Edinburgh Medical and Physical Dictionary* (Edinburgh, 1807); the definition of 'melancholia' is in volume II, not paginated. Definitions of melancholy and its cognates in the *OED* are also illuminating. On melancholy see W. Lepenies, *Melancholy and Society* (Cambridge, MA, 1992). Some

paintings by Joseph Wright of Derby could be said to touch on 'melancholy' in their exploration of the relationships between natural knowledge, the boundaries between life and death, contemplation and introspection. Indeed, Wright's *Hermit Studying Anatomy* of 1771–3 was used for the cover of the Penguin edition of *Frankenstein*. Equally interesting are *The Alchemist, in Search of the Philosopher's Stone, Discovers Phosphorus* (exh. 1771; reworked and dated '1791'), *Miravan Opening the Tomb of his Ancestors* (1772), the portrait *Brooke Boothby* (1781), and The Indian Widow (1785); see B. Nicolson, *Joseph Wright of Derby: Painter of Light*, 2 vols (London, 1968), and *Wright of Derby*, exh. cat. ed. J. Egerton; London, Tate Gallery; Paris, Grand Palais; New York, Metropolitan Museum of Art; 1990. It is perhaps significant that Wright painted Erasmus Darwin, who is so often mentioned in connection with *Frankenstein*, five times.

    3. L. S. Jacyna, 'Images of John Hunter in the Nineteenth Century', *History of Science*, XXI (1983), pp. 85–108; S. Schaffer, 'Genius in Romantic Natural Philosophy', in *Romanticism and the Sciences*, ed. A. Cunningham and N. Jardine (Cambridge, 1990), pp. 82–98; D. Knight, 'The Scientist as Sage', *Studies in Romanticism*, VI (1967), pp. 65–88. See also A. Desmond, *The Politics of Evolution: Morphology, Medicine and Reform in Radical London* (Chicago, 1989).

    4. *Frankenstein*, p. 73.

    5. It is sometimes said that Coleridge coined the term 'scientist' in 1833; for example in T. Levere, 'Coleridge and the Sciences', in *Romanticism and the Sciences* (Cambridge, 1990) pp. 295–306, especially p. 2.96, but see also R. Williams, *Keywords: A Vocabulary of Culture and Society* (revd edn London, 1983), pp. 276–80, especially p. 279, where Williams attributes it to Whewell in 1840. Williams notes that the word 'scientist' was used very occasionally in the late eighteenth century.

    6. Richard Walker, *Regency Portraits* (London, 1985), I, pp. 605–8; II, plates 516–24, NPG nos. 1075, 1075a, 1075b and 1383a.

    7. *Frankenstein*, p. 86.

    8. The most important source for scientific and medical portraits is Renate Burgess, *Portraits of Doctors and Scientists in the Wellcome Institute of the History of Medicine* (London, 1973); my impression is that signatures were particularly likely to be added to portraits when prints were published as frontispieces to be collected works of medical authors or as illustrations to obituaries. Recent work on French eulogies is also relevant: Dorinda Outram, 'The Language of Natural Power: The "Eloges" of Georges Cuvier and the Public Language of Nineteenth Century Science', *History of Science*, XVI (1978), pp. 153–78; Daniel Roche, 'Talent, Reason, and Sacrifice: The Physician during the Enlightenment', in *Medicine and Society in France*, ed. R. Forster and O. Ranum (Baltimore, 1980), pp. 66–88; C. Paul, *Science and Immortality: The Eloges of the Paris Academy of Sciences* (1699–1791) (Berkeley, 1980).

    9. Humphry Davy, *Elements of Chemical Philosophy* (London, 1811), p. 503; the 'Historical View of the Progress of Chemistry' is pp. 1–60. On Mary Shelley's reading see N. White, *Shelley* (London, 1947), II, pp. 539–45, and P. Feldman and D. Scott-Kilvert, eds, *The Journals of Mary Shelley 1814–1844* (Oxford, 1987), I, pp. 85–103. Hindle comments on her reading of Davy: *Frankenstein*, pp. 24–5.

    10. Frankenstein, p. 91.

    11. Ibid.

    12. Ibid., p. 92.

    13. C. Webster, 'The Historiography of Medicine' in *Information Sources in the History of Science and Medicine* (London, 1983), pp. 29–43; J. Christie, 'The Development of the Historiography of Science', in *Companion to the History of Modern Science*, ed. R. Olby, G. Cantor, J. Christie and M. Hodge (London, 1990), pp. 5–22.

    14. L. Rosner, *Medical Education in the Age of Improvement: Edinburgh Students and*

Apprentices, 1760–1850 (Edinburgh, 1991), conveys most effectively the ways in which medical students encountered the ancients and the more modern masters.

15. L. Jordanova, 'The Art and Science of Seeing in Medicine: Physiognomy 1780–1820', in *Medicine and the Five Senses*, ed. W. Bynum and R. Porter (Cambridge, 1993) pp. 122–33; R. Darnton, *Mesmerism and the End of the Enlightenment in France* (Cambridge, MA, 1968); R. Porter, *Health for Sale: Quackery in England, 1660–1850* (Manchester, 1989).

16. D. Allen, 'The Women Members of the Botanical Society of London, 1836–56', *British Journal for the History of Science*, XIII (1981), pp. 240–54; L. Schiebinger, *The Mind Has No Sex? Women in the Origins of Modern Science* (Cambridge, MA, 1989); L. Davidoff and C. Hall, *Family Fortunes: Men and Women of the English Middle Class, 1780–1850* (London, 1987), especially pp. 289–93; A. Morrison-Low, 'Women in the Nineteenth-century Scientific Instrument Trade', in *Science and Sensibility: Gender and Scientific Enquiry, 1780–1945* (Oxford, 1991), pp. 89–117.

17. W. Lefanu, *British Periodicals of Medicine, 1640–1899* (Oxford, 1984); I. Inkster and J. Morrell, eds, *Metropolis and Province: Science in British Culture, 1780–1850* (London, 1983); R. Emerson, 'The Organisation of Science and its Pursuit in Early Modern Europe', and J. Morrell, 'Professionalisation', both in *Companion to the History of Modern Science*, pp. 960–79 and 980–89; T. Gelfand, 'The History of the Medical Profession', in the *Companion Encyclopedia of the History of Medicine*, ed. W. Bynum and R. Porter (London, 1993), II, p. 1119–50; J. Morrell and A. Thackray, *Gentlemen of Science: Early Years of the British Association for the Advancement of Science* (Oxford, 1981).

18. For example, S.A.A.D. Tissot, *De la sante des gens de lettres* (Lausanne, 1758); *Avis aux gens de lettres et aux personnes sédentaires sur leur santé* (Paris, 1767); *An Essay on Diseases Incidental to Literary and Sedentary Persons* (London, 1768); and *An Essay on the Disorders of People of Fashion* (London, 1771). See also R. Porter, 'Diseases of Civilization', in the *Companion Encyclopedia of the History of Medicine*, I, pp. 584–600, especially 589–92.

19. S.A.A.D. Tissot, *Onanism* (London, 1766); Ludmilla Jordanova, 'The Popularisation of Medicine: Tissot on Onanism', *Textual Practice*, I (1987), pp. 68–79.

20. Details of these two pairs of prints may be found in the *Catalogue of Prints and Drawings in the British Museum* (London, 1877 and 1935). The 'Benevolent Physician' prints are discussed in volume V covering 1771–83 (nos 6347 and 6350, c. 1783), the 'Rapacious Quack' ones in volume III covering 1751–60 (nos. 3797 and 3798, c. 1760). Since the 'Physician' and the 'Quack' were pendants, the implication is that the prints were issued twice, once c. 1760 and again c. 1783. Despite the titles, these two pairs are quite different in design.

21. On this point it is suggestive that, in the preface he wrote for the 1818 edition, Percy Shelley specifically insisted that no 'inference [was] justly to be drawn from the following pages as prejudicing any philosophical doctrine of whatever kind' (*Frankenstein*, p. 58).

22. This was published in 1986, by New Orchard Editions, and is accompanied by wood engravings by Lynd Ward.

23. *Frankenstein*, p. 98.

24. J. McManners, *Death and the Enlightenment: Changing Attitudes to Death among Christians and Unbelievers in Eighteenth-century France* (Oxford, 1981); P. Ariès, *The Hour of Our Death* (Harmondsworth, 1983); R. Maulitz, *Morbid Appearances: the Anatomy of Pathology in the Early Nineteenth Century* (Cambridge, 1987); R. Richardson, *Death, Dissection and the Destitute* (London, 1987).

25. D. Ramsay, *A Review of the Improvements, Progress and State of Medicine in the XVIIIth Century* (Charleston, 1801), p. 15.

26. Ramsay, *Review*, p. 16.

27. Ibid., p. 34.

28. *Frankenstein*, p. 96.

29. K. Garlick, *Sir Thomas Lawrence. A Complete Catalogue of Oil Paintings* (Oxford, 1989).

30. Biographies of all these medical men may be found in the *DNB*, which in a significant sense constitutes a primary source, since the entries were written in the idiom of nineteenth-century heroism. Cf. the *Dictionary of Scientific Biography*, the first volume of which appeared in 1970.

31. Richardson, *op. cit.*

32. James Hall, *Dictionary of Subjects and Symbols in Art* (revd edn, London, 1979), pp. 94 ('Death'); pp. 130–1 ('Four Temperaments'); p. 185 ('Skull'). Hall stresses the direct links between melancholy, contemplation, books and a skull. (See also note 2.)

33. A. Cunningham and N. Jardine, eds, *Romanticism and the Sciences* (Cambridge, 1990).

34. Cunningham and Jardine, *op. cit.*, especially pp. 13–22 and 213–27.

35. Marten Hutt in the Wellcome Unit for the History of Medicine, University of Oxford, is currently completing a doctoral dissertation on medical biographies in the late eighteenth and early nineteenth centuries. See, for example, John Aikin, *A Specimen of the Medical Biography of Great Britain; with an Address to the Public* (London, 1775) and *Biographical Memoirs of Medicine of Great Britain* (London, 1780); Joseph Towers, *British Biography; or, an Accurate and Impartial Account of the Lives and Writings of Eminent Persons in Great Britain and Ireland*, 10 vols (London, 1766–1780).

36. For example, Thomas Garnett (1766–1802) and John Haighton (1755–1823) in the *DNB* (Oxford, 1949–50), volumes VII and VIII respectively (first published 1889–90).

37. A particularly clear example of such histories is W. Black, *An Historical Sketch of Medicine and Surgery, from their Origin to the Present Time* (London, 1782).

38. R. Baker, 'The History of Medical Ethics', in *Companion Encyclopedia of the History of Medicine*, pp. 852–87, especially pp. 861–8. These themes emerged particularly clearly in the early nineteenth-century medical reform movement: A. Desmond, *The Politics of Evolution: Morphology, Medicine and Reform in Radical London* (Chicago, 1989); I. Loudon, 'Medical Practitioners 1750–1850, and the Period of Medical Reform in Britain', in *Medicine in Society: Historical Essays*, ed. A. Wear (Cambridge, 1992), pp. 219–47; R. French and A. Wear, eds, *British Medicine in an Age of Reform* (London, 1991).

39. L. Jordanova, *Sexual Visions: Images of Gender in Science and Medicine between the Eighteenth and Twentieth Centuries* (Hemel Hempstead, 1989), ch. 5.

40. For example, Marie Roberts, 'The Male Scientist, Man-Midwife and Female Monster: Appropriation and Transmutation in *Frankenstein*', in *A Question of Identity: Women, Science and Literature*, ed. M. Benjamin (New Brunswick, 1993), pp. 59–74. For a very different view of man-midwifery see W. Bynum and R. Porter, eds, *William Hunter and the Eighteenth-Century Medical World* (Cambridge, 1985), part IV.

41. S. W. Fores, *Man-Midwifery Dissected; or, The Obstetric Family Instructor* (London, 1793).

42. P. Feldman and D. Scott–Kilvert, eds, *The Journals of Mary Shelley, 1814-1844* (Oxford, 1987), p. 100. N. Hampson, *The Enlightenment* (Harmondsworth, 1968). Buffon is still widely read as a stylist in France, and as a result today remains available in cheap editions.

43. S. Schaffer, 'States of Mind: Enlightenment and Natural Philosophy', in *The Languages of Psyche: Mind and Body in Enlightenment Thought* (Berkeley, 1990), pp. 233–90; R. Porter, *Health for Sale: Quackery in England 1660–1850*.

44. P. Feldman and D. Scott-Kilvert, eds, *The Journals of Mary Shelley, 1814–1844*, e.g. pp. 26, 39, 47, 55, 65, 67, 124, 180.

45. Nigel Leask, 'Shelley's "Magnetic Ladies": Romantic Mesmerism and the Politics of the Body', in *Beyond Romanticism: New Approaches to Texts and Contexts, 1780–1831*, ed. S. Copley and J. Whale (London, 1992), pp. 53–78.

46. Brian Easlea, *Fathering the Unthinkable: Masculinity, Scientists and the Nuclear Arms Race* (London, 1983), pp. 28–39; Maurice Hindle makes a similar point in his introduction, *Frankenstein*, pp. 41–2.

CROSBIE SMITH

Frankenstein and Natural Magic

Victor Frankenstein warns Captain Robert Walton of the dangers of a quest for god-like knowledge and power:

I see by your eagerness, and the wonder and hope which your eyes express, my friend, that you expect to be informed of the secret with which I am acquainted; that cannot be: listen patiently until the end of my story, and you will easily perceive why I am reserved upon that subject. I will not lead you on, unguarded and ardent as I then was, to your destruction and infallible misery. Learn from me, if not by my precepts, at least by my example, how dangerous is the acquirement of knowledge, and how much happier that man is who believes his native town to be the world, than he who aspires to become greater than his nature will allow.[1]

John Baptista Porta instructs his readers on 'what manner of man a Magician ought to be' (1658):

Now it is meet to instruct a Magician, both what he must know, and what he must observe; that being instructed every way, he may bring very strange and wonderful things to pass. Seeing

From *Frankenstein, Creation and Monstrosity*, ed. Stephen Bann. © 1994 by Reaktion Books, Ltd.

> Magick, as we shewed before, is a practical part of Natural
> Philosophy, therefore it behoveth a Magician, and one that
> aspires to the dignity of that profession, to be an exact and very
> perfect Philosopher.... If you would have your works appear more
> wonderful, you must not let the cause be known: for that is a
> wonder to us, which we see to be done, and yet know not the
> cause of it: for he that knows the causes of a thing done, doth not
> so admire the doing of it; and nothing is counted unusual and
> rare, but only so far forth as the causes thereof are not known.[2]

'In a fit of enthusiastic madness I created a rational creature', the dying
Victor Frankenstein confessed to Walton.[3] Mary Shelley's celebrated text
was largely structured by powerful tensions between the surface 'rationality',
associated with Enlightenment ideology, and the deeper and darker side of
nature and human beings beloved by the Romantic poets with whom the
young novelist shared a common culture. Within the text, the character of
Victor embodied these tensions. Brought up in an enlightened family whose
hallmarks were stability and happiness, Victor himself slipped inexorably into
a very different state, one characterized by instability, misery and, above all,
by secrecy. No longer a wholly 'rational creature', Victor's confessions
revealed a dangerous and even demonic side to man in which natural
philosophy, that supposed triumph of the Age of Reason, was recruited for
secret and sinister ends.

Recent *Frankenstein* scholarship has increasingly recognized the
fruitfulness of interpreting the novel in its historical contexts. We are
indebted especially to Marilyn Butler for her superb edition of the 1818 text
and for her demonstration of Mary Shelley's significant 1831 transformation
of Frankenstein himself into a character with greater appeal to contemporary
Christian audiences.[4] In this essay I also adopt a contextual approach, and
focus on the issues raised by the themes of natural magic and natural
philosophy that run through the novel. By setting the text against a broad
context of 'Enlightenment' ideology, I argue that the persistent subversion of
that ideology by Frankenstein's personal inclination towards natural and
even demonic magic, adapted to his 'Romantic' character, underpinned a
mayor textual preoccupation with questions of human knowledge and power.

Earlier studies of *Frankenstein* have sometimes drawn attention to the
conspicuous lack of scientific detail culminating in the celebrated scene in
chapter IV:

> It was on a dreary night of November, that I beheld the
> accomplishment of my toils. With an anxiety that almost

amounted to agony, I collected the instruments of life around me, that I might infuse a spark of being into the lifeless thing that lay at my feet. It was already one in the morning; the rain pattered dismally against the panes, and my candle was nearly burnt out, when, by the glimmer of the half-extinguished light, I saw the dull yellow eye of the creature open; it breathed hard, and a convulsive motion agitated its limbs.[5]

In Mario Praz's introductory essay to his anthology *Three Gothic Novels* (Walpole's *The Castle of Otranto*, Beckford's *Vathek*, and *Frankenstein*), it is claimed that although Mary Shelley's novel surpassed the others 'in its capacity of stirring our sense of horror', it nevertheless had a 'fundamental weakness which seriously hampers the suspense of disbelief', namely, that the author neither described 'the materials of the experiments' nor 'the manner of the unholy operations'.[6] In contrast, the famous 1931 film offered its audiences far more scientific detail, mainly in the form of late nineteenth-century electrical apparatus, than did the original text, while simultaneously introducing human witnesses into Frankenstein's laboratory.

A contextual approach directs attention to the cultural construction of all such artefacts as 'the suspense of disbelief' and away from a concern with universalist, timeless judgements like those of Praz. By investigating the image of the natural philosopher in historical context, we can begin to understand that the character of Frankenstein plays a very distinctive role, one which might be described as that of an 'extraordinary' rather than conventional man of science.[7] I therefore argue that Mary Shelley's central character does not conform to the image of orthodox practitioners of science in the late eighteenth century and early nineteenth, still less to that of the modern scientist. Most obviously, Frankenstein's obsession, his isolation, his individualism and his egoism are strongly suggestive of Romantic images of the mad genius, the creative artist, and the natural philosopher *qua* natural magician. Above all, as the opening quotation from Porta shows, secrecy acted to preserve that sense of wonder and mystery which the rationality of the Enlightenment had seemed, in the eyes of the Romantics, to threaten and destroy.

NATURE IN THE 'AGE OF REASON': VICTOR'S GENEVESE YEARS

Eighteenth-century Enlightenment philosophers promoted the broad assumption that Nature was ordered and rational. Natural history, concerned with the *classification* of plants, of animals, of human beings, of stars, revealed the systematic arrangements within Nature. These patterns of order sometimes formed the basis for the famous 'design argument' in British natural theology (design *in* Nature demonstrates the existence and wisdom of God), and sometimes the basis for a de-Christianized deism that recognized an omniscient Designer.[8]

Natural philosophy, the study of the *laws* by which Nature acted or moved, complemented natural history. Investigations of the principles of regularities or uniformities of Nature, rather than Nature's hidden and ultimate causes, became standard for academic natural philosophers of the Age of Reason, with 'reason' itself being redefined as Natural Law. The Laws of Nature themselves, such as Newton's Law of universal gravitation, stood as the exemplars of Reason. Any further attempts to probe the causes 'behind' the law were then assigned to an ancient metaphysics (such as that of natural magic) and thus to *forbidden* territory.[9] Combining natural history (the arrangements) with natural philosophy (the laws of operation) yielded Nature's *economy*. In fact, Nature consisted of many economies or systems— the solar system, for example, or the plant economy. All of these natural economies, characterized by orderly arrangements and governed by immutable laws, acted in harmony with one another.

By the late eighteenth century, these various economies of Nature shared a common characteristic. They were all 'equilibrium systems', exemplified by the simple case of the lever or balance. The important feature was that in such systems slight disturbances would be compensated and adjusted in such a way that the equilibrium (or average) position was restored. Thus the phrase 'balance of Nature' was not just an empty cliché, but one that was related to actual systems in Nature.[10] Examples are numerous: Lavoisier's chemical equations that balanced quantitatively; D'Alembert's and Lagrange's reduction of the whole of the science of dynamics to that of statics or equilibrium through a so-called 'principle of virtual velocities', which was also exemplified in the Law of the lever; and Laplace's and Lagrange's new model of the solar system, in which planetary perturbations (thought by Newton to require God's restoring power) were shown to be periodical and self-restoring, such that the solar system would never fall into disorder.[11]

It followed that each system was a perfect system, operating like a perfect machine and capable of self-restoration. Such natural systems could thus form a model for the reform of other systems that showed anything but perfection, especially human institutions and societies. Nature stood as the exemplar of perfection amid human imperfection, but doctrines of the 'perfectibility of man' meant that human beings could at least aspire to such perfection by reforming or even overthrowing unnatural tyranny and authoritarian systems in favour of free individuals in a new state of nature, with each individual pursuing life, liberty and happiness and thereby maximizing the sum total of human happiness.[12]

These doctrines presupposed that man, thus set free, would act as a rational creature, seeking to optimize his own interests but not at too great an expense to other rational creatures. In John Locke's words (*pace* Hobbes), 'the state of Nature has a law of Nature to govern it, which obliges everyone ... that being all equal and independent, no one ought to harm another in his life, health, liberty or possessions'.[13] A perfect human economy would also act like a balanced machine, and small variations would only lead to fluctuations around a natural mean.

The notion of a balanced economy of nature, however, carried with it something more than benevolent harmony: Nemesis, the goddess of retribution. Traditional views persisted in the work of, for instance, the celebrated eighteenth-century botanist-classifier Carl Linnaeus (1707–78). *Divine nemesis* would act to prevent a loss of equilibrium in Nature's economies. All levels of Nature and society needed to be maintained within their 'proper limits' so as to prevent evil—entailing chaos and disorder—triumphing over good, the latter understood in terms of order, balance and happiness.

The clergyman Thomas Robert Malthus (1766–1834) offered a similar perspective around 1800. The sexual appetites of living creatures led to a tendency towards ever-expanding populations according to a geometrical increase. But the arithmetical increase in food supply provided a natural check on any given population, such that a balance was always maintained with respect to a given species. The benefits to the whole economy of nature were obvious: no single species could overrun the world. But the price paid in terms of suffering, starvation and death by individuals (especially human individuals) by allowing free reign to their populating urges could be very high indeed. This kind of nemesis derived principally from God through the system established by Him for ordering Nature and society. But more radical 'secular' philosophers tended to view the laws of Nature as sufficient guides to morality. Violation of natural law and disobedience to her systems would bring Nature's retribution on the 'evil-doer'.[14]

From the opening of the very first chapter of Victor Frankenstein's personal account, readers learn that his family origins combined all the values of enlightened Swiss respectability and stability:

> I am by birth a Genevese; and my family is one of the most distinguished of that republic. My ancestors had been for many years counsellors and syndics [legislators]; and my father [Alphonse] had filled several public situations with honour and

reputation. He was respected by all who knew him for his integrity and indefatigable attention to public business. He passed his younger days perpetually occupied by the affairs of his country; and it was not until the decline of life that he thought of marrying, and bestowing on the state sons who might carry his virtues and his name down to posterity.

And, as Victor added later, the 'republican institutions of our country have produced simpler and happier manners than those which prevail in the great monarchies that surround it'.[15] Victor's father, then, was a man of impeccable republican credentials, a man prepared to sacrifice self-promotion and self-gratification for the public good. Even marriage was to serve the interests of the state by allowing the perpetuation of virtue, embodied in the name of Frankenstein, to posterity. Indeed, the Frankensteins were construed as guardians of virtue rather than individuals employing, as Victor would employ, virtue as a means to power and self-aggrandisement.

Alphonse Frankenstein displayed those very qualities of nobility and honour in the events that led to his marriage to Caroline Beaufort, daughter of an old merchant friend. Beaufort's slide from prosperity into poverty prompted the merchant, following honourable settlement of his debts, to retreat into a wretched state of isolation from society. Sacrificing all self-interest in the search for his friend, Alphonse arrived too late to save the old man from death, but 'came like a protecting spirit to the poor girl, who committed herself to his care'.[16] Following marriage to Caroline, Alphonse sacrificed his public employments to the call of domestic duty, devoting himself to the education of his children. Victor, the eldest child, expressed the state of family stability and happiness thus: 'No creature could have more tender parents than mine. My improvement and health were their constant care, especially as I remained for several years their only child'.[17]

Into this ideal domestic state came the abandoned Elizabeth, Victor's cousin and future fiancée. Indeed, it was Victor's mother who, desiring 'to bind as closely as possible the ties of domestic love', had decided 'to consider Elizabeth as my future wife'. The immediate result was a powerful reinforcement of domestic equilibrium and happiness:

> If the servants had any request to make, it was always through her intercession. We [Elizabeth and Victor] were strangers to any species of disunion and dispute; for although there was a great dissimilitude in our characters, there was a harmony in that very dissimilitude. I was more calm and philosophical than my companion; yet my temper was not so yielding. My application

was of longer endurance; but it was not so severe whilst it endured. I delighted in investigating the facts relative to the actual world; she busied herself in following the aerial creations of the poets. The world was to me a secret, which I desired to discover; to her it was a vacancy, which she sought to people with imaginations of her own.[18]

Already, of course, Victor's listeners are given a hint that something dark lurked in Victor's nature, perhaps even within Nature itself, in contrast to the outward stability, harmony and delights of conventional and enlightened domestic society, where even the servants could share in the state of happiness. But in the meantime, 'No youth could have passed more happily than mine. My parents were indulgent, and my companions amiable'.[19]

The talented Henry Clerval, Victor's best friend, was also rescued from the perils of social isolation by the Frankenstein family: 'for being an only child, and destitute of companions at home, his father was well pleased that he should find associates at our house; and we were never completely happy when Clerval was absent'. Together with Victor's younger brothers, the domestic balance was almost perfect:

Such was our domestic circle, from which care and pain seemed for ever banished. My father directed our studies, and my mother partook of our enjoyments. Neither of us possessed the slightest pre-eminence over the other; the voice of command was never heard amongst us; but mutual affection engaged us all to comply with and obey the slightest desire of each other.[20]

Again, however, Victor was concerned to show that the origins of his later misfortunes were contemporaneous with the bright childhood 'visions of extensive usefulness', visions ultimately transmuted 'by insensible steps' into 'gloomy and narrow reflections upon self'. What Victor, with the benefit of hindsight, called 'the birth of that passion which afterwards ruled my destiny', had in his view arisen 'like a mountain river, from ignoble and almost forgotten sources; but, swelling as it proceeded, it became the torrent which, in its course, has swept away all my hopes and joys'. That source of disequilibrium was natural philosophy, 'the genius that has regulated my fate'.[21]

In its earliest form, this historical river of natural philosophy had begun when inclement weather disrupted a 'party of pleasure to the baths near Thonon', confining the Frankenstein family to the inn. Victor, then thirteen, 'chanced to find a volume of Cornelius Agrippa'. Agrippa (1486–1535) was a

natural magician whose activities were to inspire the famous tale of the
sorcerer's apprentice. Fired with enthusiasm, and undaunted by his father's
dismissal of the work as 'sad trash', Victor returned home to devour still
more of Agrippa's works, complemented by those of the alchemist Paracelsus
(c. 1493–1541) and the Aristotelian natural magician Albertus Magnus (c.
1192–1280).[22]

It was thus that Victor 'entered with the greatest diligence into the
search of the philosopher's stone and the elixir of life'. The latter especially
drew his undivided attention, for 'wealth was an inferior object; but what
glory would attend the discovery, if I could banish disease from the human
frame, and render man invulnerable to any but a violent death'.

Medieval alchemy had often been concerned with the relatively
ordinary practices of metallurgy and medicine. But the strong mystical
dimensions, blended from several ancient cultures into Christianity, meant
that there was also a concern with material and spiritual perfection.
Perfection would be achieved by the liberation of material and other earthly
substances from a temporal existence in which all objects, living and non-
living, were subject to ageing and decay.

Gold represented perfection for metals. Base metals turned into gold
would have achieved material perfection, for gold, unlike other metals, did
not rust or decay. Hence came the ancient search for the so-called
Philosopher's Stone, which would bring to its possessor unlimited wealth.
Immortality or eternal youth would achieve material perfection for human
beings. Hence, too, came the quest for the elusive Elixir of Life. Spiritual
perfection, on the other hand, related to salvation of the individual soul.
Consistent also with the practices of such medieval and Renaissance natural
magicians, Victor did not limit his concerns to matters of health and disease:
'The raising of ghosts or devils was a promise liberally accorded by my
favourite authors, the fulfilment of which I most eagerly sought'.[23]

As Victor came of age, the early streams gradually yielded to a wider and
less passionate river of eighteenth-century natural philosophy. A spectacular
lightning strike (lightning was traditionally associated with powers outside the
ordinary course of Nature) elicited instead a very 'modern' explanation from
Victor's father. Rather than offer anything like an occult or causal explanation,
he followed an eighteenth-century experimental natural philosopher's
practice of describing only 'the various effects of that power' and of
constructing 'a small electrical machine', exhibiting 'a few experiments' and
flying a kite to draw down 'electrical fluid' from the clouds.[24]

In his *History and Present State of Electricity* (1767), the English natural
philosopher and chemist Joseph Priestley (1733–1804) had similarly asserted
modern man's power over nature:

> What would the ancient philosophers, what would Newton himself have said, to see the present race of electricians imitating in miniature all the known effects of that tremendous power, nay, disarming the thunder of its power of doing mischief, and, without any apprehension of danger to themselves, drawing lightning from the clouds into an private room and amusing themselves at their leisure by performing with it all the experiments that are exhibited by electrical machines.[25]

Such claims tended, of course, to elevate the power of the experimental natural philosopher well beyond that of ordinary mortals, and to give him, in the eyes of his audience, something approaching god-like status.

As Simon Schaffer has shown, the concomitant physical dangers of electricity could readily be linked to the myth of Prometheus: his punishment for the presumptuous act of stealing fire from the gods. The death of the Russian-based theorist G.W. Richmann during thunderstorm experiments into electricity in 1753 thus occasioned *The Gentleman's Magazine* to comment that 'we are come at last to touch the celestial fire, which if ... we make too free with, as it is fabled Prometheus did of old, like him we may be brought too late to repent of our temerity'. Likewise referring to lightning experiments, the French electrician Mazeas wrote concerning 'that Wonderful Matter which Nature has kept hid from us since the Creation of the World. The fable of Prometheus is verify'd—what after this can mortals find difficult?'[26]

As a result of his father's electrical demonstrations, conveying as they did a sense of modern mastery even over Nature's most mysterious powers, Victor abandoned his allegiance to the 'old lords of my imagination'. But, thanks in part to the incomprehensibility of a local chemistry lecturer, he also discontinued his interest in natural philosophy in favour of mathematics and languages.[27]

Just prior to Victor's departure, in accordance with his parents' wishes, for the University of Ingolstadt, 'the first misfortune of my life occurred'. Disease, in the form of scarlet fever, not only introduced instability into the family but also, as his mother sickened and died, demonstrated to Victor the imperfections of the human frame:

> On the third day my mother sickened; her fever was very malignant, and the looks of her attendants prognosticated the worst event. [...] I need not describe the feelings of those whose dearest ties are rent by that most irreparable evil, the void that

presents itself to the soul.... [When] the lapse of time proves the reality of the evil, then the actual bitterness of grief commences. Yet from whom has not the rude hand rent away some dear connexion; and why should I describe a sorrow which all have felt, and must feel?[28]

Although temporarily restored by Elizabeth's devotion to the duty of 'rendering her uncle and cousins happy', Victor's ties to the stable social world of his family were entirely broken as he finally set out for Ingolstadt three months late. In contrast to Victor's parents, Clerval's father insisted that he 'became a partner with him in business' on the grounds that 'learning is superfluous in the commerce of ordinary life'. Safely placed in the world of trade, Clerval was thus spared the corrupting and disturbing influence of the pursuit of knowledge. And as he journeyed to Ingolstadt, Victor, separated from all his social protectors, 'indulged in the most melancholy reflections'.[29]

NATURE IN THE AGE OF ROMANTICISM: VICTOR'S INGOLSTADT YEARS AND AFTER

As Victor himself confessed, 'life had hitherto been remarkably secluded and domestic; and this had given me invincible repugnance to new countenances'. He therefore believed himself 'totally unfitted for the company of strangers'. Yet as he proceeded further, his 'spirits and hopes arose' and he 'ardently desired the acquisition of knowledge'.[30] The way therefore seemed open for the new student to forge fresh social links with peers and professors alike.

The signs, however, were inauspicious. On arrival, Victor was conducted to his 'solitary apartment'. Furthermore, he had entered Ingolstadt three months later than his peers. All of these factors would compromise his stability. Worst of all, the possibility of throwing aside subjective anxieties in the common cause of the pursuit of objective knowledge was almost immediately thwarted by his reaction against the character of the professor of natural philosophy, M. Krempe. Foolishly admitting that his reading on the subject had been limited to Paracelsus and Albertus Magnus, Victor was treated to a heated diatribe from his prospective master:

Every minute ..., every instant that you have wasted on those books is utterly and entirely lost. You have burdened your memory with exploded systems, and useless names. Good God! in what desert land have you lived, where no one was kind enough to inform you that these fancies, which you have so greedily imbibed, are a thousand years old, and as musty as they are ancient? I little expected in this enlightened and scientific age to find a disciple of Albertus Magnus and Paracelsus. My dear Sir, you must begin your studies entirely anew.[31]

Having already abandoned his faith in ancient science, Victor's response was less a matter of disappointment at Krempe's invective, and more one of contempt for the moderns, personified in the 'gruff voice and repulsive countenance' of this 'squat little man'. Furthermore, Victor felt more strongly than ever an utter contempt for the mundane uses of modern natural philosophy. How very different 'when the masters of the science sought immortality and power; such views, although futile, were grand'. Now the 'ambition of the inquirer seemed to limit itself to the annihilation of those visions on which my interest in science was chiefly founded. I was required to exchange chimeras of boundless grandeur for realities of little worth'.[32]

The indications here of Victor's latent enthusiasm for grand visions strongly suggest that he would not conform to 'safe' Enlightenment models of 'scientific' man as a 'rational' creature who knew that the best interests, happiness, pleasure and wealth of himself as an individual, and of society as a sum of individuals, lay in obedience to Nature's laws and systems and that deviations from those conventions would only bring disorder upon society and nature, as well as inevitable retribution upon himself. Victor would slip imperceptibly from his place in 'rational society' (exemplified both by his home and by his academic masters) into a state of enthusiasm, radicalism and even madness, a state that threatened the social order itself. Such 'enthusiasts' for natural philosophy, often associated with radical religious sects, with superstition and even with magic, were commonplace in late eighteenth-century England. Given access to the powers of nature, these dangerous individuals were themselves powers for social, political and religious instability. Natural philosophy itself, which offered a route to stability and perfection, could, if left unpoliced, easily function as a path to chaos and revolution.[33]

Through the second half of the eighteenth century, the official voice of European science issued from the prestigious scientific academies. As Thomas Hankins has argued, the constructed image of establishment science had been initiated by Fontenelle (1657–1757), whose eulogies of deceased members of the French Academy of Sciences were moral biographies, emphasizing the virtues of these dead heroes of science. Such natural philosophers embodied qualities of simplicity, humility, austerity, love of nature, want of ambition and an unselfish pursuit of truth. The pursuit of natural science was regarded as the highest moral good: the motives were pure, the objectivity stood opposed to self-interest and ambition, and the virtues (such as 'duty' and 'courage') were Stoic, as in the classical world.[34]

While Victor's own father possessed such classical virtues of self-sacrifice and devotion to duty, it was evident that the mundane Professor Krempe did not at all conform to this constructed image. But Victor soon encountered another very different scientific character at the university. Neither a paragon of classical virtue nor a pedantic man of science, the charismatic professor of chemistry, Waldman, would provide the inspirational spark which ignited the obsessive genius of Victor Frankenstein.

From Victor's account, it is evident that Waldman's appearance and manner, 'expressive of the greatest benevolence', and a 'voice the sweetest I had ever heard', contrasted dramatically with his natural philosophy colleague. But it was Waldman's 'panegyric upon modern chemistry' that really fired Victor's dormant enthusiasm for natural science:

> 'The ancient teachers of this science [chemistry]', said he, 'promised impossibilities, and performed nothing. The modern masters promise very little; they know that metals cannot be transmuted, and that the elixir of life is a chimera. But these philosophers, whose hands seem only made to dabble in dirt, and their eyes to pore over the microscope or crucible, have indeed performed miracles. They penetrate into the recesses of nature, and shew how she works in her hiding places. They ascend into the heavens; they have discovered how the blood circulates and the nature of the air we breathe. They have acquired new and almost unlimited powers; they can command the thunders of heaven, mimic the earthquake, and even mock the invisible world with its own shadows'.[35]

In part, Waldman's powerful rhetoric reflected the dramatic impact of the 'chemical revolution', usually associated with the French chemist Antoine Lavoisier (1743–94). Towards the end of the eighteenth century, Lavoisier's identification of 'oxygen' as a constituent of the 'air we breathe' formed a centrepiece of the language of chemical elements that offered a whole new system of classification for material substances. As Waldman privately told Victor, the ancients had 'left to us, as an easier task, to give new names, and arrange in connected classifications, the facts which they in a great degree had been the instruments of bringing to light'. Furthermore, 'Chemistry is that branch of natural philosophy in which the greatest improvements have been and may be made; it is on that account that I have made it my peculiar study; but at the same time I have not neglected the other branches of science'.[36]

More broadly, therefore, Waldman's public rhetoric also presented the most triumphant vision of spectacular scientific achievements since the Scientific Revolution of the seventeenth century. First, the ascending of the modern masters into the heavens simultaneously suggested a Christ-like power *and* referred specifically to the dramatic and dangerous hot-gas balloon ascents of the late eighteenth century, notably those of Pilâtre de Rozier from 1783 (hailed by Lavoisier as the year of the first human flight) until his death two years later in a spectacular crash at Boulogne. Typically, these balloon ascents were linked to scientific investigations, for example meteorology.[37]

Second, the modern masters, from William Harvey (1578–1657) onwards, had 'discovered' how the heart pumps the blood of animals in circular and regular fashion through arteries and veins. Third, these masters (notably Lavoisier) had analysed the nature of the air that creatures breathe. Prometheus-like too, they 'command the thunders of heaven' in electrical experiments. Furthermore, in an allusion to the attempts of Priestley and others to model or imitate earthquakes using electrical discharges, the moderns had begun to 'mimic the earthquake'.[38]

Uniting animal physiology with grand electrical phenomena by means of a single natural economy, that of the atmosphere, Waldman emphasized the consequent 'new and almost unlimited powers' acquired by the chemists and natural philosophers. He thus privately counselled Victor that 'A man would make but a very sorry chemist, if he attended to that department of human knowledge alone'. In order to 'become really a man of science, and not merely a petty experimentalist', Victor would need to apply himself to 'every branch of natural philosophy'.[39]

Waldman's sympathetic and sensitive personality appealed to Victor. Rather than dismiss the ancients with contempt, the professor had referred to them as 'men to whose indefatigable zeal modern philosophers were indebted for most of the foundations of their knowledge'. Indeed, he asserted that the 'labours of men of genius, however erroneously directed, scarcely ever fail in ultimately turning to the solid advantage of mankind'. But he also pointed to the spectacular performance of the modern chemists, understood not as 'petty experimentalists' but as masters with a vision. Not surprisingly, Victor overcame his prejudices against modern chemists and at once became apprentice to Ingolstadt's charismatic chemist.

Waldman's private remarks on the dichotomy between a 'petty

experimentalist' and a true 'man of science' were also symptomatic of a cultural shift within German-speaking lands at the close of the eighteenth century. As Schaffer has argued, 'ingenuity' was an epithet by which to characterize the inventive craft skills of seventeenth- and eighteenth-century experimenters and instrument makers. But 'genius', as a term used by Romantic natural philosophers, implied not simply a special capacity of the creative artist or philosopher, but the power which possessed him.[40]

In this sense, the imagery of 'genius' was related to excessive, and even divine, power: the genius was a 'modern Prometheus'. Waldman could thus refer with approval to the ancients' 'indefatigable zeal' and 'labours of genius', even though they 'promised impossibilities and performed nothing'. Victor too would soon 'read with ardour those [modern] works, so full of genius and discrimination, which modern inquirers have written' on natural philosophy and especially chemistry. It was thus that natural philosophy became the 'genius that has regulated my fate'.[41]

Although Waldman provided something of an ideal role-model for Victor, it soon emerged that 'an intrinsic love for the science [of chemistry] itself' had taken possession of the aspiring natural philosopher. If Waldman served as an ideal for Victor, the reality was that Victor's pursuit of the science 'became so ardent and eager, that the stars often disappeared in the light of morning whilst I was yet engaged in my laboratory'. After two years, throughout which he remained at Ingolstadt, he 'made some discoveries in the improvement of some chemical instruments, which procured me great esteem and admiration at the university'.[42]

Up to this point, Victor had been acting in relation to the Ingolstadt science professors. Now, however, he felt himself 'as well acquainted with the theory and practice of natural philosophy as depended on the lessons of any of the professors at Ingolstadt'. To paraphrase his later remarks, he could no longer rank himself 'with the herd of common projectors'. No petty experimentalist, Victor had been thoroughly grounded in the principles and practice of a unified natural philosophy embracing everything from human physiology to atmospheric electricity. And as he shifted from matters of chemistry to those of physiology, he began seeking an answer to the ancient question: 'Whence ... did the principle of life proceed?'[43]

Motivated by 'an almost supernatural enthusiasm', yet with no fear of 'supernatural horrors', Victor had indeed been possessed by the genius of natural philosophy. His fate would therefore be controlled, not by supernatural forces or evil spirits from without, but by that enthusiasm within himself which would make him aspire 'to become greater than his nature will allow'.[44] This 'supernatural' possession, then, would be productive of all his subsequent misery and tragedy.

Moving from investigations of the structure of the human frame (anatomy) to 'observe the natural decay and corruption of the human body', Victor now sought to control the causes of imperfection in living creatures:

Now I was led to examine the cause and progress of this decay, and forced to spend days and nights in vaults and charnel houses.... I paused, examining and analysing all the minutiae of causation, as exemplified in the change from life to death, and death to life, until from the midst of this darkness a sudden light broke in upon me—a light so brilliant and wondrous, yet so simple, that while I became dizzy with the immensity of the prospect which it illustrated, I was surprised that among so many men of genius, who had directed their inquiries towards the same science, that I alone should be reserved to discover so astonishing a secret.... What had been the study and desire of the wisest men since the creation of the world, was now within my gras.[45]

Finding 'so astonishing a power placed within my hands', Victor now 'possessed the capacity of bestowing animation' upon lifeless matter. Ultimately undaunted by the difficulties of applying that power in practice, he was none the less equivocal concerning the precise status of the project. When, therefore, he spoke of giving 'life to an animal as complex and wonderful as man', his words suggested either the creation of an animal *like* man or of man himself. But, having begun 'the creation of an human being', a desire for rapid completion of the project prompted him to 'make the being of a gigantic stature; that is to say, about eight feet in height, and proportionably large'.[46] His impatience was to cost him dear, for the less than perfect end-product would, in appearance at least, emerge as nothing less than a monster, an outcast from any natural species of being.

Driven onwards by a variety of feelings 'like a hurricane', Victor indeed seemed possessed by powers outside human nature. The visionary goals of making a new species that would 'bless me as its creator and source', and perhaps ultimately of renewing 'life where death had apparently devoted the [human] body to corruption', supported him in a task undertaken 'with unremitting ardour'. So single-minded indeed was he that he again envisaged no tensions between the divergent aims of creating a new species and the renewal of life in the existing human species. The former goal, of course, not only violated God's prerogative to have fixed all species 'in the beginning', but also promised to introduce a disturbing and inherently unnatural force into the balanced economy of living nature. The latter goal similarly challenged a traditional Christian acceptance of human imperfection, manifested in sin and suffering, disease and death, with a presumptuous conviction that nature's imperfections could be made perfect by human genius.[47]

Victor's initial goal of creating a new human being coincided in part with an Enlightenment dream of a 'new man', capable of perfection through reason and free from the inherited encumbrances of the past, such as noble rank or religious dogma. One of the most stirring and popular advocates of Reason, the Marquis de Condorcet (1743–94), believed that the 'new man' and his rights would derive from 'the single truth, that man is a sentient being, capable of reasoning and of acquiring moral ideas'. All that had to be done to initiate the process was to strip away the inheritance of status and property. In its conception, Victor's creature was to have been just such a 'new man'. But as the creature later explained to Victor, this 'new man' was likely to find himself outside existing eighteenth-century human society:

> I heard [from the De Lacey family] of the division of property, of immense wealth and squalid property; of rank, descent, and noble blood.
>
> The words induced me to turn towards myself. I learned that the possessions most esteemed by your fellow-creatures were, high and unsullied descent united with riches. A man might be respected with only one of these acquisitions; but without either he was considered, except in very rare instances, as a vagabond and a slave, doomed to waste his powers for the profit of the chosen few. And what was I? Of my creation and creator I was absolutely ignorant; but I knew that I possessed no money, no friends, no kind of property. I was, besides, endowed with a figure hideously deformed and loathsome; I was not even of the same nature as man ... Was I then a monster, a blot upon the earth, from which all men fled, and whom all men disowned?[48]

In the process of creation, Victor had been driven by enthusiasm rather than motivated by a quest for perfection. Like Walton, Frankenstein was 'too ardent in execution, and too impatient of difficulties'.[49] Early on, he admitted that he had 'prepared myself for a multitude of reverses; my operations might be incessantly baffled, and at last my work be imperfect'. However much he might hope that his 'present attempts would at least lay the foundations of future success', the source of his less than perfect creation lay in the *unnatural* and *secretive* character of his scientific approach. His whole experimental practice seemed to violate nature and natural law:

... with unrelaxed and breathless eagerness, I pursued nature to her hiding places. Who shall conceive the horrors of my secret toil, as I dabbled among the unhallowed damps of the grave, or tortured the living animal to animate the lifeless clay? [...] a resistless, and almost frantic impulse, urged me forward; I seemed to have lost all soul or sensation but for this one pursuit. It was indeed but a passing trance, that only made me feel with renewed acuteness so soon as, the unnatural stimulus ceasing to operate, I had returned to my old habits. I collected bones from charnel houses; and disturbed, with profane fingers, the tremendous secrets of the human frame.[50]

All these activities were conducted in Victor's 'workshop of filthy creation', a 'solitary chamber, or rather cell, at the top of the house'. Victor's original natural magic had been transmuted into a form of demonic magic, less a perversion of religion than of Nature.

Victor confessed that at this stage in his work his eyes had been 'insensible to the charms of nature' and that likewise he had forgotten 'those friends who were so many miles absent'. He therefore moralized retrospectively:

A human being in perfection ought always to preserve a calm and peaceful mind, and never to allow passion or a transitory desire to disturb his tranquillity. I do not think that the pursuit of knowledge is an exception to this rule. If the study to which you apply yourself has a tendency to weaken your affections, and to destroy your taste for those simple pleasures in which no alloy can possibly mix, then that study is certainly unlawful, that is to say, not befitting the human mind. If this rule were always observed; if no man allowed any pursuit whatsoever to interfere with the tranquillity of his domestic affections, Greece had not been enslaved; Caesar would have spared his country; America would have been discovered more gradually and the empires of Mexico and Peru had not been destroyed.[51]

Very soon, however, the first signs of *nemesis* appeared. Victor began to be 'oppressed by a slow fever', and 'became nervous to a most painful degree; a disease that I regretted the more because I had hitherto enjoyed most excellent health, and had always boasted of the firmness of my nerves'. Indeed, we recall that in happier times Victor was supposedly more calm and philosophical than his cousin Elizabeth. But these symptoms were as nothing compared to the succession of nervous disorders that followed his infusion of life into the inanimate body of his unnatural and imperfect creation: 'the beauty of the dream vanished, and breathless horror and disgust filled my heart'.[52]

Initially 'disturbed by the wildest dreams', he was then confined by a nervous fever during which the 'form of the monster on whom I had bestowed existence was for ever before my eyes'. His balance temporarily restored through Clerval's efforts and by the sight of 'a divine spring', he nevertheless remained in a very unstable condition: 'When I was otherwise quite restored to health, the sight of a chemical instrument would renew all the agony of my nervous symptoms'.[53]

Throughout his tale Victor continually contrasted the tranquil face of external Nature, with its Wordsworthian capacity to restore peace and stability to the troubled human mind, and the underlying powers of that Nature which, in their intensity and in their capacity to produce instability, mirrored the dark, disturbing forces within human beings. As he returned to Geneva Victor 'contemplated the lake: the waters were placid; all around was calm.... By degrees the calm and heavenly scene restored me'. Yet the combination of mountain and lake prompted him to question whether the scene was 'to prognosticate peace, or to mock at my unhappiness'.[54]

As night closed around, Victor saw only 'a vast and dim scene of evil' and 'foresaw obscurely that I was destined to become the most wretched of human beings'. An electric storm of increasing violence 'appeared at once in various parts of the heavens', presaging Victor's first encounter with his creature since the fateful night: 'A flash of lightning illuminated the object, and discovered its shape plainly to me; its gigantic stature, and the deformity of its aspect, more hideous than belongs to humanity, instantly informed me that it was the wretch, the filthy deamon to whom I had given life'.[55] Victor's dark passion for natural philosophy had created this being. Now Nature herself, with passionate intensity, was angrily displaying to Victor the unnatural product of his perverted genius.

The creature, embodiment of the genius of natural philosophy, mirrored the personality of his creator with its qualities of intense passion and power. Thus with respect to the impossibility of pursuing the suspected murderer of his brother William, first casualty of the creature's revenge on its creator and on the unjust human society that had rejected him, Victor admitted that 'one might as well try to overtake the winds, or confine a mountain-stream with a straw'.[56]

Similarly, Victor described the approach to the valley of Chamounix: 'we beheld immense mountains and precipices overhanging us on every side, and heard the sound of the river raging among rocks, and the dashing of waterfalls around'. Towering over this display of Nature's passionate intensity, the Alpine pyramids and domes belonged 'to another earth, the habitations of another race of beings'. Significantly, it was within these unearthly regions that the creature had taken up habitation and from which it threatened to unleash 'the whirlwinds of its rage' upon Victor, his family and all mankind. Much later, a wind rising 'with great violence in the west', accompanied by 'restless waves' on the lake and then a sudden 'heavy storm of rain', heralded the murder of Elizabeth at the hands of Victor's creation.[57]

In contrast, the creature himself would recall an earlier stage in his existence when the coming of spring had given him new hope: 'Happy, happy earth! fit habitation for gods, which, so short a time before, was bleak, damp, and unwholesome. My spirits were elevated by the enchanting appearance of nature ... the present was tranquil'. But the creature could find no place in this natural order, this Garden of Eden:

> Like Adam, I was created apparently united by no link to any other being in existence.... [But Adam] had come forth from the hands of God a perfect creature, happy and prosperous, guarded by the especial care of his Creator; he was allowed to converse with, and acquire knowledge from beings of a superior nature: but I was wretched, helpless, alone.... God in pity made man beautiful and alluring, after his own image; but my form is a filthy type of yours, more horrid from its very resemblance. Satan had his companions, fellow-devils, to admire and encourage him; but I am solitary and detested ... no Eve soothed my sorrows, or shared my thoughts; I was alone.[58]

Discovering that 'the unnatural hideousness' of his person was the 'chief object of horror' to human beings, he became 'an outcast in the world for ever'. The creature, 'miserable and the abandoned', was 'an abortion, to be spurned at, and kicked, and trampled on'. He therefore 'declared everlasting war against the [human] species, and, more than all, against him who had formed me, and sent me forth to this insupportable misery'. He soon identified with the violent and discordant powers of Nature, the deeper, darker and secret Nature that destroyed rational and stable order:

> As the night advanced, a fierce wind arose from the woods, and quickly dispersed the clouds that had loitered in the heavens: the blast tore along like a mighty avalanche, and produced a kind of insanity in my spirits, that burst all bounds of reason and

reflection. I lighted the dry branch of a tree, and danced with fury around the devoted cottage, my eyes still fixed on the western horizon, the edge of which the moon nearly touched. A part of its orb was at length hid, and I waved my brand; it sunk, and, with a loud scream, I fired the straw.... The wind fanned the fire, and the cottage was quickly enveloped by the flames, which clung to it, and licked it with their forked and destroying tongues.[59]

The creature had indeed become a fiend. This ritual was akin to demonic magic, destroying the cottage, that symbol of human tranquillity and harmony with nature. Although his heart had been 'fashioned to be susceptible of love and sympathy', the misery brought about by rejection and injustice produced the creature's desire for evil: 'The completion of my demoniacal design became an insatiable passion' which would only end with the death of Victor Frankenstein.[60] That death represented the conclusion to Victor's nightmare journey from the 'Enlightenment' stability of his Genevese childhood to the 'Romantic' instability of Ingolstadt and after.

Following the deaths of William and Justine, Elizabeth 'often conversed of the inconstancy of fortune, and the instability of human life'. She simultaneously renounced all belief in Enlightenment optimism regarding the progress and perfectibility of man and society: 'I no longer see the world and its works as they before appeared to me. Before [Justine's death], I looked upon the accounts of vice and injustice ... as tales of ancient days, or imaginary evils ... but now misery has come home, and men appear to me as monsters thirsting for each other's blood'.[61] But it was Victor himself who would embody most vividly the shift from stability to instability.

Once again, Victor's journey towards increasing mental instability often contrasted with Nature's tranquillity: 'I [was] the only unquiet thing that wandered restless in a scene so beautiful and heavenly ... often, I say, I was tempted to plunge into the silent lake, that the waters might close over me and my calamities for ever'. Initially diverted from all such easy options by the commitment to create a companion for his creature in return for the creature's promise to leave humanity in peace, Victor was nonetheless haunted by the potential for even greater discord and misery. As he asked Walton; 'Can you wonder, that sometimes a kind of insanity possessed me, or that I saw continually about me a multitude of filthy animals inflicting on me incessant torture, that often extorted screams and bitter groans'.[62]

Setting up his laboratory on one of the remotest parts of the Orkney Islands, Victor no longer had the consolation of Switzerland's tranquil lakes: 'Its fair lakes reflect a blue and gentle sky; and, when troubled by the winds, their tumult is but as the play of a lively infant, when compared to the roarings of the giant ocean'. The ocean also acted as almost 'an insuperable barrier between me and my fellow-creatures'. In this mood of desolation Victor 'thought with a sensation of madness on my promise of creating another like him, and, trembling with passion, tore to pieces the thing on which I was engaged'.[63] From then on, creator and creature were locked in mortal combat.

Victor's continuing slide from stability to instability was hastened by his fear of being designated mad by society: 'I had a feeling that I should be supposed mad, and this for ever chained my tongue, when I would have given the whole world to have confided the fatal secret'.[64] Unable therefore to call upon human assistance, he attempted to enlist unearthly powers in a crusade against his creature:

> By the sacred earth on which I kneel ... I swear; and by thee, O
> Night, and by the spirits that preside over thee, I swear to pursue
> the daemon.... And I call on you, spirits of the dead; and on you,
> wandering ministers of vengeance, to aid and conduct me in my
> work. Let the cursed and hellish monster drink deep of agony; let
> him feel the despair that now torments me.[65]

But such rituals of demonic magic, together with his passionate denials of insanity, served only to reinforce a sense of instability. 'I am not mad', he told his father as he called the sun and the heavens to testify to his past deeds. 'I am the assassin of those most innocent victims; they died by my machinations'. Unable to find lasting tranquillity of mind, Victor himself ultimately admitted that soon 'a real insanity possessed me'.[66]

Just prior to commencing his story, Frankenstein had told Walton that he believed 'the strange incidents connected with it will afford a view of nature, which may enlarge your faculties and understanding'. Through that story Mary Shelley expressed in prose fiction a dramatic shift from late eighteenth-century Enlightenment philosophies of Nature, society and man that emphasized Nature's balance, stability and perfection, to early nineteenth-century Romantic perspectives that probed beneath the tranquil face of Nature and man to confront the dark and passionate powers therein. By the close of the story Walton could thus summarize the condition of Frankenstein, the modern Prometheus, as that of one who sometimes

> commanded his countenance and tones, and related the most
> horrible incidents with a tranquil voice, suppressing every mark
> of agitation; then, like a volcano bursting forth, his face would
> suddenly change to an expression of the wildest rage, as he
> shrieked out imprecations on his persecutor.[67]

For his part Walton had introduced Frankenstein's tale with reference to his own polar voyage to a 'country of eternal light', whereby he might benefit mankind by finding 'in those undiscovered solitudes' and 'unexplored regions' a North-west passage to the Pacific or by 'ascertaining the secret of the magnet'. Clerval also, in obtaining his father's permission to have leave of absence from bookkeeping to visit Ingolstadt, spoke of 'a voyage of discovery to the land of knowledge'.[68] Victor's story, then, was a voyage of discovery that imaginatively explored the mysterious and dark side of Nature and man, especially in relation to an individual's quest for god-like power and knowledge through natural philosophy. As the scientific knowledge of the nineteenth and twentieth centuries gained power and credibility, can we wonder that the story of *Frankenstein* assumed mythic status?

NOTES

I am especially grateful to Ludmilla Jordanova, Ian Higginson, Michael Neal and Michael Griffiths for their comments and assistance during the drafting of this essay. I must also acknowledge a debt to undergraduates at the University of Kent, too numerous to mention individually, who have participated in discussions on *Frankenstein* in my Humanities course 'Literature and Science'.

1. M. W. Shelley, *Frankenstein or The Modern Prometheus. The 1818 Text*, ed., with introduction and notes, Marilyn Butler (London, 1993), p. 34 (references below are to Shelley, *The 1818 Text*).
2. J. B. Porta, *Natural Magick*, ed. D. J. Price (New York, 1957), pp. 3–4. First published as *Natural Magick by John Baptista Porta, a Neapolitane: in Twenty Books ... Wherein are Set Forth All the Riches and Delights of the Natural Sciences* (London, 1658).
3. Shelley, *The 1818 Text*, p. 192.
4. Marilyn Butler in Shelley, *The 1818 Text*, pp. 199–201 (Appendix A).
5. Shelley, *The 1818 Text*, p. 38.
6. Mario Praz, 'Introductory Essay', in *Three Gothic Novels*, ed. Peter Fairclough (Harmondsworth, 1968), pp. 25–7.
7. See J. A. Secord, 'Extraordinary Experiment: Electricity and the Creation of Life in Victorian England', in *The Uses of Experiment*, ed. David Gooding et al. (Cambridge, 1989), pp. 337–83. This stimulating paper examines in the historical context of British science of the 1830s the claims of Andrew Crosse, an eccentric English experimentalist, to have created life in his private laboratory. Located outside the legitimate boundaries set by the British Association for the Advancement of Science, Crosse's 'extraordinary' practices invite comparison with Mary Shelley's earlier positioning of Victor Frankenstein as an isolated genius working well beyond orthodox science.
8. Crosbie Smith, 'From Design to Dissolution: Thomas Chalmers' Debt to John Robison', *British Journal for the History of Science*, XII (1979), pp. 59–70 (on natural history, natural philosophy and natural theology); J. H. Brooke, *Science and Religion: Some Historical Perspectives* (Cambridge, 1991), pp. 191–225 (on the fortunes and functions of natural theology in the early nineteenth century).
9. T.L. Hankins, *Science and the Enlightenment* (Cambridge, 1985), pp. 3–7 (on Reason and natural law); Richard Kieckhefer, *Magic in the Middle Ages* (Cambridge, 1989), p. 9 (on natural magic as a science of hidden powers).
10. M. N. Wise (with the collaboration of Crosbie Smith), 'Work and Waste: Political

Economy and Natural Philosophy in Nineteenth-century Britain (1)', *History of Science*, XXVII (1989), pp. 263–301 (pp. 266–8).

11. Ibid., pp. 268–75.

12. Ibid., pp. 272–5, 288.

13. John Locke, *Of Civil Government* (1690), cited in Gerd Buchdahl, *The Image of Newton and Locke in the Age of Reason* (London, 1961), pp. 91–2.

14. Wise (with Smith), *op. cit.*, pp. 278, 281–2.

15. Shelley, *The 1818 Text*, pp. 17, 46.

16. Ibid., pp. 17–19.

17. Ibid., p. 19.

18. Ibid., p. 29.

19. Ibid., p. 21.

20. Ibid., p. 25.

21. Ibid., p. 21.

22. Ibid., pp. 21–3, 269–61 (notes 8–9 by Marilyn Butler).

23. Ibid., p. 23. See, especially, 'Alchemy' in *Dictionary of the History of Science*, ed. W. F. Bynum, E. J. Browne and Roy Porter, pp. 9–10 (a summary of alchemical goals and practices); Kieckhefer, *Magic in the Middle Ages*, pp. 133–39 (on alchemy); pp. 151–75 (on demonic magic).

24. Shelley, *The 1818 Text*, pp. 23–4.

25. Cited in Simon Schaffer, 'Natural Philosophy and Public Spectacle in the Eighteenth Century', *History of Science*, XXI (1983), pp. 1–43 (8).

26. Cited in Schaffer, *op. cit.*, p. 9.

27. Shelley, *The 1818 Text*, p. 24.

28. Ibid., p. 26.

29. Ibid., p. 27.

30. Ibid., p. 28.

31. Ibid.

32. Ibid., pp. 28–9.

33. Schaffer, *op. cit.*, pp. 9–15.

34. Hankins, *op. cit.*, pp. 7–8.

35. Shelley, *The 1818 Text*, p. 30.

36. Ibid., pp. 30–31. See, especially, C. E. Perrin, 'The Chemical Revolution', in *Companion to the History of Modern Science*, ed. R. C. Olby, G. N. Cantor, J. R. R. Christie and M. J. S. Hodge (London, 1990), pp. 264–77.

37. Schaffer, *op. cit.*, pp. 28–9.

38. Ibid., pp. 6–15 (on electricity); pp. 15–21 (on earthquake imitation).

39. Ibid., p. 21; Shelley, *The 1818 Text*, p. 31.

40. Simon Schaffer, 'Genius in Romantic Natural Philosophy', in *Romanticism and the Sciences*, ed. A. Cunningham and N. Jardine (Cambridge, 1990), pp. 82–98 (82–3).

41. Shelley, *The 1818 Text*, pp. 11, 30–31.

42. Ibid., pp. 31–2.

43. Ibid., pp. 32–3, 186.

44. Ibid., pp. 33–4.

45. Ibid.

46. Ibid., p. 35.

47. Ibid.

48. Ibid., pp. 99–100. On Condorcet, see Hankins, *op. cit.*, pp. 188–90. On radical political contexts for Mary Shelley, see Lee Sterrenburg, 'Mary Shelley's Monster: Politics and Psyche in *Frankenstein*', in *The Endurance of Frankenstein*, ed. G. Levine and U. C. Knoepflmacher (Berkeley, 1979), pp. 143–71.

49. Shelley, *The 1818 Text*, p. 7.
50. Ibid., pp. 35–6.
51. Ibid., p. 37.
52. Ibid., pp. 37–9.
53. Ibid., pp. 39–44, 48.
54. Ibid., p. 55.
55. Ibid., pp. 55–7.
56. Ibid., p. 59.
57. Ibid., pp. 74–81, 170–71.
58. Ibid., pp. 95, 108–10.
59. Ibid., pp. 111, 115, 196, 117.
60. Ibid., pp. 194–5.
61. Ibid., p. 73.
62. Ibid., pp. 72, 127.
63. Ibid.,pp. 142–4.
64. Ibid., p. 162.
65. Ibid., p. 178.
66. Ibid., pp. 162, 166.
67. Ibid., pp. 116, 185.
68. Ibid., pp. 4, 9, 12, 41. British public enthusiasm for the search for a North-west passage linking the Atlantic and the Pacific was rekindled in 1817 when the whaling captain William Scoresby reported finding whales in the Atlantic with harpoons of a type characteristic of Pacific whalers embedded in them. A year later Captain John Ross led two ships on a scientific expedition that made extensive measurements of terrestrial magnetism in Arctic regions. But they failed to find a North-west passage. See Brendan Lehane, *The North-West Passage* (Amsterdam, 1981), especially pp. 94–100.

DEBRA E. BEST

The Monster in the Family: a reconsideration of Frankenstein's domestic relationships

ABSTRACT   Reading *Frankenstein* not as Gothic fiction but as a domestic novel, it is argued that Mary Shelley was, even at this early point in her career, concerned with the complex workings of the English middle-class family, which blurred the boundaries of gender, family, and social roles. The radical instability and multiplicity of family roles, it is argued, tempts Victor to stabilize domesticity by actually creating a relative. The creature, ironically, becomes the embodiment of the family's multivalence and its potential destruction. Moreover, the reader's and the author's relationship to the novel, developed through a multivalent narrative structure and language, recapitulates Victor's unstable relationship to family. Mary Shelley thus expresses her own concerns with language's potential failure to create meaning, with her abilities as an author, with self-definition, and with her relationships to both her family and her creation, the novel itself.

Most readers are unlikely to remember that the seven years prior to *Frankenstein*'s publication in 1818 also saw the publication of all Jane Austen's novels. Traditionally, *Frankenstein* has been viewed as science fiction or as Gothic, and we see Mary Shelley in the company of William Godwin, Percy Shelley, and Lord Byron, not to mention Mary Wollstonecraft's memory. But we might just as easily picture her surrounded by the domestic novels popularized during her time. Although her book lists and journals do not

From *All the World's a Stage: Dramatic Sensibility in Mary Shelley's Novels.* © 2002 by Routledge.

mention Austen, they do reveal that in the years before and during *Frankenstein*'s composition, Mary Shelley had read Maria Edgeworth, Charlotte Smith, and Samuel Richardson, with *Clarissa* listed three times during this period. In addition, since some journal notebooks are lost, she may also have read novels we do not know about.[1] Considering Mary Shelley in the company of these domestic novelists, and *Frankenstein* in the context of her long literary career, I shall argue that *Frankenstein*, like many of Mary Shelley's works, is very much concerned with the search for and the definition of family, critiquing and questioning both the ideal and the demographics of the nineteenth-century English middle-class family. In particular, Mary Shelley interrogates the fragile combinations and recombinations resulting from the period's typically large extended families.

It might seem strange to call *Frankenstein* a "domestic novel", particularly if one defines the genre in terms of romantic relationships; *Frankenstein* certainly does not focus on Victor's courtship of Elizabeth. But the domestic novel typically concerns a much broader web of relations within and between families. In this light, Victor's family, the DeLaceys, Walton and Margaret, and the orphaned creature all assume increased importance (as do *Frankenstein*'s often ignored early chapters), and Victor becomes a well-developed character in himself as opposed to one psychological function playing his part in a psychomachia, as is commonly argued.[2]

Mary Shelley demonstrates her concern with domestic relationships more obviously in her later novels. The entire third part of *The Last Man* involves the gradual loss of family and friends, reenacting Victor's loss of his family. As Anne K. Mellor argues, *Lodore* and *Falkner* "assert Mary Shelley's conviction that a woman finds her greatest fulfillment within the family."[3] One might reasonably expect that some of this concern with family might also surface as early as *Frankenstein*. This is evident in the preface to the 1818 edition, in which Mary Shelley states that "my chief concern [with morals] has been limited to ... the exhibition of the amiableness of *domestic affection*, and the excellence of universal virtue",[4] echoing the importance of "domestic affections" described in Mary Wollstonecraft's *A Vindication of the Rights of Woman*, which she also had read during *Frankenstein*'s composition.[5]

For the most part, *Frankenstein* scholarship does not consider the family as a whole. When it considers the domestic space at all, it is usually in terms of the Gothic elements of doppelgängers, incest, and Oedipal relations. Ellen Moers, for example, provides a biographical account of the monster's creation, arguing that Mary Shelley "transform[s] the standard Romantic matter of incest, infanticide, and patricide into a phantasmagoria of the nursery".[6] Janet Todd observes that Mary Shelley develops Wollstonecraft's concern with exclusion from society and family. But Todd, Mellor, and Sandra

M. Gilbert & Susan Gubar, among others, focus mainly on mother–child relationships: between Mary Shelley and Mary Wollstonecraft, between Victor and Caroline Frankenstein, and between Victor and the monster.

Several readers do, however, observe that Mary Shelley critiques the bourgeois family. Furthering Gilbert & Gubar's statement that *Frankenstein* shows women's alienation from male society, Mellor, Katherine Ellis, and Johanna M. Smith state that Mary Shelley reveals the potential damage which can result from the bourgeois family's typical separation of the masculine public sphere and the feminine domestic sphere.[7] Such readings are notable for observing Mary Shelley's concern with the middle-class family and for pointing out the division within those families. But critics have yet to account for the complex roles male characters play in the novel's domestic space. If we examine the workings of all domestic roles, we find that *Frankenstein* interrogates multivalent domestic relationships between characters of varying gender in order to suggest that these large extended households generate a sense of uncertainty and a longing for a stable family.

VICTOR'S DOMESTIC RELATIONSHIPS AND THE NINETEENTH-CENTURY FAMILY

With Victor Frankenstein's family, Mary Shelley transfers the demographics of the typical early nineteenth-century English middle-class family to a Swiss setting in order to explore the potential for conflict within these typically large extended families. According to Leonore Davidoff & Catherine Hall, in *Family Fortunes*, "Inclusion of relationships further from the nuclear core helped to create the dense network which gave security to individuals". Each family member would assume several roles so that multiple bonds strengthened family ties.[8] In portraying Victor's family, however, Mary Shelley exaggerates the multiplicity until the roles themselves conflict and thus create confusion concerning one's proper role. As a result, the roles not only fail to provide Victor a sense of security, but they also lead the family to violate social and familial taboos. With Elizabeth, for example, Mary Shelley juxtaposes cousin, sister, mother, and wife so that elements of incest become apparent. According to Davidoff & Hall, families frequently adopted cousins or orphaned children of close friends, as the Frankensteins do Elizabeth, and step siblings, such as Elizabeth and Victor, often married. Moreover, in preparation for the day when she would look after her own family, a daughter such as Elizabeth or even Justine would assume motherly duties, particularly if the mother died, which was fairly common given the high mortality rate during childbirth.[9] One might not expect, however, one person to assume all of these roles, but Elizabeth does. Victor thus becomes engaged to his cousin/sister/mother, an incestuous problem which Mary Shelley certainly knew, as she presented the issue in depth in Matilda, just a few years later.

In Justine, too, Mary Shelley exaggerates multiplicity, as the roles of sister and mother conflict with that of servant. According to Davidoff & Hall, despite dictates against it, servants commonly nursed children, as Justine does William, received Justine's level of education, and might imitate the manner of the family they represented. Nevertheless, the distinction between family relation and servant remained.[10] In *Frankenstein*, however, Justine's "endeavour[s] to imitate [Caroline Frankenstein's] phraseology and manners" (p. 81) go beyond the mere imitation of the family's manner, suggesting the breakdown of class distinctions. Unlike Justine, a servant would never be considered as a sister or mother, but the Frankenstein family adopts Justine and loves and esteems her as a sister, just as it does Elizabeth (p. 81). She serves as a "continual remind[er]" of the mother (p. 61), and acts towards William "like a most affectionate mother" (p. 80). Mary Shelley does explain that "a servant in Geneva does not mean the same thing as a servant in France and England", that the condition "does not include the idea of ignorance, and a sacrifice of the dignity of a human being" (p. 60), but the rest of the Frankenstein family does conform to English demographics, and kindness towards a servant does not mean that she joins the family. Mary Shelley reminds us of that fact as soon as Justine is accused of William's murder. The society and the family, except for Victor and Elizabeth, then dismiss this "sister" as a servant and see her inferior status as the motive for the crime. Lake Elizabeth, Justine fulfills all her potential roles to such a degree that they come into conflict, but here Mary Shelley shows not the potential for incest, but the potential for class distinctions to blur as servants begin to fulfill familial roles.

In Victor's relationships with his brothers, Mary Shelley depicts a multiplicity which crosses gender boundaries, so that Victor fulfills socially inappropriate roles. According to Davidoff & Hall, "the emphasis on certain relationships and their close association with stereotyped gender characteristics provided a stable framework".[11] Yet, when Victor helps nurse the ill William, he fulfills a duty which fell primarily upon the mother, and when he educates Ernest and William at a young age, he again assumes a feminine role, since a father did not educate his son until he became older. Appropriately, Victor enters the medical profession, which had a close relationship to women, nursing children and acting as advisors during childbirth.[12] Gilbert & Gubar, Susan Winnett, and Anne Mellor, among others, recognize Victor's feminine characteristics when they observe that he "gives birth" to the creature. Colleen Hobbs goes so far as to describe Victor's feminine hysteria.[13]

Mary Shelley was aware of issues of transvestitism, depicting them more obviously in other works. In *The Last Man*, for example, Evadne disguises herself as a man in order to be near Raymond. In "A Tale of the Passions", Ricciardo is actually the female Despina. Mary Shelley, moreover, would later help arrange the "elopement" of Isabel Robinson and Mary Diana Dods, disguised as "Mr Sholto Douglas".[14] In *Frankenstein*, Victor assumes not the mother's clothes but her duties. The multiple domestic roles of brother and mother thus transgress social boundaries, and as a result, the "stable framework" ordinarily provided by the bonds does not exist.

Clerval also fulfills inappropriate roles, but in this case Mary Shelley suggests how the transgression affects other families and the roles of other family members. Clerval's absorption into the Frankenstein household as friend and brother conforms to the demographics, but he also at times acts as Victor's father and son, roles which peers the same age did not ordinarily adopt.[15] Victor refers to him as "my friend, my benefactor" (p. 174), the latter term invoking the father's duty towards his children. Victor, moreover, conceals from Clerval "those feelings that overpowered me", just as he does from Alphonse both after Caroline's funeral and prior to the wedding (p. 92; cf. p. 156). These father/son roles also reverse, with Victor acting as benefactor, following Clerval "as his shadow, to protect him from the fancied rage of his destroyer" (p. 160). If Clerval thus acts as friend, brother, father, and son in Victor's family, then one must ask, who is performing his duties in his own family? Although Clerval's position does not cause conflict in the Frankenstein household, it must disrupt his own domestic circle.

Clerval's inappropriate role as Victor's father also suggests that Alphonse Frankenstein, the only living character with a single role, does not perform his primary duties. Mary Shelley's depiction of Victor's father shows the seeds of her complaints that English family affections focus on the husband and wife, which she develops further in *Rambles in Germany and Italy* when she mounts an attack against English policies of primogeniture: "Our affections and domestic duties begin and end there—with the exception of those exercised by the parents towards their *very young* children".[16] In *Frankenstein*, Alphonse has not fulfilled his duties since Caroline's death and the children's maturation. Fathers did nurse sick children, especially when the mother was absent, yet Alphonse waits nearly 2 months before visiting Victor when he becomes ill after Clerval's death. The father's primary duty was "as protector and guide", and he was expected to advise the boy beginning his career and to take him into his own business or settle him elsewhere.[17] Yet Ernest becomes a farmer, and Victor becomes a doctor. In addition, when Victor converses with Alphonse about his interests in alchemy, Alphonse simply dismisses the study.[18]

Mary Shelley, moreover, uses the relationship between Victor's parents to emphasize the potential for incest, which she introduces with Victor and Elizabeth's relationship. When Caroline's father dies, Alphonse takes his place and arranges for her protection, and then marries her 2 years later. Although a man often became either the father or the husband of his friend's daughter, he did not generally do both. In assuming the two roles, Alphonse in essence marries his own daughter. As Victor relates the history of his parents' relationship, he demonstrates his knowledge of its multiplicity; that is, on some level, he recognizes that Alphonse acts as Caroline's husband, friend, and father, and this realization would have enhanced his sense of multivalence, particularly with respect to Alphonse and Elizabeth.

In addition, Mary Shelley makes the parents ultimately responsible for the family's conflicted multiplicity, since they instigate much of its structure. They inappropriately bring Clerval into the family circle, even though he already has a family. They adopt both Elizabeth and Justine, yet make only the latter a "servant", whom Alphonse abandons when she most needs familial support. Furthermore, when Caroline brings Elizabeth into the family, she "gives" her to Victor, and, in her dying request, she simultaneously refers to her in all four of her roles: "My *children* ... my firmest hopes of future happiness were placed on the prospect of your *union*. This expectation will now be the consolation of your father. Elizabeth, my love, you must supply *my place* to your younger *cousins* (p. 38, emphasis added). After identifying Victor and Elizabeth as her "children", as brother and sister, she requests their marriage, while also assigning Elizabeth the role of mother and emphasizing her position as cousin. The father also encourages Elizabeth, as well as Justine, to assume the mother's role, and he does not fulfill his own duties, leading Clerval to assume the role of father. Victor suggests his parent's culpability in the 1831 edition when he says, "I was ... their child ... whose future lot it was in their hands to direct to happiness or misery, according as they *fulfilled their duties* towards me" (p. 234, emphasis added). Victor's "future lot" is one of misery.

Throughout the novel, Mary Shelley suggests the perplexity that these multiple relations cause Victor. It clearly emerges, for example, in the dream after the monster's creation:

> I thought I saw Elizabeth, in the bloom of health, walking in the streets of Ingolstadt. Delighted and surprised, I embraced her; but as I imprinted the first kiss on her lips, they became livid with the hue of death; her features appeared to change, and I thought that I held the corpse of my dead mother in my arms. (p. 53)

Elizabeth fades into the corpse of the mother, reflecting Victor's inability to sort out the multiple roles and accept Elizabeth in one (that of lover) without her slipping into another (that of mother). In addition, the dream equates the mother and Elizabeth with death, the most intense sign of life's ultimate uncertainty.

This perplexity persists even when Victor should be most certain about a relationship—when he commits himself to marriage. He tells his father to set the wedding date, saying, "On it I will consecrate myself, in life or death, to the happiness of my cousin" (pp. 187–188); notice, he does not say, "to the happiness of my wife". Victor responds to the marriage with contradictory emotions, at first saying, "My future hopes and prospects are entirely bound up in the expectation of our union", remarking immediately afterwards, "To me the idea of an immediate union with my cousin was one of horror and dismay" (pp. 148–149). The wedding night is "dreadful, very dreadful" (p. 192), not only because of the monster's impending visit but also because it means the consummation of a multivalent and potentially incestuous relationship. Will Victor be sleeping with his wife, his sister, his cousin, or his mother?

Through Victor Frankenstein's family, Mary Shelley thus examines the potentially destructive aspects of the multiple relations in early nineteenth-century English families. Rather than creating a complex network of bonds to pull the family together, Victor's domestic relationships create confusion concerning one's proper role in the family, while also leading one towards social and familial taboos, such as incest and gender transgression. Rather than "defusing potential conflict from intense intra-family attachments" as a family should, Victor's family binds everyone so closely together that it self-destructs.

THE DELACEYS AND THE SEARCH FOR FAMILY

At the center of the novel's narration, Mary Shelley places the DeLaceys as a counterpoint to Victor's family, showing how a family is supposed to function. Although French in origin and living in Germany, the DeLaceys represent the typical but idealized family demographics for nineteenth-century England. Anne Mellor calls them "'an alternative ideology': a vision of a social group based on justice, equality, and mutual affection".[19] The creature emphasizes their identity as a family by describing the roles each person plays: "The youth and his companion had each of them several names, but the old man had only one, which was *father*. The girl was called *sister*, or *Agatha*; and the youth Felix, *brother*, or *son*" (pp. 107–108). He defines each person in terms of his or her relationship to the others. As he details how each person performs his or her duties, it becomes clear that their roles do not conflict, unlike the situation in Victor's family.

By presenting the idealized family only in isolation, Mary Shelley suggests its vulnerability to forces outside the finite domestic unit. Interestingly, Mary Shelley's other idealized family, Lionel's and Adrian's in *The Last Man*, is similarly removed from society and ultimately destroyed, in this case by the intrusion of the plague. The DeLacey family falls because of Safie's father, who refuses to assume a role in their family and transgresses his roles in his own by forming a master/slave relationship with both his wife and his daughter. Yet, although these events cause the DeLaceys' financial ruin and exile, their final destruction does not come until they themselves neglect their social duties. Like Safie's father, they accept the good deeds, as the creature gathers their wood, but they refuse to perform their reciprocal duties and adopt the orphan. When the creature attempts a full integration into the family, they reject him, even though it means abandoning their home. This family's failings and destruction thus reveal the tenuousness of even this family, which, despite the absent mother, represents stability.

At the same time, though, Mary Shelley shows the importance of stable domestic relations. Until they reject him, the DeLaceys provide the creature with some sense of family, while they increase his desire for a relationship such as one of theirs. He asks, "But where were my friends and relations?" (p. 117), and he generalizes about the importance of "all the various relationships which bind one human being to another in mutual bonds" (pp. 116–117). When the DeLaceys leave, they "[break] the only link that held me to the world" (p. 134). They had provided him with a place in the world and a sense that he belonged in it. This certainty departs with them, leaving him hostile because of its absence.

The monster's narrative as a whole describes the search for a stable family such as the DeLaceys. He asks Victor to fulfill his duties and allow him to feel a son's "gratitude" (p. 142), but he does not want a gather" so much as he wants some stable domestic relationship; the request comes as he demands a companion like himself. He also approaches William with this desire in mind, reasoning, "This little creature was unprejudiced ... If, therefore, I could seize him, and educate him as my companion and friend, I should not be so desolate in this peopled earth" (p. 138). When the child's response reveals that he already has a father, "My papa is a Syndic—he is M. Frankenstein" (p. 139), the monster kills William because he denies him the relationship he needs. In search of a motivation behind the murder, readers describe the animosity between Victor and the monster and point to the monster's succeeding line to William: "Frankenstein! you belong then to my enemy—to him towards whom I have sworn eternal revenge" (p. 139).[20] While this motivation is important, one should not disregard the creature's attempt at a relationship, and William's rejection immediately before this line. Although William's acceptance of the monster or Victor's assumption of his parental responsibilities might have prevented the violence, these acts in themselves are not the cause.

The outer narrator, Walton, also searches for a stable relationship, repeating his desire for a friend who will "approve or amend [his] plans" (p. 13) and accept him as he is. Mary Shelley places him, as she does the creature, outside a domestic circle, aware of what a family is, yet unable to find a companion like himself. His only apparent relation, *Mrs* Saville, presumably has her own family circle, which would not include her brother. Furthermore, the relationship that he does have with her has some of the same multivalence as Victor's family. The novel's framework of letters to Margaret subtly reveals that she helped raise Walton, which might be expected of an older sibling, particularly of a daughter after the mother's death. But their relationship transcends expected multiple roles, as it, like Victor and Elizabeth's, contains elements of incest. Walton's second letter ends, "I *love* you very *tenderly*. Remember me with *affection*, should you never hear from me again" (p. 16, emphasis added). A later letter dramatizes Margaret's "anxious wait" for his return: "Oh! my *beloved* sister, the sickening failings of your *heart-felt* expectations are, in prospect, more terrible to me than my own death" (p. 210, emphasis added). Few siblings, particularly married ones, would be so anxious about their separation, and the language of both letters suggests that Walton addresses a lover rather than a sister.[21]

Although *Frankenstein* does not concern the search for a member of the opposite sex, as do most domestic novels, it does concern the search for "a companion like one's self, a theme developed throughout Mary Shelley's works. *Matilda* comments that while an outcast, her father searched for someone "superior or equal to himself [who] could aid him in unfolding his mind". In "Valerius", the title character develops a friendship with Isabel, the one person who understands and can sympathize with his position. In *Valperga*, Castruccio longs for someone to whom he can "pour out his full heart". This theme's most developed statement appears in *Lodore* where FitzHenry "knew, or rather believed, that while we possess one real, devoted, and perfect friend, we cannot be truly miserable".[22] All of these characters, including *Frankenstein*'s three narrators, seek a clear and steady relationship which will provide a sense of stability, certainty, and self-identity.

THE MONSTER AND THE CREATION OF FAMILY

In *Frankenstein*, Mary Shelley has her protagonist search for such a relationship by actually creating another being. Ordinarily, the child of a potentially self-destructive domestic circle such as Victor's might seek clarification by starting his own, but Mary Shelley sets up the family structure such that if Victor marries, he must marry within this same family circle. The mother's death triggers Victor's response because it enhances the multivalence already present by emphasizing the ambiguity of the family's existence, extinguishing the stable mother/son relationship, and increasing Elizabeth's duties as mother. Victor never resolves these feelings because he does not take sufficient time to grieve, to deal with loss and gain. Rather, when he most needs his family's support, he goes to the university and begins his formal studies regarding the causes of life and death.

In the novel's early chapters, Mary Shelley details Victor's childhood, his family situation, and his early studies in order to suggest that the combination of Victor's scientific studies and his desire to relieve the tensions caused by multivalence culminates in the monster's creation. While working, Victor equates his success with certainty, saying after one setback, "Sometimes, on the very brink of certainty, I failed" (p. 49). The creature offers this potential because he represents the clear, stable, domestic relationship which Victor believes absent; he becomes Victor's child. As Mellor argues, Victor Frankenstein is a man who wants to have a baby without a woman: "In his attempt to create a new species, Victor Frankenstein substitutes solitary paternal propagation for sexual reproduction".[23] Sexual *double entendre* and images of birth occur throughout Victor's descriptions of the creation, which he refers to as "labour", "the most gratifying consummation", "the cause of generation and life", and "the summit of my desires" (p. 47). By replacing sex with science Victor avoids both the incestuous relationship with Elizabeth and the unknown relationship with a member of the opposite sex, while he seeks the clear, stable parent/child bond by means that lead to certitude—science as narrowly defined by a "modern Prometheus".

The monster also offers the potential for certainty by enacting Victor's darkest desires and destroying the sources of multivalence in his life, his family and friends. Mary Shelley shows Victor's culpability in the murders by having him identify himself with the monster, who, he says, acts as "the light of my own vampire, my own spirit let loose from the grave and forced to destroy all that was dear to me" (p. 72), because of a survival instinct, because of a need to destroy the sources of multivalence before they destroy him. Furthermore, the murderer's method reflects the desire for stable human relationships. Victor wishes to keep his family and friends in one position with respect to himself, so each person dies because of too strong a hold around the neck. The neck also contains the organs of speech, which utter the defining terms of "son", "brother", and "friend".

Mary Shelley orders the murders so that they reflect the family's degrees of multivalence. William, the first victim, only plays two roles in Victor's life, brother and son. Justine has three roles: servant, sister, and mother. The final two victims, Clerval and Elizabeth, each play four roles, with Elizabeth's being the most intimate. The multivalence's potential to destroy the family also increases with each victim. Victor's relationship with William suggests the potential for gender roles to cross, which might deviate from social norms, but would not necessarily lead to the family's disintegration. Justine represents the possibility of class distinctions blurring, which might destroy the family's self-definition as middle class, but would not necessarily explode the domestic unit. Clerval fulfills inappropriate roles, which in itself would not harm the Frankenstein household, since the roles are at least fulfilled, yet his transgression might disrupt another family. Victor's relationship with Elizabeth, on the other hand, suggests both incest and Oedipal desires for the mother, both of which do have the potential to ruin the family. This destruction would culminate with its members no longer fulfilling their duties, just as Victor's father does not. As William Veeder has pointed out, the victim's primary roles in Victor's life proceed from "a tie with a child, then with a peer, then with the closest male peer, then with the still closer female peer", and then, I might add, with the parent. Veeder says that the progression culminates with "the ultimate bond with the father", but I do not think that Mary Shelley would place the father's role above the mother's, since *Frankenstein*, *Lodore*, and *Falkner*, among other works, specifically explore the effects of absent mothers.[24] Regardless, as the relationships become closer, the potential for disaster increases.

Ironically, the sequence also establishes the family order, with the parents' deaths occurring at the beginning and end, echoing their positions at each end of the domestic unit, with their bond holding together all the sibling relationships. Emphasizing this placement, "Alphonse", as Veeder points out, has an etymological connection with "alpha", signifying the beginning.[25] Furthermore, the sequence alternates between mother-figure and father-figure, reflecting the parents' role in establishing the multivalent relationships which the sequence now obliterates.

Victor's brother Ernest survives the attacks largely because he is 16. In *Falkner*, Mary Shelley suggests the age's significance: "If a time is to be named when the human heart is nearest moral perfection, most alive and yet most innocent, aspiring to good, without a knowledge of evil, the period at which Elizabeth had arrived,—from thirteen to sixteen,—is it".[26] Since Ernest is "without a knowledge of evil, he lacks knowledge of murder. Since he is "nearest moral perfection", Victor's relationships with him, unlike his others, cannot be morally or socially subversive. By idealizing the age, Mary

Shelley defends her own relationship with Percy Shelley, having eloped at age 16. Perhaps to emphasize Ernest's innocence, she places him in the idealized pastoral role of farmer. In addition, Ernest's age positions him at the border between innocence and sexual maturity and at the cusp of a new kind of social interaction, so Victor may attribute any instabilities in their relationship to Ernest's age. Perhaps most importantly, when Ernest becomes older, his relationship with Victor ceases to transgress social norms. According to Davidoff & Hall, the father assumed responsibility for the older son's education, since it was improper for the mother to discuss sexual matters, and she presumably lacked knowledge of worldly affairs.[27] Hence, although Victor still acts as Ernest's parent, their relationship no longer crosses gender boundaries. The alternation of mothers and fathers thus concludes without the extra male's participation.

The murders also create certainty by allowing Victor to replace these multivalent relationships with his family with stable ones. Mary Shelley shows the family entering Victor's mind, where his imagination forms the relationships he desires: "He believes, that, when in dreams he holds converse with his friends, and derives from that communion consolation for his miseries, or excitements to his vengeance, that they are not the creations of his fancy, but the real beings who visit him from the regions of a remote world" (p. 208). In this passage from the end of the novel, Walton explains how Victor convinces himself that these idealized, imagined beings are real, and they fulfill for him the familial duties of consolation and encouragement. They thus provide Victor with certainty and, Walton's tone implies, strength.

THE MONSTER AND UNCERTAINTY

Mary Shelley brings Victor's attempts at certainty into question by depicting the creature, ironically, as the embodiment of the family's multivalence and its potential destruction. Victor had sought a clear relationship with a creature "like himself". The mirror, shadow, or double, however, may be seen either as an exact reflection of oneself or as the exact opposite in which everything is reversed.[28] Hence, although Victor attempts to make him "after his own image", the monster's form is instead "a filthy type of [his], more horrid from its very resemblance" (p. 126). With this reversal, the monster comes to represent the doubts the scientist had hoped to expel. Significantly, his deformed appearance parallels the deformed structure of Victor's family. Each domestic role, when taken by itself, conforms to social expectations and appears "beautiful" and "in proportion", as Victor describes the inanimate creature (pp. 52–53). But taken as a whole, the combination of elements becomes exaggerated, transgressing the conventional bounds of family or human formation. Hence, Victor runs from the newly animated creature, the embodiment of multivalent relationships among human parts, and he never establishes his own relationship with it.

Denied the stable parent/child bond, the creature instead imitates Victor's family and fulfills contradictory roles. This newborn child and Victor reverse their roles, as the creature causes Victor to share his feelings of revenge, hatred, and desolation to such an extent that he "creates" Victor, as living Massey & Peter McInerney have noted.[29] While traveling across the ice, he also performs the parental duty of protecting his "child", "extricat[ing Victor] from seemingly insurmountable difficulties" and leaving provisions behind so that Victor can continue the pursuit (p. 201).

Through the creature, Mary Shelley shows the family destruction that can result from multivalent relationships. Victor's own changing feelings, at first thinking the monster beautiful but then remarking that "the beauty of the dream vanishe[d]" when it became animated (pp. 52–53), parallel the potential disintegration of any relationship. Furthermore, in the creation of life out of death, death and life cease to be clear and distinct, suggesting the small gap between the family's survival and its death. The murders themselves, of course, literally bring the family's survival into question. Finally, when Victor physically experiences the creature's grasp when he is not present, the nature of reality and the imagination become uncertain.

Narrative Structure and the Reader's Uncertainty

Mary Shelley designs *Frankenstein* so that not only Victor and the other narrators experience this uncertainty, but the reader does as well. Multivalence occurs at every level of the novel, from the plot to the language to the narrative structure. Since its first reviews, critics of *Frankenstein* have observed the plot's improbable coincidences and events.[30] Victor lands at the exact spot where the monster left Clerval's body, the monster watches the cottagers for months without detection, and Safie conveniently receives the language instruction from which the monster benefits. Just as each individual domestic role works within Victor's family, but taken all together they result in multivalence and the family's potential destruction, so each event in the novel works by itself but taken together they result in coincidences and the plot's potential explosion. Readers have also complained that Mary Shelley does not distinguish the novel's characters adequately, but this "problem", again, creates a multivalent relationship among the narrators, who appear to be both separate entities and doppelgängers.

Moreover, throughout the text, Mary Shelley places ambiguous images which duplicate themselves. For example, the creature, the embodiment of multivalence, generally appears in shadows. While working on the female monster, Victor sees "by the light of the moon, the demon at the casement" (p. 163). In the Arctic, he views him when "the night was nearly dark", in the shadows of twilight (p. 199). In the novel's last line, Walton watches the creature disappear against the snowy white horizon, "lost in darkness and distance" (p. 221). Furthermore, beginning immediately after the monster's creation, Victor's dreams duplicate known images so vividly that the relationship between dream and reality become difficult to distinguish.

This multivalence occurs even on the level of language. The creature seems to describe systematically how he learns a language, yet a close examination reveals that he learns French in Germany by reading, presumably translations, of works originally written in English (*Paradise Lost*), Latin (Plutarch's *Lives*), and German (*The Sorrows of Werther*). Furthermore, the creature narrates his words in French, yet we read them, through the English Walton, in English. Even the monster's words directly to Walton appear in English. Again, like the domestic roles, each language by itself presents no difficulties, but when taken together reveal an impossible linguistic relationship.

Similar difficulties appear on the syntactic level of language, as sentences suggest multiple meanings, leading to the possibility of misinterpretation. For example, when Victor says, "My ardour was indeed the astonishment of the students; and my proficiency, that of the masters" (p. 45), one wonders if his "proficiency" is the astonishment of the masters or if it is equal to the proficiency of the masters. Mary Shelley uses similarly ambiguous syntax at times throughout the novel. The multivalent language becomes most apparent with the repeated utterance, "I shall (or will) be with you on your wedding-night". Victor applies the words to himself, forming a personal relationship with them and interpreting them as a foreboding of his own murder, when he should instead apply them to Elizabeth. The multiplicity of meaning becomes such that the sign and the signifier no longer correspond. The meaning explodes with the ramification that Victor's last links to his family disintegrate.

Language's failure to create meaning affects both the family relationships and personal identity. On a linguistic level, the family's multivalence is a conflict between such defining terms as "mother" and "lover" which are necessary to establish both personal identity and a relationship to the community. Mary Shelley fully develops this concept in *Rambles in Germany and Italy*. Her account of Bavaria's atrocities against Tyrol focuses to a large extent on the injunctions to change their language and to erase Tyrol's name from maps. The community in effect unites to preserve the terms which define them as "Tyrolese".[31] In *Frankenstein* the creature's search for a companion like himself is also a search for such defining terms. Noting the creature's difficulties in communicating, Stephen C. Behrendt, Richard J. Dunn, and Peter Brooks have related his isolation to the breakdown of language.[32] Unlike the DeLaceys, he is not "father", "sister", "brother", "son", or even "Agatha" or "Felix". Even the terms of reference, such as "monster", "fiend", and "wretch", do not remain constant, as the creature remains nameless throughout the novel. The dramatis personae for Richard Brinsley Peake's *Presumption* (1823) emphasizes this fact by listing *** in his place.[33] After seeing this play, Mary Shelley commented, "This nameless mode of naming the unnamable is rather good".[34] In *Rambles*, she remarks that "A name is often everything; on me it has a powerful effect",[35] and she communicates this effect in *Frankenstein* where the names themselves have meaning; "Felix", for example, represents "happiness", "Agatha" represents "goodness", and "Sophie" represents "Wisdom".[36] The creature, though, is left asking, "What was I?" (p. 117). Notice that he asks "What" and not "Who was I?" He emphasizes not the name's but the domestic role's absence. Without a domestic role and the terms associated with one, his own existence remains undefined.

Through this plot, imagery, and language, the reader experiences the multivalence which causes Victor to create the monster. Mary Shelley designs a narrative structure which enhances the reader's involvement in the textual ambiguities. Described in terms of "concentric circles" or "Chinese boxes", it moves outward to the reader, who shares Margaret's experience in reading Walton's letters, as well as the experience of each individual listener.[37] Hence, the reader shares Walton's doubts concerning Victor's and the monster's reliability, while also perhaps questioning Walton. The reader thus has a multivalent relationship with the novel, acting as both active participant and passive audience.

As the reader becomes involved in the novel, he or she experiences a world filled with questions and begins to realize that Victor fails because he seeks an impossible world without any multiplicity, a world in which doubts and questions are absent. Just as the reader must revise his or her expectations for the novel and accept its improbabilities and coincidences, Victor must revise and accept his relationships with each family member and the creature. When he does not, his quest for certitude leads to his own self-destruction.

MARY SHELLEY'S RELATIONSHIP TO THE NOVEL

Like the reader, Mary Shelley has dual roles with respect to the novel. She places herself in the positions of both author and reader by having Walton send the story to Margaret Walton Saville, MWS, as Mellor points out.[38] Mary Shelley's multiple definitions of herself further arise with respect to her own name, which at various times appeared as Mary Wollstonecraft Godwin and Mary Godwin Shelley before she settled on Mary Wollstonecraft Shelley.[39] In addition, Percy Shelley and Thomas Hogg referred to her as "Maie", "Pecksie", and "Dormouse", names which Mary Shelley herself used in her letters.[40] Since multivalent domestic relationships lead Victor to create the monster in the hopes of providing himself with clarification, then Mary Shelley perhaps created the novel for a similar reason.

Like Victor's monster, however, the novel instead becomes "my hideous progeny", as her insecurities as an author arise. Mellor suggests that such insecurities led Mary Shelley to accept Percy Shelley's revisions to the text even though he occasionally distorted the meaning or added incongruous passages.[41] Moreover, despite the success of the first edition, Mary Shelley continued to revise the text, producing two later editions in 1823 and 1831. With the latter, she bowed to both her sentiments for Percy Shelley and the sensibilities of a Victorian audience. She, for example, reduced the level of incest by making Elizabeth no longer literally Victor's cousin. To modern readers, such changes have made the text itself ambiguous, as we must decide which edition is *Frankenstein*. Interestingly, the text has continued to change, as screen writers continue to create their own monstrous versions.

Mary Shelley distrusted her own ability to use language. As the novel's language demonstrates, words can carry multiple meanings, be misinterpreted, and often fail to communicate. This multiplicity translates into the creature's lack of a name and Mary Shelley's uncertainty about her own name. Gilbert & Gubar, Ellen Moers, and David Collings, among others, have remarked that without a name, the creature in *Frankenstein* sits on the margins of language, just as Mary Shelley, as a woman, sat on the margins of male conversations.[42] Although this may be true, Mary Shelley's other writings suggest that this marginalization is part of a more universal, non-gender-oriented problem with language—its insufficiency to communicate human thoughts clearly. In "Valerius" both Mary Shelley's narrators complain about language's insufficiency to communicate human thoughts, saying, "Human language sinks under the endeavour to describe the tremendous change operated in the world" and "Why cannot human language express human thoughts? ... the feeling is far too intense for expression".[43] This inadequacy surfaces in *Frankenstein* when the creature is instantaneously rejected even though he speaks well. Stephen C. Behrendt notes that all *Frankenstein*'s major characters repeatedly stress language's inadequacy, with "phrases such as 'I cannot describe to you,' [and] 'It is impossible to communicate' ... (pp. 20–21) echo[ing] in speeches throughout the novel".[44] Words, it seems, often fail one and often cannot overcome appearances.

Committing oneself to writing also can mean opening oneself to public view, something that Mary Shelley knew and wished to avoid after the scandalized response to Godwin's *Memoirs of the Author of the Vindication of the Rights of Women*.[45] Her elopement with Percy Shelley had already made her a social outcast, and she did not wish to worsen the situation. Reflecting her reticence, her journal entries are generally brief, often appearing as no more than a reading list, in large part because servants were known to read such documents and blackmail the writer. Paolo Foggi's later attempt at blackmail certainly lends credence to any such worries that Mary Shelley might have had.

Nevertheless, *Frankenstein*, like all her writings, to some extent commits her domestic relationships to writing. Mary Shelley's family was not multivalent, but it did transgress the demographic norm. The four children in the Godwin household had four different fathers. Living with just Godwin and Fanny for the first 4? years of her life, the sudden addition of Mrs Godwin and her two children must have led to some uncertainty, especially since Mary Shelley did not get along with Mrs Godwin; in her 28 October 1814 journal entry, she remarks, "Mrs. Godwin—she is a woman I shudder to think of".[46] Mary Shelley also knew that the creation of one stable relationship can lead to uncertainties elsewhere. Eloping with Percy Shelley strained her relationships with Godwin, Isabel Baxter Booth, who would not speak to her, and her half-sister Fanny, who, as the mediator between Mary Shelley and Godwin, became both friend and foe. Just as the novel does not concern Victor's relations with just his mother or his father, it also does not reflect Mary Shelley's relations with just Percy Shelley or William Godwin or Mary Wollstonecraft. Rather, it reflects her relationships with her entire family.

FRANKENSTEIN AS DOMESTIC NOVEL

Although Mary Shelley does not focus on romantic relationships in *Frankenstein*, she does explore the workings of domestic relationships, both Victor's and her own. According to Nancy Armstrong, the domestic novel's basic plot concerns the transformation of morally or socially subversive relationships into something acceptable.[47] Victor Frankenstein's domestic relationships are morally or socially subversive, but instead of reforming them, Victor looks elsewhere. In contrast, Safie and Walton transform their relationships. Safie allows herself to depend first upon her mother and then upon Felix and his family. After Victor's death, Walton fulfills his responsibility to his men, and he maintains his relationship with Victor by "creating" the manuscript that preserves his story, much as Mary Shelley, after Shelley's death, edits her husband's works and fictionalizes him in such characters as *The Last Man*'s Adrian. Unlike these relationships and those of other domestic novels, Victor Frankenstein's story is tragic, because he neither transforms his family into one with multiple but not multivalent roles, nor accepts other relationships, particularly that with the creature.

In some respects, *Frankenstein* might best be described as an anti-domestic novel. According to Armstrong, domestic fiction "helped to formulate the ordered space we now recognize as the household, made that space totally functional, and used it as the context for representing normal behavior. In so doing, fiction suppressed alternative bases for human relationships".[48] In *Frankenstein* Mary Shelley shows the results of alternative bases for relationships, for its household space does not function as it should, and she uses it as the context for representing abnormal behavior. But this results not because the household space is disordered so much as because it is ordered in excess; that is, if one takes the domestic household that one finds in what we might ordinarily consider a domestic novel, and orders it to the extreme, such that the relationships become multivalent rather than multiple, then one has the world of *Frankenstein*. The Promethean overreacher in the novel, to draw on its subtitle, is not just Victor Frankenstein, but rather the domestic unit itself.

NOTES

1. Paula R. Feldman & Diana Scott-Kilvert's compilation of the reading lists reveals that between 1814 and Mary Shelley's completion of *Frankenstein* on 14 May 1817, she had read Edgeworth's *Castle Rackreu, an Hibernian Tale* (8 November 1816), Smith's *Letters of a Solitary Wanderer* (15 September 1816), and Richardson's *Clarissa; or the History of a Young Lady* (1815, 20–23 September 1816, 1816), *The History of Sir Charles Grandison* (6–15 November 1816), and *Pamela; or Virtue Rewarded* (20–30 November 1816). The journals do not begin until 1814, and some 1816 journal notebooks are lost. Paula R. Feldman & Diana Scott-Kilvert, "The Shelleys' Reading List", in *The Journals of Mary Shelley, 1814–1844*, ed. Paula Feldman & Diana Scott-Kilvert (Baltimore: Johns Hopkins University Press, 1987), pp. 631–684.

2. Detailed discussions of the doppelgänger in *Frankenstein* include Masao Miyoshi, *The Divided Self: A Perspective on the Literature of the Victorians* (New York: New York University Press, 1969); Morton Kaplan & Robert Moss, "Fantasy of Paternity and the Doppelgänger: Mary Shelley's *Frankenstein*", in *The Unspoken Motive A Guide to Psychoanalytic Literary Criticism* (New York: Free Press, 1973), pp. 119–145; Hartley S. Spatt, "Mary Shelley's Last Men: The Truth of Dreams", *Studies in the Novel*, 7 (1975), pp. 526–537; and Irving Massey, "Singles and Doubles: *Frankenstein*", in *The Gaping Pig: Literature and Metamorphosis* (Berkeley: University of California Press, 1976), pp. 124–137.

3. Anne K. Mellor, *Mary Shelley: Her Life, Her Fiction, Her Monsters* (New York: Methuen, 1988), p. 186.

4. Mary Wollstonecraft Shelley (1818) *Frankenstein or the Modern Prometheus*, ed. James Rieger (Chicago: University of Chicago Press, 1982), p. 7, emphasis added. All subsequent references to *Frankenstein* will refer parenthetically to page numbers from this edition.

In the introduction to the 1831 text of *Frankenstein*, Mary Shelley ascribes these words to her husband, saying, "As far as I can recollect, it was entirely written by him" (p. 229). Johanna M. Smith convincingly argues, however, that Mary Shelley did actually write the Preface: Johanna M. Smith, "'Cooped Up': Feminine Domesticity in *Frankenstein*", in *Mary Shelley: Frankenstein*, ed. Johanna M. Smith (New York: St Martin's, 1992), pp. 270–285.

5. Mary Wollstonecraft (1792) "A Vindication of the Rights of Women", in *Frankenstein: or The Modern Prometheus*, ed. D. L. MacDonald & K. D. Scherf (Detroit: Broadview Press, 1994), p. 258. The reading lists reveal that Mary Shelley read *A Vindication of the Rights of Woman* on 6–9 December 1816: Feldman & Scott-Kilvert, "The Shelleys' Reading List".

6. Ellen Moers, "Female Gothic", in *The Endurance of "Frankenstein"*, ed. George Levine & U. C. Knoepflmacher (Berkeley: University of California Press, 1979), pp. 77–87, p. 87. See also Robert D. Hume, "Gothic Versus Romantic: A Revaluation of the Gothic Novel", *PMLA*, 84 (1969), pp. 282–290; Eve Kosofsky Sedgwick, *The Coherence of Gothic Conventions* (New York: Methuen, 1986); and Lee E. Heller (1992) "*Frankenstein* and the Cultural Uses of Gothic", in Smith, *Mary Shelley: Frankenstein*, pp. 325–341.

For the remaining references in this paragraph, see Janet M. Todd, "Frankenstein's Daughter: Mary Shelley and Mary Wollstonecraft", *Women and Literature*, 4 (1976), pp. 18–27; Anne K. Mellor, "Possessing Nature: The Female in *Frankenstein*", in *Romanticism and Feminism*, ed. Anne K. Mellor (Bloomington: Indiana University Press, 1988), pp. 220–222; Sandra M. Gilbert & Susan Gubar, "Horror's Twin: Mary Shelley's Monstrous Eve", in Sandra M. Gilbert & Susan Gubar, *The Madwoman in the Attic* (New Haven: Yale University Press, 1979), pp. 213–247.

7. Gilbert & Gubar, "Horror's Twin", Mellor, "Possessing Nature"; Mellor, *Mary Shelley*; Katherine Ellis (1979) "Monsters in the Garden: Mary Shelley and the Bourgeois Family", in Levine & Knoepflmacher, *The Endurance of 'Frankenstein'*, pp. 123–142; Johanna M. Smith, "Cooped Up".

8. Leonore Davidoff & Catherine Hall, *Family Fortunes* (Chicago: University of Chicago Press, 1987), pp. 321–322. Unless otherwise stated, all information concerning the demographics of the typical early nineteenth-century English middle-class family is from Davidoff & Hall.

9. Ibid., pp. 322, 329, 342, 353.

10. Ibid., pp. 392–394.

11. Ibid., p. 322.

12. Ibid., pp. 330, 335, 339, 340–341.

13. Gilbert & Gubar, "Horror's Twin"; Susan Winnett, "Coming Unstrung: Women, Men, Narrative, and Principles of Pleasure", *PMLA*, 105 (1990), pp. 505–518; Mellor, "Possessing Nature"; Colleen Hobbs, "Reading the Symptoms: An Exploration of Repression and Hysteria in Mary Shelley's *Frankenstein*", *Studies in the Novel*, 25 (1993), pp. 152–169. See also Barbara Frey Waxman, "Victor Frankenstein's Romantic Fate: The Tragedy of the Promethean Overreacher as Woman", *Papers on Language and Literature*, 23 (1987), pp. 14–26.

14. For a brief account, see Emily W. Sunstein, *Mary Shelley: Romance and Reality*

(Boston: Little, 1989), pp. 280–289. See also Betty T. Bennett, *Mary Diana Dods, a Gentleman and a Scholar* (Baltimore: Johns Hopkins University Press, 1994).

15. Davidoff & Hall, *Family Fortunes*, p. 329.

16. Mary Wollstonecraft Shelley (1844) *Rambles in Germany and Italy, in 1840, 1842, and 1843* (Folcroft, PA: Folcroft Library Editions, 1975), vol. 3, p. 107.

17. Davidoff & Hall, *Family Fortunes*, pp. 330–332.

18. Several critics, most notably William Veeder and Johanna M. Smith, have observed Victor's hostilities towards his father. Smith argues that Victor's conflicts with Alphonse result from him being a "Good Father", and thus enforcing the patriarchy (pp. 278–280). This reading, however, does not explain the places where Alphonse does not fulfill his duties, and it conflicts with Mary Shelley's statements in *Rambles*. See William Veeder, "The Negative Oedipus: Father, Frankenstein, and the Shelleys", *Critical Inquiry*, 12 (1986), pp. 365–387; Smith, "Cooped Up".

19. Mellor, "Possessing Nature", p. 23.

20. See, for example, Martin Tropp, *Mary Shelley's Monster: The Story of "Frankenstein"* (Boston: Houghton, 1976), p. 26; and Veeder, "The Negative Oedipus"; pp. 374, 384.

21. Supporting this reading, Kaplan & Moss and Gilbert & Gubar discuss the elements of incest in Walton and Margaret's relationship: Kaplan & Moss, "Fantasy of Paternity and the Doppelgänger", pp. 134–135; Gilbert & Gubar, "Horror's Twin", p. 228.

22. Mary Wollstonecraft Shelley (1819; pub. 1959) "Matilda", in *The Shelley Reader*, ed. Betty T. Bennett & Charles E. Robinson (New York: Oxford University Press, 1990), p. 177; Mary Wollstonecraft Shelley, *Valperga* (London: Whittaker, 1823), vol. 1, p. 120; and Mary Wollstonecraft Shelley (1835) *Lodore* (Hartford: Silas Andrus, 1846), vol. 1, p. 13.

23. Mellor, *Mary Shelley*, p. 100.

24. Veeder, "The Negative Oedipus", p. 385. Sharon L. Jowell discusses in detail the theme of the absent mother in Mary Shelley's later works: Sharon L. Jowell, "Mary Shelley's Mother's: The Weak, the Absent, and the Silent Mothers in *Lodore* and *Falkner*", *European Romantic Review*, (1997) 8(3), pp. 298–322.

25. Veeder, "The Negative Oedipus", p. 386.

26. Mary Wollstonecraft Shelley, *Falkner* (London: Saunder & Otley, 1837), p. 169.

27. Davidoff & Hall, *Family Fortunes*, p. 341.

28. Jane Gallop's reading of Lacan is particularly useful here: Jane Gallop, *Reading Lacan* (Ithaca: Cornell University Press, 1985), especially p. 59.

29. Massey, "Singles and Doubles: *Frankenstein*", pp. 125, 134; and Peter McInerney, "Frankenstein and the Godlike Science of Letters", *Genre*, 13 (1980), p. 467.

30. See, for example, Sir Walter Scott's review in *Blackwood's Edinburgh Magazine*, 2 (1818), pp. 613–620, which Macdonald & Scherf reprint in their edition of *Frankenstein*.

31. Shelley, *Rambles in Germany and Italy*.

32. Steven C. Behrendt (1990) "Language and Style in *Frankenstein*", in *Approaches to Teaching Shelley's Frankenstein*, ed. Steven C. Behrendt (New York: Modern Language Association of America, 1990), p. 81; Richard J. Dunn, "Narrative Distance in *Frankenstein*", *Studies in the Novel*, 6 (1974), p. 417; and Peter Brooks, "Godlike Science/Unhallowed Arts: Language and Monstrosity in *Frankenstein*," *New Literary History*, 9 (1978), pp. 591–605.

33. Richard Brinsley Peake (1823) "Presumption; or, The Fate of Frankenstein", in *Hideous Progenies: Dramatizations of "Frankenstein" from Mary Shelley to the Present*, ed. Steven Earl Forry (Philadelphia: University of Pennsylvania Press, 1990), pp. 135–160.

34. Shelley to Leigh Hunt, 9 September 1823, in *The Letters of Mary Wollstonecraft Shelley*, ed. Betty T. Bennett (Baltimore: Johns Hopkins University Press, 1980), vol. 1, p. 378.

35. Shelley, *Rambles in Germany and Italy*, p. 174.

36. Mellor, "Possessing Nature", p. 23.

37. See in particular the following early descriptions of the novel's narrative structure: Hirsch, "The Monster Was a Lady"; Gerhard Joseph, "Frankenstein's Dream: The Child as Father of the Monster", *Hartford Studies in Literature*, 7 (1975), pp. 97–115; and Charles Schug, "The Romantic Form of Mary Shelley's *Frankenstein*", *Studies in English Literature, 1500–1900*, 17 (1977), pp. 607–619.

38. Mellor, *Mary Shelley*, p. 54.

39. Although one might expect her to assume her maiden and married names, Mary Shelley never signs herself "Mary Godwin Shelley". Rather, her mother's name always appears in the middle, as she signs herself "Mary W. G." and, after her marriage, "M. W. S."

40. See Bennett, *The Letters of Mary Wollstonecraft Shelley*, vol. 1, p. 10, n. 3.

41. Mellor, *Mary Shelley*, pp. 57–69.

42. Gilbert & Gubar, "Horror's Twin", p. 238; Moers, "Female Gothic"; p. 94; and David Collings (1992) "The Monster and the Imaginary Mother: A Lacanian Reading of Frankenstein" in Smith, *Mary Shelley: Frankenstein*, p. 253.

43. Mary Wollstonecraft Shelley, "Valerius: The Reanimated Roman", in *Collected Tales and Stories*, ed. Charles E. Robinson (Baltimore: Johns Hopkins University Press, 1976), pp. 337, 342.

44. Behrendt, "Language and Style in *Frankenstein*", p. 80.

45. See Sunstein, *Mary Shelley: Romance and Reality*, pp. 19–20 for an account of the public response.

46. Feldman & Scott-Kilvert, *The Journals of Mary Shelley*, p. 40.

47. Nancy Armstrong, *Desire and Domestic Fiction: A Political History of the Novel* (New York: Oxford University Press, 1987), p. 6.

48. Ibid., pp. 23–24.

Character Profile

Volume I is primarily Victor Frankenstein's story. It contains a description of and a reaction to the circumstances of his birth, the history of a happy domestic life, his childhood friends and liberal education at home, and through his experiences at the University at Igolstadt. It is also the story of how a young man becomes obsessed with probing the fundamental secrets of human life, his seduction by obsolete and often discredited scientific writings, his unwavering determination to create life in a laboratory, and the fatal consequences of an unethical experiment with which he must live with for the rest of his life.

The first impression we receive of the monster and his creator, Victor Frankenstein, occurs in Letter IV from Robert Walton on a ship headed to an icy cold hinterland beyond St. Petersburg. Walton reports that his men have first sited a being of gigantic stature on a rapidly moving dog sled on their telescope and, the following morning, the sailors discovered a man, Victor Frankenstein, floating on a large fragment of ice. Curiously, however, the shivering and sickly Frankenstein will not board their vessel until he is told of their destination. Walton records his impression. "His limbs were nearly frozen, and his body dreadfully emaciated by fatigue and suffering. I never saw a man in so wretched a condition." Nevertheless, despite his appearance, Walton describes Frankenstein as a benign man, possessing a sweet disposition, "a celestial spirit, with a halo around him," susceptible to any act of kindness he receives from others. Though unhappy most of the

237

time and preferring solitude during these bouts of sullen humour, he nevertheless displays an interest in others. Once he regains his strength under Walton's care, Frankenstein makes anxious inquiry regarding the creature whom he refers to as "the daemon" and begins to narrate his strange fate to Walton, emphasizing that he is seeking that which has run away from him, and, moreover, that he himself is indeed beyond help.

The actual tale of Victor Frankenstein, whom the reader first encounters as the mysterious stranger stranded at sea, begins with the first chapter. He was born in Geneva to a well-respected family, his father having served admirably in various public functions. His father, Alphonse, is very devoted, having married late in life to Catherine Beaufort, the daughter of a close friend. Frankenstein is brought up in a loving household, enjoying a liberal education. As he explains to Walton, "'[n]o youth could have passed more happily than mine.'" Two close companions are with him all the time, Henry Clerval, the son of his father's merchant friend, and his niece, Elizabeth Lavenza, who is adopted into the household when Frankenstein is four years old. Both parents hope to see Frankenstein married to Elizabeth one day. While his friends are interested in poetry and books of chivalry and romance, Frankenstein becomes immersed "investigating the facts relative to the real world." Indeed, natural philosophy captures his imagination as does thoughts of raising ghosts. He reads the works of various outdated occult and scientific writers, Cornelius Agrippa, Paracelsus and Albertus Magnus. As he readily admits, his greatest dream was to search for the philosopher's stone and elixir of life, and his vision was undeterred by reality.

At the age of seventeen, Victor Frankenstein becomes a student at the university of Ingolstadt, and shortly after his arrival he receives news that his mother has died as a result of nursing Elizabeth through scarlet fever. Thus, Frankenstein begins his studies in a depressed state. Though he feels lonely leaving his friends behind, he immediately becomes immersed in his scientific studies. When Professor Krempe invalidates his previous readings, Frankenstein finds him to be repulsive. "'I was required to exchange chimeras of boundless grandeur for realities of little youth.'" However, he takes an immediate liking to Professor Waldman, a scholar who appreciates the modern scientific masters whose work has the potential for uncovering miracles, while allowing that the philosophers of old made valuable contributions for their time. Waldman becomes his mentor, inviting his student into his laboratory, which contains a variety of machines. From this point on, Frankenstein becomes engaged, heart and soul, in conducting his experiments, so much so that he isolates himself from the rest of the world, neglecting his family and friends back home. Driven by a special curiosity with the structure of the human frame, and principle of life, Frankenstein becomes obsessed with death. "'I became acquainted with the science of anatomy: but this was not sufficient; I must also observe the natural decay and corruption of the human body.'" To this end, he spends days and nights in cemeteries and charnel houses collecting bones and materials he will eventually use in crafting new life. "'I became myself capable of bestowing animation upon lifeless matter.'"

One dreary November night, Frankenstein's experiment comes to fruition and succeeds in generating a new being in his laboratory. It is an ugly creature indeed, a being larger than man, with black lips, yellow eyes, and skin which scarcely covers the muscles and arteries beneath the skin. But this realization of a dream brings terror and revulsion towards that which he has created. "'I had desired it with an ardour that far exceeded moderation; but now that I finished, the beauty of the dream vanished, and breathless horror and disgust filled my heart.'" Frankenstein immediately flees the room, abandoning the monster at the hour of its birth. In so doing, Frankenstein condemns both the monster and himself to a tortured existence that will become progressively worse with each passing day, a never-ending agony which can only be relieved in their mutual demise.

That Frankenstein is destined for unabated misery is made clear when his dear friend Henry Clerval arrives at Ingolstadt to begin his studies. Though he is initially joyful at Clerval's arrival at the university, Frankenstein becomes very nervous when he brings Clerval to his home, fearing that the creature might still be there to greet them. "'I was unable to remain for a single instant in the same place; I jumped over the chairs, clapped my hands, and laughed aloud.'" Frankenstein soon succumbs to a nervous fever, especially since he cannot divulge the terrible secret of what he has done.

The consequences of Frankenstein having banished the monster is first manifested in the death of his younger brother, William. When a miniature portrait of Caroline Frankenstein, that William used to carry, is found on Justine Moritz, the latter is accused of murder. Frankenstein cannot believe that she is capable of committing such a crime. Nevertheless, the evidence is incriminating and, though Frankenstein is sure that the monster is behind the evil deed, he is enjoined from testifying on her behalf because to do so would reveal his unspeakable secret. As a result, Justine is executed, the first of several beloved relationships that are forever endangered by an angry being who will continue to redress his grievances by destroying all that his creator loves. As Volume I ends, Frankenstein is beyond all hope and redemption, in a world reminiscent of Dante's *Inferno*. "'Anguish and despair had penetrated into the core of my heart; I bore a hell within me, which nothing could extinguish.'"

VOLUME II

Volume II is primarily the monster's story as he confronts his creator, Victor
Frankenstein. It contains a description of and a reaction to the circumstances
of his most unnatural birth, his tragic abandonment by his "father," and his
gross anatomy and fearful aspect that excludes him from human society and
companionship. It also contains the details of his education through the
observation of strangers who likewise are compelled to live in the wilderness,
how he learns to speak, and the books he has read from which he learns
sympathy, compassion and acceptance of the solitary life to which he is
condemned. The monster's story is also about his rage against Frankenstein
for refusing to create his female equivalent, which would have granted his
"progeny" a loving companion to share the burden of his life as a pariah, and
the desperate revenge and murderous acts he commits against the injustices
wrought by Victor Frankenstein. What is patently clear from the monster's
moral outrage and Frankenstein's absolute culpability is that both are
condemned to an eternal state of hopelessness and utter despair.

Volume II opens with Frankenstein's description of his own inner
torment following the execution of Justine Moritz and the consequent
misery it has brought upon Elizabeth. "'I was seized by a remorse and sense
of guilt, which hurried me away to a hell of intense tortures, such as no
language can describe.'" He even contemplates suicide, but the thought of
further distressing his family dissuades him. Instead, he becomes determined
to take revenge on the monster. A family excursion to the beautiful valley of
Chamounix offers only a temporary reprieve as Frankenstein can run away
from neither himself nor his monstrous creation. From a vantage point upon
a glacier, Frankenstein sees a field of ice and the "awful majesty" of Mont
Blanc in the distance. It is at this juncture that Frankenstein encounters his
hideous daemon. "[H]is countenance bespoke bitter anguish, combined with
disdain and malignity, while its unearthly ugliness rendered it almost too
horrible for human eyes." For his part, the monster states that he expected
such a miserable reception from his despising creator. Nevertheless, he is not
deterred and, once again, pleads with Frankenstein to fashion him a suitable
female companion. "'Do your duty towards me, and I will do mine towards
you and the rest of mankind.'" It is also very significant that the monster has
the benefit of the superior language skills he has acquired during his exile.
Indeed, the monster proves to be a consummate rhetorician in pleading his
cause with a "father" who has thus far failed to respond to his plea for justice.
"'Remember, that I am thy creature. I ought to be thy Adam, but I am rather
the fallen angel, whom thou drivest from joy for no misdeed.'" That the
monster has at least succeeded in getting his attention is attested to by

Frankenstein's statement that he "'weighed the various arguments that he had used, and determined at least to listen to his tale. I was partly urged by curiosity and compassion confirmed my resolution.'" And thus begins the monster's narration of what has transpired since he was banished by Victor Frankenstein.

Since leaving Ingolstadt, the monster is forced to wander in the forest near Ingolstadt while attempting to become acquainted with his various senses. Before quitting Frankenstein's apartment, the monster covered himself with some clothes, but these proved insufficient. Having lived thus far in darkness, daylight is at first difficult to get used to. Eventually, the monster learns to enjoy the pleasant sounds of nature and the sweet song of birds. Having discovered the materials for a fire, the monster then spends the daylight hours foraging for food and is forced to endure a great deal of endure hunger and cold in the process until he stumbles upon a small shepherd's hut in the woods. When the monster enters the hut, an old man inside shrieks with horror and runs away. Nevertheless, the monster is charmed by what he discovers. "'[I]t presented to me then as exquisite and divine a retreat as Pandemonium appeared to the dæmons of hell after their sufferings in the lake of fire,'" an allusion to Book I of *Paradise Lost*, which the monster has read before his encounter with Victor Frankenstein.

Having quit the shepherd's hut, the monster walks until he reaches a village of neat cottages and stately homes, and settles into an vacant yet comfortable cottage from which he observes the De Lacey family. "'[F]or the present, I would remain quietly in my hovel, watching, and endeavouring to discover the motives which influenced their actions.'" The monster becomes enchanted with these "lovely creatures" and soon discovers, from a distance, what he discerns to be language as the medium of their communication. "'I perceived that the words they spoke sometimes produced pleasure or pain, smiles or sadness, in the minds and countenances of the hearers.'" He also observes Felix De Lacey, the old man's son, teaching his beautiful and exotic companion, Safie, to learn their language. "'While I improved in speech, I also learned the science of letters, as it was taught to the stranger.'" Thus, the monster is introduced to Volney's *Ruins of Empire* (1791), a work chosen for its affinity to eastern authors, which affords him with "an insight into the manners, governments and religions of the different nations of the earth." A little further in his narration, the monster tells Frankenstein that he discovered a leather bag containing *Paradise Lost*, a volume of *Plutarch's Lives* (a Greek biographer (c. 46–119) who wrote of Greek and Roman heroes) and the *Sorrows of Young Werther* (1774), Goethe's novel of a sensitive young artist in love with a woman who is engaged to someone else. From *Paradise Lost*, the monster becomes acquainted with sublime thoughts. "'It moved every feeling of wonder and awe, that the picture of an omnipotent God warring with his creatures was capable of exciting.'" And, though the monster has learned despondency from Werther's imagination, he finds Plutarch spiritually uplifting in recounting the stories of past heroes. He also states that he has read the writings of some ancient Greek and Roman statesmen and poets, such as Numa, Solon and Lycurgus, from whom he learns benevolence in law and government.

However, as a result of his ennobling education and close observation of the loving and nurturing De Lacey family, the monster's bitterness is heightened and continually inflamed as he is excluded from the gifts of social contact and communion. "'But where were my friends and relations? No father had watched my infant days, no mother had blessed me with smiles and caresses.'" His attempts at helping strangers are met only with revulsion. At first, the monster's rage is manifested by a destruction of inanimate objects, setting fire to the cottage and destroying the beauty of its garden. However, this method of expression proves unsatisfactory. And, so, the monster finally confesses to the murder of Frankenstein's youngest brother, William, and the deliberate placing of incriminating evidence into the pockets of the loving and innocent Justine Moritz. Volume II ends with the monster finally capturing Frankenstein's sympathetic attention and promises to provide him with a female companion. However, there is no absolute certainty that Frankenstein can or will deliver on his promise for he appears to have retreated into a disinterested routine of everyday life. "'I entered again into the every-day sense of life, if not with interests, at least with some degree of tranquility.'"

Volume III

The character profile in Volume III focuses on a heightened sense of the dual aspect of Frankenstein's nature—with Frankenstein and his monster locked in mortal combat. Though the duality of characterization must be assumed from the beginning of the novel, in this third and last volume of *Frankenstein*, the monster and his creator are inextricably intertwined in thought and deed. Frankenstein and his hideous progeny are hopelessly enslaved by one another. Volume III begins with a very anxious Victor Frankenstein, afraid of the monster, yet deeply concerned about unleashing yet another being capable of delivering more tragedy and destruction. "'I feared the vengeance of the disappointed fiend, yet I was unable to overcome my repugnance to the task which was enjoined me.'" As a result of his inner conflict, Frankenstein procrastinates as much as possible. Feeling pressure from his father to act on his promise to marry Elizabeth, Frankenstein consents, but only after he returns from two years of travel on the continent with his dear friend Henry Clerval. Though he harbors the secret agenda of using the time to create a female monster, both Elizabeth and his father consent to the delay. "'I must perform my engagement, and let the monster depart with his mate, before I allowed myself to enjoy the delight of a union from which I expected peace.'"

While on tour, Frankenstein expresses a desire to visit Scotland alone and finds a desolate place in the northern highland as the scene of his laboratory, an abode which mirrors his desperate solitude and utter hopelessness. But Frankenstein has serious misgivings and finds himself paralyzed with fear at the thought of creating another creature, especially with the unthinkable prospect that the two monsters will be able to reproduce. After close observation, the monster learns of his Frankenstein's hesitation and confronts his creator. He threatens further consequences, including a promise to disrupt Frankenstein's wedding night. For his part, Frankenstein resolves to dispose of the "body" he has begun working on and dumps it into the sea late one night. When Frankenstein awakens in his boat the next morning, he is completely lost in a strange land. He is rudely greeted and told to appear before a magistrate whereupon he learns that a dead body has been found in Perth, and that he, a stranger, is accused of a crime which he did not commit. When he learns that the victim is his cherished friend, Henry Clerval, he is filled with inconsolable remorse. "'But I was doomed to live.'" Following an arrest and trial, Frankenstein is released.

Now that his friend and traveling companion is gone, Frankenstein returns home with the intention of marrying Elizabeth. He is extremely paranoid about the monster attacking him at any moment and arms himself with many weapons and, based on prior events, it is a foregone conclusion that the monster will keep his promise of visiting Frankenstein on his wedding night. Frankenstein is agonizingly aware of this. "'I had been calm during the day; but so soon as night obscured the shapes of objects, a thousand fears arose in my mind.'" And those dark forebodings soon come to pass as Frankenstein returns to his room only to find that Elizabeth had been strangled and the monster was indeed the murderer. "'The murderous mark of the fiend's grasp was on her neck.'" Immediately upon making this horrible discovery, Frankenstein looks up at the window to find the fiend grinning at him; he makes an unsuccessful attempt to shoot the monster and then collapses into unconsciousness for a brief time. Upon regaining consciousness, he decides to return home only to have his father die in his arms of a broken heart.

And so Victor Frankenstein is left with no other purpose to live than to pursue and destroy his monster. It is this purpose alone which calms and sustains him. "'My present situation was one in which all voluntary thought was swallowed up and lost ... revenge alone endowed me with strength and composure....'" Indeed, Frankenstein's raging obsession assumes the mechanical aspect of his machine-like creation. "'I pursued my path towards the destruction of the daemon, more as a task enjoined by heaven, as the mechanical impulse of some power of which I was unconscious.'" Everywhere that he turns in the stillness of night, he imagines that he is being tormented by the monster's evil laughter. Frankenstein's pursuit continues for several months with the monster managing to evade capture while stealing his food supply. Eventually, Robert Walton rescues him and brings him on board his vessel. Hoping to find a friend in Victor Frankenstein, Walton gives enthusiastic attention and credence to his incredible tale, but is never given the satisfaction of learning the secret of this creature's formation. Steadily declining in health each day, Frankenstein asks Walton to completed his unfinished task of destroying the monster, and then he dies while the monster yet lives. Shortly thereafter, the monster appears in Walton's cabin to tell the story of what motivated his murderous deeds. After telling his story, the monster makes his final declaration, vowing to end his mischief and depart for the northernmost extremities of the globe. "'I shall die, and what I now feel be no longer felt. Soon these burning miseries will be extinct.'"

Contributors

HAROLD BLOOM is Sterling Professor of the Humanities at Yale University. He is the author of over 20 books, including *Shelley's Mythmaking* (1959), *The Visionary Company* (1961), *Blake's Apocalypse* (1963), *Yeats* (1970), *A Map of Misreading* (1975), *Kabbalah and Criticism* (1975), *Agon: Toward a Theory of Revisionism* (1982), *The American Religion* (1992), *The Western Canon* (1994), and *Omens of Millennium: The Gnosis of Angels, Dreams, and Resurrection* (1996). *The Anxiety of Influence* (1973) sets forth Professor Bloom's provocative theory of the literary relationships between the great writers and their predecessors. His most recent books include *Shakespeare: The Invention of the Human* (1998), a 1998 National Book Award finalist, *How to Read and Why* (2000), *Genius: A Mosaic of One Hundred Exemplary Creative Minds* (2002), and *Hamlet: Poem Unlimited* (2003). In 1999, Professor Bloom received the prestigious American Academy of Arts and Letters Gold Medal for Criticism, and in 2002 he received the Catalonia International Prize.

PERCY BYSSHE SHELLEY was the husband of Mary Shelley and one of the canonical Romantic poets and literary critics. Among his chief works which influenced *Frankenstein* are his lyrical drama, *Prometheus Unbound*, and his poem "Mutability."

ROBERT KIELY has been a Professor of English at Harvard University. He is the author of *Reverse Tradition: Postmodern Fictions and the Nineteenth Century Novel*, and *Beyond Egotism: The Fiction of James Joyce, Virginia Woolf, and D. H. Lawrence.*

DAVID KETTERER is Professor Emeritus of English, Concordia University. He is the author of *Canadian Science Fiction and Fantasy*, and *Edgar Allan Poe: Life, Work and Criticism*.

SANDRA M. GILBERT is Professor of English at the University of California, Davis. Along with Susan Gubar, she has published *The Madwoman in the Attic: The Woman Writer and the 19th-Century Literary Imagination* in 1979, a runner-up for both The Pulitzer Prize and the National Book Critics Circle Award. Gilbert is the author of a prose memoir, *Wrongful Death: A Medical Tragedy*, and many books of poetry including *Ghost Volcano, Inventions of Farewell: A Book of Elegies*, and *Kissing the Bread: New and Selected Poems*.

SUSAN GUBAR is Distinguished Professor of English and Women's Studies at Indiana University. Along with Sandra M. Gilbert, she published *The Madwoman in the Attic: The Woman Writer and the 19th-Century Literary Imagination* in 1979, a runner-up for both The Pulitzer Prize and the National Book Critics Circle Award. Gilbert and Gubar also co-authored *No Man's Land: The Place of the Woman Writer in the Twentieth Century: The War of the Words, Sexchanges*, and *Letters from the Front*. Gubar is the author of *Racechanges: White Skin, Black Face in American Culture*, and the editor of *Critical Condition: Feminism at the Turn of the Century*.

LAURA P. CLARIDGE has taught at the United States Naval Academy. She is the author of *Romantic Potency: The Paradox of Desire*, and *Norman Rockwell: A Life*.

WILLIAM VEEDER is a Professor of English and the Humanities at the University of Chicago. He is the author of *Henry James: The Lessons of the Master: Popular Fiction and Personal Style in the Nineteenth Century*, and *W.B. Yeats: The Rhetoric of Repetition*.

BARBARA FREY WAXMAN is a Professor of English at the University of North Carolina, Wilmington. She is the author of "Reader-Response Theory, Social Criticism, and Personal Writing," and *To Live in the Center of the Moment: Literary Autobiographies of Aging*.

MATTHEW C. BRENNAN has been a Professor of English at Indiana State University. He is the author of "Coleridge, Friedrich, and the 'Hymn' to Mountain Glory," and *Wordsworth, Turner, and Romantic Landscape: A Study of the Traditions of the Picturesque and the Sublime*.

IAIN CRAWFORD has been a Professor of English and Dean of the School of Liberal Arts at the University of Southern Indiana. He is the author of "'Nature ... Drenched in Blood': Barnaby Rudge and Wordsworth's 'The Idiot Boy'" and "Shades of the Prison-House: Religious Romanticism in *Oliver Twist*."

PAUL A. CANTOR has been a Professor of English at the University of Virginia and a member of the National Council on the Humanities. He is the author of numerous books on Shakespeare and Romanticism, including *Creature and Creator: Myth-making and English Romanticism*.

MARY LOWE-EVANS is the Chair and a Professor of English at the University of West Florida in Pensacola. She is the editor of *Critical Essays on Mary Wollstonecraft Shelley*, and author of *Crimes Against Fecundity: Joyce and Population Control*.

LUDMILLA JORDANOVA is Professor of Visual Arts, School of World Art Studies and Museology at the University of East Anglia, and Dean of the Schools of World Art Studies and Music. She is the author of *Nature Displayed: Gender, Science, and Medicine, 1760–1820: Essays*, and co-author of *The Quick and the Dead: Artists and Anatomy*.

CROSBIE SMITH is a Professor of the History of Science at the University of Kent, Canterbury. He is the author of *The Science of Energy: A Cultural History of Energy Physics in Victorian Britain*, and co-author of *Energy and Empire: A Biographical Study of Lord Kelvin*.

DEBRA E. BEST has taught at the University of North Carolina, Chapel Hill. She is the author of "Villains and Monsters: Enacting Evil in Beves of Hamptoun."

Bibliography

Baldick, Chris. *In Frankenstein's Shadow: Myth, Monstrosity, and Nineteenth-century Writing*. Oxford and New York: Oxford University Press, 1987.

Bann, Stephen, ed. *Frankenstein, Creation and Monstrosity*. London: Reaktion Books, 1994.

Bewell, Alan. "An Issue of Monstrous Desire: Frankenstein and Obstetrics." *The Yale Journal of Criticism* 2, no. 1 (Fall 1988): 105–128.

Bloom, Harold. "Frankenstein or the New Prometheus." *Partisan Review* XXXII (1965): 611–18.

_____, ed. *Mary Shelley's Frankenstein*. New York: Chelsea House Publishers, 1987.

Blumberg, Jane. *Mary Shelley's Early Novels: "This Child of Imagination and Misery."* Iowa City: University of Iowa Press, 1993.

Botting, Fred. *Making Monstrous: Frankenstein, Criticism, Theory*. Manchester, UK and New York: Manchester University Press, 1991.

Burton, Pollin R. "Philosophical and Literary Sources for Frankenstein." *Comparative Literature* XVII/2 (Spring 1965): 97–108.

Cantor, Paul. *Creature and Creator: Myth-making and English Romanticism*. Cambridge and New York: Cambridge University Press, 1984.

Claridge, Laura P. "Parent-Child Tensions in Frankenstein: The Search for Communion." *Studies in the Novel* 17, no. 1 (1985 Spring): 14–26.

Clemit, Pamela. *The Godwinian Novel: The Rational Fictions of Godwin, Brocken Brown, Mary Shelley*. Oxford: Clarendon Press, 1993.

Engar, Ann. "Mary Shelley and the Romance of Science." *Jane Austen and Mary Shelley and Their Sisters*. Edited by Laura Dabundo. Lanham, MD: University Press of America (2000): 135–46.

Fisch, Audrey A., Anne K. Mellor, and Esther H. Schor, eds. *The Other Mary Shelley: Beyond "Frankenstein."* New York: Oxford University Press, 1993.

Gilbert, Sandra M. and Susan Gubar. *The Madwoman in the Attic: The Woman Writer and the Nineteenth-Century Literary Imagination*. New Haven: Yale University Press (1979): 213–47.

Gillin, Edward. "The 'Frightful Darkness' of Melville and Shelley." *Mid-Hudson Language Studies 12*, no. 2 (1989): 55–64.

Homans, Margaret. "Bearing Demons: Frankenstein's Circumvention of the Maternal." *Bearing the Word: Language and Female Experience in Nineteenth Century Women's Writing*. Chicago and London: The University of Chicago Press (1986): 100–19.

Huet, Marie-Hélène. "Unwonted Paternity: The Genesis of Frankenstein." From *Monstrous Imagination*. Cambridge, Mass.: Harvard University Press, 1993.

Jacobus, Mary. "Is There a Woman in This Text?" *New Literary History* 14 (1982): 117–41.

Johnson, Barbara. "My Montser/My Self." *Diacritics* 12 (1982): 2–10.

Ketterer, David. "(De)Composing Frankenstein: The Import of Altered Character Names in the Last Draft." *Studies in Bibliography* 49 (1996): 232–76.

————. *Frankenstein's Creation: The Book, The Monster, and Human Reality*. Victoria, BC: University of Victoria Press, 1979.

Kiely, Robert. "Frankenstein." From *The Romantic Novel in England*. Cambridge, Mass.: Harvard University Press (1972): 155–73.

Kranzler, Laura. "Frankenstein and the Technological Future." *Foundation* 44 (Winter 1988–1989): 42–49.

Levine, George. *The Realistic Imagination: English Fiction from Frankenstein to Lady Chatterley*. Chicago: The University of Chicago Press, 1981.

————. and U.C. Knoepflmacher, eds. *The Endurance of* Frankenstein. Berkeley: University of California Press, 1979.

McWhir, Anne. "Teaching the Monster to Read: Mary Shelley, Education, and *Frankenstein.*" *The Educational Legacy of Romanticism.* Edited by John Willinsky. Waterloo, Canada: Wilfrid Laurier University Press, 1990.

Mellor, Anne K. *Mary Shelley: her Life, her Fiction, her Monsters.* New York: Routledge, 1988.

_____. "Possessing Nature: The Female in Frankenstein." From *Romanticism and Feminism.* Edited by Anne K. Mellor. Bloomington: Indiana University Press (1988): 220–32.

Ping, Tang Soo. "Frankenstein, *Paradise Lost,* and 'The Majesty of Goodness.'" *College Literature* 16, no. 3 (Fall 1989): 255–260.

Smith, Johanna M. *Mary Shelley.* New York: Twayne Publishers, 1996.

Spark, Muriel. *Mary Shelley.* London: Penguin, 1987.

Sunstein, Emily W. *Mary Shelley: Romance and Reality.* Baltimore: Johns Hopkins University Press, 1989.

Thornburg, Mary K. Patterson. *The Monster in the Mirror: Gender and the Sentimental/Gothic Myth in* Frankenstein. Ann Arbor, MI: UMI Research Press, 1987.

Waxman, Barbara Frey. "Victor Frankenstein's Romantic Fate: The Tragedy of the Promethean Overreacher as Woman." *Papers on Language and Literature* 23, no. 1 (Winter 1987): 14–26.

Youngquist, Paul. "*Frankenstein*: The Mother, the Daughter, and the Monster." *Philological Quarterly* 70 (1991): 339–59.

Acknowledgments

"On Frankestein" by Percy Bysshe Shelley. From *Frankenstein: The 1818 Text Contexts, Nineteenth-Century Responses, Modern Criticism* (A Norton Critical Edition): 185. © 1996 by W.W. Norton & Company, Inc. Originally published in *The Athenaeum Journal of Literature, Science and the Fine Arts*, Nov. 10, 1832. Reprinted by permission.

"Frankenstein" by Robert Kiely. From *The Romantic Novel in England*. Cambridge: Harvard University Press (1972): 155–73. © 1972 by the President and Fellows of Harvard College. Reprinted by permission.

"Thematic Anatomy: Intrinsic Structures" by David Ketterer. From *Frankenstein's Creation: The Book, The Monster and Human Reality*. Victoria, British Columbia: University of Victoria Press (1979): 45–65. © 1979 by David Ketterer. Reprinted by permission.

"Horror's Twin: Mary Shelley's Monstrous Eve" by Sandra M. Gilbert and Susan Gubar. From *The Madwoman in the Attic: The Woman Writer and the Nineteenth-Century Literary Imagination*. New Haven and London: Yale University Press (2000): 227–47. © 1984 by Sandra M. Gilbert and Susan Gubar. Reprinted by permission.

"Parent-Child Tensions in *Frankenstein: The Search for Communion*" by Laura P. Claridge. From *Studies in the Novel*, vol. XVII, no. 1 (Spring 1985): 14–26. © 1985 by North Texas State University. Reprinted by permission.

"*Frankenstein*: Self-Division and Projection" by William Veeder. From *Mary Shelley and Frankenstein: The Fate of Androgyny*. Chicago and London: The University of Chicago Press (1986): 81–82 and 89–102. © 1986 by The University of Chicago. Reprinted by permission.

"Victor Frankenstein's Romantic Fate: The Tragedy of the Promethean Overreacher as Woman" by Barbara Frey Waxman. From *Papers on Language and Literature*, vol. 23, no. 1 (Winter 1987): 14–26. © 1987 by The Board of Trustees, Southern Illinois University. Reprinted by permission.

"The Landscape of Grief in Mary Shelley's *Frankenstein*" by Matthew C. Brennan. From *Studies in the Humanities*, vol. 15, no. 1 (June 1988): 33–44. © 1988 by Indiana University of Pennsylvania. Reprinted by permission.

"Wading Through Slaughter: John Hampden, Thomas Gray, and Mary Shelley's *Frankenstein*" by Iain Crawford. From *Studies in the Novel*, vol. XX, no. 3 (Fall 1988): 249–61. © 1988 by the University of North Texas. Reprinted by permission.

"Mary Shelley and the Taming of the Byronic Hero: 'Transformation' and *The Deformed Transformed*" (1993) by Paul A. Cantor. From *The Other Mary Shelley: Beyond* Frankenstein, eds. Audrey A. Fisch, Anne K. Mellor and Esther H. Schor: 89–104. © 1993 by Oxford Unviersity Press. Reprinted by permission.

"The Groomsmen" by Mary Lowe-Evans. From *Frankenstein: Mary Shelley's Wedding Guest*. New York: Twayne Publishers (1993): 73–82. © 1993 by Twayne Publishers. Reprinted by permission.

"Melancholy Reflection: Constructing an Identity for Unveilers of Nature" by Ludmilla Jordanova. From *Frankenstein, Creation and Monstrosity*. Edited by Stephen Bann. London: Reaktion Books, Ltd. (1994): 60–76. © 1994 by Reaktion Books, Ltd. Reprinted by permission.

"Frankenstein and Natural Magic" by Crosbie Smith. From *Frankenstein, Creation and Monstrosity*. Edited by Stephen Bann. London: Reaktion Books, Ltd. (1994): 39–59. © 1994 by Reaktion Books, Ltd. Reprinted by permission.

"The Monster in the Family: a reconsideration of *Frankenstein's* Domestic Relationships" by Debra E. Best. From *Women's Writing*, vol. 6, no. 3 (1999): 365–84. © 1999 by Triangle Journals, Ltd. Reprinted by permission.

Index

Characters in literary works are indexed by first name followed by the name of the work in parentheses.